This Is

THE NEWFOUNDLAND

SECOND EDITION

Distributed in the U.S.A. by T.F.H. Publications, Inc., 211 West Sylvania Avenue, P.O. Box 27, Neptune City, N.J. 07753; in England by T.F.H. (Gt. Britain) Ltd., 13 Nutley Lane, Reigate, Surrey; in Canada to the book store and library trade by Clarke, Irwin & Company, Clarwin House, 791 St. Clair Avenue West, Toronto 10, Ontario; in Canada to the pet trade by Rolf C. Hagen Ltd., 3225 Sartelon Street, Montreal 382, Quebec; in Southeast Asia by Y.W. Ong, 9 Lorong 36 Geylang, Singapore 14; in Australia and the south Pacific by Pet Imports Pty. Ltd., P.O. Box 149, Brookvale 2100, N.S.W., Australia. Published by T.F.H. Publications Inc. Ltd., The British Crown Colony of Hong Kong.

Official Breed Book of

The Newfoundland Club of America

MAP OF NEWFOUNDLAND

LABRADOR

QUEBEC

GULF OF ST. LAWRENCE

BELLE ISLE ST

WHITE BAY

WHI

BONNE BAY

BONNE B.

BEAR Hd

ST. GEORGE'S BAY

ST. GEORGE'S
BAY

C. RAY

P. BASQUE

PENGUIN Is

GREAT
MIQUELO

N

ATLANTIC

OCEAN

BELLE ISLE

C. NORMAN

C. BAULD

GOOSE C.

BELL I.

NOTRE DAME BAY

FOGO

C. FOGO

PENQUIN I^s

SEAL COVE

GANDER

BONAVISTA

C. BONAVISTA

TRINITY BAY

CONCEPTION BAY

HEARTS CONTENT

HEARTS DELIGHT

CARBONEAR

ST JOHNS

FORTUNE BAY

GREAT GARNISH

MERASHEEN I.

PLACENTIA BAY

TOPSAIL

FERRYLAND

ST PIERRE I.

MARY'S BAY

EY BAY

C. RACE

Dedicated to the Newfoundland dog,
without which there would have been
no reason for such a book.

Ch. Dryad's Christine of Glenora, owned by Edenglen Kennels, and Dryad's Goliath of Gath, owned by Dryad Kennels.

Black and Landseer
Newfoundlands
By Louis Agassiz Fuertes ©

This Is

THE NEWFOUNDLAND

Official Breed Book of

The Newfoundland Club of America

SECOND EDITION

Edited By

Mrs. MAYNARD K. DRURY

Illustrated by

ERNEST H. HART

Contents

THIS IS THE NEWFOUNDLAND

Foreword

We are proud to present the second edition of:

This Is the Newfoundland

The Newfoundland Club of America has again shown "the unity of purpose that is in itself a tribute to the quality of the breed which inspired it." Contributions from members of the club, friends of the breed, and the coordinating efforts of the Committee have culminated in this edition. It includes much new material, pictures of most of the outstanding Newfoundlands of the past fourteen years, an expanded chapter on European dogs, and explanations of the breeding practices that have benefited the breed to date.

There have been two events in the past fourteen years which will greatly influence the modern history of our breed.

First was the National Specialty Show that was held at the Lenox School in March 1967. There were 117 dogs entered in the conformation classes and an equal number in the "fun" classes. The excellent judging by Mrs. D. D. Power and Mrs. N. Demidoff, the fine quality of the dogs entered, the cooperative efforts of all the Committees, the camaraderie of those present, and the graciousness of our hosts, the Rev. and Mrs. Robert Curry, made it a milestone in Newfoundland history. Today we are reaping the results in better breeding programs, more interest in the breed, and larger entries at shows.

Second is the Revised Standard, as approved by the A.K.C., and printed herein. It is the result of many years of hard work and much research. We present it with pride and hope it will be a guide to breeding and judging Newfoundlands for many years.

We hope that this edition of *This Is the Newfoundland* will bring pleasure to all who read it and help all owners and breeders, as well as all prospective owners and breeders, of our noble breed.

MRS. MAYNARD K. DRURY
President
The Newfoundland Club of America
Phelps, New York
October 28, 1969

Acknowledgments

We would like to thank again all those who contributed to the first edition of *This Is the Newfoundland.* They made the second edition possible.

We are grateful to all those who sent us pictures of their dogs. We are as proud of them as they are. However, many of the pictures we received we could not use because of limited space. Therefore, the pictures included in this book are of Newfoundlands who have won a Newfoundland Specialty Show, placed in a Group, or were of particular significance to the breed.

New material has come from many sources. Suggestions for improvements and changes have come from members and non-members of the Newfoundland Club of America. Our special thanks go to the following persons who have been of particular help: Charles D. Webster (our delegate to the American Kennel Club for sixteen years and a member of their board of directors for eight years), author of the chapter on literature and lore; Adrian van Sijl, who compiled and wrote the chapter "The Newfoundland in Europe"; Mrs. Robert Curry, who helped translate and edit the European chapter; Donn Purdy, author of "The Newfoundland in Canada"; and Mrs. S. J. Navin, Mrs. Alan Fulton, Mrs. Fred Peterson, Mr. Joseph Reinisch, Mrs. Willis Linn, Mr. and Mrs. James Schmoyer, Mrs. Don Jager, Mr. and Mrs. C. Y. Smith, Mrs. Alan Riley, Doremus & Co., Mr. and Mrs. Al Duffett and Mr. and Mrs. David Suckling.

The Book Committee
CHARLES D. WEBSTER, Chairman
WILLIS LINN, Vice-Chairman

Chapter I

Origin

Even after thousands of years of speculation and much intensive study, scientists are far from agreement regarding the origin of the human species. Legends, recorded history, archaeological discoveries, modern laboratory testing facilities, all leave the origin of *Homo sapiens*, man himself, the articulate "master of the universe," a much-debated and debatable question. How infinitely more difficult the task of trying to tie down with certainty the origin of "man's best friend," *Canis familiaris*; and, compounding the difficulty, the origin of *one* breed among hundreds whose tortuous lifelines disappear into the remote mists of antiquity! Nevertheless, speculations are always enjoyable and often fruitful. Although not all inclusive by any means, we present in the following paragraphs some of the most thoughtful speculations relative to the subject of this chapter, the origin of the Newfoundland dog.

From the inevitable conflict of information and opinion about the origin of the Newfoundland we can draw one conclusion: owners and supporters down through the ages have not been very interested in recording the history of their canine companions. Even the early explorers, such as Cabot, failed to mention their dogs. They were apparently just taken for granted (much as friends are often so taken!). Of course there were exceptions, and on these exceptional historians we must rely for our information.

In 1620, Captain Richard Whitbourne of Exmouth wrote that while exploring Newfoundland in the year 1615 it was well known to forty-eight persons of his company and "diverse other men that three several times" the wolves and beasts of the country came down near them to the seaside, where they were laboring about their fish, howling and making a noise "so that at each time my mastiffe-dogge went unto them (as the like in that country hath not been seen) the one began to fawn and play with the other, and so went together into the woods, and continued with them, every one of these times, nine or ten days, and did return unto us without any hurt."

Later, Sir Joseph Banks, did considerable to enhance the name of our breed. He was a member of the Royal Geographic Society and succeeded in including himself as a member of many of the famous explorations of the 1700's under such memorable leaders as Captain Cook on his trip to Australia. The famous Captain Bligh was outfitted under Sir Joseph's direction. He was the King's Representative in Charge of Exploration. We have access to his *Journal of a Voyage to Newfoundland*. He writes:

"I had thought I should meet with a sort of dog differing from any I had seen, whose peculiar excellence was taking the water freely. I was, therefore, the more surprised when told that there was no distinct breed. Those I met with were mostly curs with a cross of the Mastiff in them. Some took the water well, others not at all. The thing they are valued for here is strength, as they are employed in winter to draw in sledges whatever is wanted in the woods. I was told indeed that at Trepassy lived a man who had a distinct breed which he called an original Newfoundland dog but I had not the opportunity of seeing any of them."

Obviously the story of the "man of Trepassy" with the "distinct breed" stayed in Sir Joseph's mind so that later, in his mercantile expeditions, he succeeded in acquiring specimens of this breed because, by report, he became so fond of the breed that he succeeded in interesting many famous personalities, such as George III, Napoleon, Captain Cook, Boswell, Byron, and Scott to the extent of their acquiring one or more of the breed.

In more recent years, Professor Albert Heim of Switzerland, Johann Pieterse of Holland, and the Honorable Harold Macpherson of Newfoundland, have recorded as much as is known about the origin of the breed. These men have considered the conflicting historical testimony. Each supports a different conclusion. Many of the less literary lovers of the breed hold equally interesting theories. We present some of these in the hope that you can select the one that appears most logical or interesting to you.

As indicated in the opening paragraph, even the origin of dogs in general is shrouded by uncertainty. There are theories of origin from wolves or jackals, as a separate species, or from other species. Dr. Heim tells us that "The Greeks and Romans knew of five different breeds of dogs. Because of their isolation and varied living conditions in different parts of the world, and primarily because of their association with different human beings, about 200 different types of dogs have come into being. These crossbreedings usually have produced dreadful offspring with poor bodies and low mentality. Only after controlled breeding for hundreds of years has it been possible to breed out these poor characteristics and obtain uniformly good points. No living breed of dog can be

Honorable Harold
Macpherson, LL.D.

traced back to its wild form. In early civilizations the dog was taken for granted and no breeding records maintained. The bone structure of various types indicates their possible backgrounds, but there is no positive source of information."

Even when data have been recorded, one must bear in mind that the use of such broad geographical terms as North America, or even Newfoundland, can be very misleading. For instance, we can refer to the export of dogs from Newfoundland, but until we study and break down the general data of 1800 to 1850 we do not discover that the black dogs were primarily from the southern islands of St. Pierre and Miquelon, whereas the exports from the main island of Newfoundland were primarily Landseers (the black-and-white variety of Newfoundland that takes its name from the famous animal painter, Sir Edwin Landseer).

The most generally accepted theory among the experts (and this agreement is by no means unanimous) is that the Newfoundland dog descends from the Tibetan mastiff which in turn developed from the ancient Malossian dog. So let us start with this as an assumption and see how it fits into the pattern of the various conflicting theories.

Let us consider first the testimony of Dr. Albert Heim (*Der Newfundlanderhunde*, pp. 5–7, circa 1925) who says that when Th. Studer examined the skulls of Newfoundland dogs he found "ray rows" of the prehistoric *Canis familiaris* Inostranzewi, the ancestor of the Tibetan and Malossian dog. This is a group of dogs of a type that includes Elkhounds, St. Bernards, Mastiffs, Tibetan, and Pyrenees dogs. Studer tries to prove that all these dogs developed by themselves and that the Newfoundland, being of this type, did not develop alone, but must have come from somewhere else to the island of Newfoundland. Finally, being introduced to the isolation of the island with its raw and rugged coastal conditions, there gradually was fixed the type of dog we call the Newfoundland. He was black in color, of good size, and possessed a massive head formation. The question is: "How did the black dog get to Newfoundland?"

Dr. Heim goes on to say that Dr. Trager has proved conclusively that, whereas the blacks came from Newfoundland or North America about 1600, the Landseer type appeared later and was of European origin. He believes that they are two distinct breeds of different origin which have now been frequently interbred.

Honorable Harold Macpherson in 1937 writes (*The Newfoundland Dog*, pp. 5 and 6) of his theory of the origin of the Newfoundland:

"The Newfoundland's chief ancestor must have been that most beautiful of dogs whose conformation is identical with his own, the Pyrenean sheep-dog.

"The Basque fishermen, reported to have visited Newfoundland as early as 1506, would naturally bring as ship's dogs these white or cream-colored Pyrenean sheep-dogs. . . .

"The English, being a sporting people, would naturally take water spaniels, bird-dogs and Mastiffs; likewise, the French, Spanish and Portuguese would bring their large dogs on salt trips from Cadiz to Newfoundland and

Here where the ponderous breakers plunge and roar
And dart their hissing tongues high up the shore

has evolved and developed a new type of dog named the Newfoundland."

His theory envisions a crossing of the Great Pyrenees and the English imports.

Johann Pieterse, well-known breeder of Newfoundlands in Holland and president of the Netherlands Club since 1932, holds a belief quite similar to that of Mr. Macpherson when he states (*The Newfoundland* (as translated by R. H. Brandon) p. 6):

"I tend to agree with the Newfoundland authorities who claim that the Newfoundland descends from French Dogs, brought to Newfoundland by the first French colonists.

"In that way the Newfoundland is descended from the large Pyrenean mountain dog, and a spaniel from the northern part of Spain, and similarly the Newfoundland would be a close kin to our spaniel and setter. Since the other races from the northern part of Canada all resemble the Husky, or all seem to be related to the wolf, it is highly improbable that the Norsemen, on their trips to the coast of Labrador, left dogs there that could be progenitors of the present-day Newfoundlands."

The only specific flaw in this hypothesis which has been expressed to date is that many of our principal American breeders state that they have never been seriously troubled with dewclaws —much less double dewclaws—which is a strong characteristic of the Pyrenean dogs. Some say that if the Great Pyrenees was really an ancestor, then many of our pups should still show this unusual evidence inasmuch as such a characteristic is not likely to disappear completely.

At a meeting of the Newfoundland Club of America, Mr. Fred Stubbart of Columbia, South Carolina, voiced his theory that the Newfoundland dog originated in America. He based his theories on bone studies made of native Indian dogs discovered in old Appalachian ruins. He evidently presumed that the Tibetan Mastiff, or his progeny, came over from the Orient via the Aleutians and Alaska along with the ancestors of the American Indian.

Still another ancient theory and one favored by Mrs. Maynard Kane Drury revolves about the travels of the Norsemen. She states that according to old Norse data, Leif Ericson brought to America about the year A.D. 1000 a large black "Bear Dog." These dogs had been previously used in Norway not only in hauling but also for guardian work. Undoubtedly they derived from the Tibetan Mastiff. This information is found in the 1888 writings of Professor Eben Horsford of Harvard who discovered and proved that the Norsemen came to Massachusetts. Professor Horsford even went on to say that the big black dog that Leif Ericson brought with him was called "Oolum." He also states that when the Norsemen left these shores, they also left their cattle and other domestic animals. It is logical, therefore, that they may have left their dogs.

If this theory is true, it may well be the link which is missing in Dr. Heim's theory as to how the dog originally got to the island of its name. Such a theory provides the time required for the animal to develop through inbreeding on the basis of "survival of the fittest," the distinct, water-dog characteristics which he developed during this isolated stay on the island of Newfoundland. It may also explain the fact that Mr. Stubbart finds similar bone structures in eastern America. It may provide the original dogs to which the new dogs mentioned in the Honorable Harold Macpherson's theory were bred. At any rate, it is certainly a fact that the Norsemen, traveling and trading along the Atlantic seaboard, brought their "Bear Dogs" from Norway. Whether they were forebears of our breed we may never know, but it does seem possible. (Within the past two years Dr. Helge Ingsted of Oslo, Norway has found bones at the L'Anse aux Meadows excavation site in Newfoundland that resemble those of dogs. This was a Viking settlement and is further proof of the possible Newfoundland heritage.)

Around these major theories there revolve innumerable minor variations, such as one finds in *The Dog*, p. 16, by Youatt in 1876 "the Spaniel is evidently the parent of the Newfoundland Dog and the Setter." One must bear in mind that considerable confusion may have been added to these theories over the centuries by talking about two distinct breeds—the blacks and the Landseers. Since that time they have been interbred so frequently that they are no longer two breeds.

To that confusion must be added the havoc created by the uncontrolled natural breeding which must have taken place during the period 1500–1700 when apparently dogs introduced from every part of Europe were bred to the native island dog. No wonder we have trouble finding records which agree.

The most probable early history, therefore, seems to have been that the black Newfoundland derived from the Tibetan Mastiff and that he came to his island home at least by the year A.D. 1000, either brought by the Norsemen or others. Until "New-foundlande" was rediscovered in 1497 by Giovanni Caboto (John Cabot), the Newfoundland dog remained isolated, developing into a distinct type. During this 500-year period there was an opportunity for at least 100 generations of breeding among limited lines. Either inbreeding or line-breeding, probably both, took place. In any event, the type was set. It was so strongly set that when the Pyrenees, the Spaniels, the Mastiffs, and whatever other dogs were brought to the island, were bred to the native Newfoundland, a predominantly black animal with a strong inclination to be a web-footed water dog resulted.

Even today the black Newfoundland is one of the most prepotent of our larger dog breeds. Breed him to a Shepherd or a Setter and you get a large black dog with the unmistakable expression and water-loving characteristics of the Newfoundland.

Now, assuming that the above discussion settles most of the questions regarding the origin of the black Newfoundland, let us consider the origin of the Landseer.

The best-documented research on this topic appears in Dr. Heim's treatise. He explains that, as the Honorable Harold Macpherson believes, the English imported their favorite dogs when they emigrated to Newfoundland, between 1550 and 1700. Dr. Heim believes that many of these dogs were the large white or brown-and-white Butcher dogs sometimes known as Estate dogs. They were apparently even bigger than the Newfoundland dog himself. Whatever the dog was, he did breed with the smaller black native dog, producing what we know today as the Landseer. Following this 200-year period of crossbreeding, there began a period of exportation back to England. From 1780 to 1850 it was almost wholly confined to the exportation of Landseers. Toward the last, blacks were exported as the Landseer supply became virtually exhausted. Other European countries, however, concentrated on the importation of blacks.

On the other hand, even this hypothesis is under question. No less an authority than Johann Pieterse dismisses this thought as "sheer fable."

So it is that the reader and the student of Newfoundland lore must either accept one of the theories expressed above, generate his own, based on some of these facts, or realize that there may well be more than one of them that applies, at least in part.

Bo Lande ("The Newfoundland" in the June 1947, *Field and Stream*) summed up the problem of origin rather neatly when he wrote, "Whatever his origin, he came into the ken of men as a large dog with size and strength to perform the tasks required of him." And we may with pardonable pride and affection add "one of man's noblest companions."

Chapter II

History

Now let us proceed from the realm of fascinating speculation into the light of documented fact. The misty era of unrecorded origin comes to an end with the naming of our established breed by George Cartwright about 1775, when he first applied the island name to his own dog. Even in this early mention, the Newfoundland was a sturdy working dog helping to draw his "Esquimaux sled" and much like his present-day offspring.

The first careful measurements of the breed occurred about 1779 when Bewick, the well-known English naturalist and engraver, provided us with the following description of what has been termed a very fine specimen at Eslington, Northumberland, in England.

The length of the dog from nose to end of tail is	6 feet 2 inches
the length of its tail	1 foot 10 inches
the girth behind shoulder	3 feet 2 inches
round its head over its ears	2 feet 0 inches
and round the upper foreleg	9½ inches

It is web-footed and swims extremely fast, dives with ease, and brings up anything from the bottom of the water.

What makes the description above all the more valuable to us is the fact that we also have Bewick's accompanying engraving of the dog which was later to be known as a Landseer.

While the breed thrived in his newly adopted home in England, his relatives on the home island of Newfoundland were having trouble even surviving. Not only were the dogs being exported in quantity, but, quite suddenly, they were legislated out of existence. Governor Edwards in 1780 issued a proclamation forbidding ownership of more than one dog per family. The theory behind this was to promote more sheep raising. However, in the opinion

A very fine specimen at Eslington.

of the Honorable Harold Macpherson, the net result was destructive and not constructive in that there was a near extermination of the Newfoundland but no great increase in sheep raising.

Probably the only thing that saved the Newfoundland from complete extinction in his homeland was the fact that many inhabitants resisted the proclamation because they felt that he was simply too useful to shoot. Not only was he used in hauling sledges in the winter (be they for the King's mail or his master's firewood) but he was also available to help with the hauling of the fish nets during the warmer months. Many Newfoundland dogs more than paid for their keep by diving to retrieve articles which fell overboard from the fishing vessels. In addition, the case histories of lifesaving, simply too innumerable to recount, exerted a great influence on the islander to save his canine treasure at any cost.

Even the sportsman of Newfoundland found time to train this versatile dog to retrieve birds and to carry supplies on hunts. So, in spite of the official stigma on him, the harassed Newfoundland did not disappear from his island home. The proclamation did, nevertheless, have far-reaching effects, for in 1901 Honorable Harold Macpherson was hard pressed to find a suitable specimen to present to the Duke and Duchess of Cornwall and York (later King George and Queen Mary of England). However, he secured the best available, trained him to harness with a specially made cart, and hoped that he had something to present which would serve to amuse the children of the royal household (which it certainly did by later report).

However, even though the Newfoundland did not have his true worth recognized in his native land, he was attaining fame in other countries besides England, his adopted land. In our own early colonial history we have records of the esteem in which he was held. The first mention of the breed as yet unnamed by Cartwright is contained in Bailey's *Long Island, Nassau and Suffolk,* Volume 1, p. 235:

"In 1639, a year before either Southold or Southampton was founded, Lion Gardiner explored his little wooded island and purchased it from the Wyandanch Indians. He named it the Isle of Wight (now Gardiner's Island). The price paid included one large, black, woolly dog, one flintlock gun, powder and ball, some Jamaica rum and several Dutch blankets."

The famous dog of Samuel Adams presents us with an interesting historical facet. Although the Colonies had a law forbidding dogs as large as a Newfoundland, Samuel Adams owned one of the animals named QueQue. He was obviously never bothered by the law because QueQue, during the occupation of Boston by the Redcoats, developed such an intense dislike for these soldiers that whenever they made an appearance he harassed them in every way possible.

During this same period we have the sad record of a Newfoundland who accompanied the ill-starred expedition of Benedict Arnold to attempt to surprise and capture Quebec. During the terrible days of near starvation on this wilderness trek, the American soldiers finally in desperate circumstances were forced to kill and eat their faithful canine companion to stay alive.

At a slightly later date we have the record of a Newfoundland that accompanied the Lewis and Clark expedition of 1802. On this we quote Charles Collins of the Chicago *Tribune* in his column, "A Linotype or Two":

"Lewis' Newfoundland, named Scannon, was stolen by Indians whose intention was to get him into cooking pots as soon as possible. This dog had been the life of the party, helping in retrieving game, killing deer, chasing buffaloes out of the camp, and keeping watch for grizzly bears. Scannon ate as much as a man, but even when starvation was close, his companions never begrudged him a hearty meal. So an angry rescue party found the trail of the Indian thieves and overtook them. The Indians surrendered Scannon without fighting, which was lucky, because the annals say that at this point the rank and file were well disposed to kill a few of them."

The Newfoundland was meanwhile making two very important contributions to the American dog fancy. He was assisting in the founding of both the Labrador and the Chesapeake Bay Retrievers. It is usually agreed that the Labrador Retriever did not

Newfoundland donated to Duke and Duchess of Cornwall and York.

come from the country of his name but rather from the area of St. Johns, Newfoundland. It can reasonably be presumed that the smaller, smooth-coated dog was related to the bigger, long-coated dog not only because of the mutual identification of water-loving characteristics but also because of their similarity in design for handling water. For many years these short-coated dogs were known as "Lesser Newfoundlands."

It is very difficult for us to separate the real Newfoundland from the "Lesser Newfoundland" in the early writings of dogs and dog breedings on the island. It must be assumed, therefore, that the dogs not only had common ancestors but developed in the same area to be two distinct breeds with many common qualities.

Regardless of which of these two "Newfoundland" dog types were aboard the foundering English brig in the fall of 1807 when the crew and live cargo were saved by those aboard the *Canton*, the dogs were definitely of Newfoundland descent. George Law in a letter written in January, 1845, describes the rescued dog called Sailor and the slut called Canton as follows:

". . . a pair of pups of the most approved Newfoundland breed, but of different families. . . . The dog was of a dingy red color; and the slut black. They were not large; their hair was short, but very thick coated; they had dewclaws. Both attained great reputation as water dogs. They were most sagacious in everything; particularly so in all duties connected with duck shooting." These two dogs are generally credited with founding the breed of Chesapeake Bay Retrievers we know today.

In 1854 the breed as a whole was duly recognized as noted in the chapter on working dogs. Dr. Elisha Kent Kane, a United States Navy officer, organized and commanded the second Grinnell expedition to search north of Baffin Bay in what is now known as Kanes Basin for the lost polar exploration party under Sir John Franklin. In Dr. Kane's two-volume narrative, *Arctic*

The Original Breed.

Exploration, he describes the use of his team of Newfoundlands which hauled his sled during the rescue and exploration work. He writes with great affection for his dogs, which included some gray specimens along with blacks and Landseers. An interesting note—Dr. Kane is an ancestor of Mr. Maynard Kane Drury, former president of the Newfoundland Club of America.

There are records in French history of a Newfoundland that was owned by Napoleon I and has been called, because of his heroic behavior, "the dog that changed history."

At the same period there are records of the heroism of Lord Nelson's Newfoundland at Trafalgar in the battle between the *Cleopatra* and the *Nymph*. Both of these are described in more detail in the chapter on working dogs.

Justifiably he has been named the hero dog.

Space prohibits the recital of all the heroic exploits of the animal. Certainly we know that in our own country's history he has played his part and has always been popular. We have many cast-iron models of the venerable creature giving us an idea of what he looked like and to indicate how popular he has been here. We hear many stories that he was the *most* popular breed during the Gay Nineties—the boon companion of the large households of that day. Since relatively few dogs were registered in those days, their actual number is difficult if not impossible to determine. We know that a great many families do remember with considerable nostalgic pride the big black dog that used to adorn their wide Victorian porches or grace their lawns along with the iron deer in that happy era.

Other countries besides England, Canada, and America were according him just recognition. In Switzerland, this was for his breeding value in fortifying the dogs at the Hospice of St. Bernard. During the winter of 1830 and again in 1856 the St. Bernard dogs came near to extinction. According to Dr. Heim, Newfoundlands were imported about this time for crossbreeding to instil new strength and disease resistance in the St. Bernard. Not long thereafter the first long-haired St. Bernard appeared. These were the only times that the St. Bernard was ever crossbred.

Other countries in Europe also have noted the exceptional qualities of the Newfoundland. A later chapter will deal with the Newfoundland in other countries.

To consider the history of the Newfoundland from the time his pedigrees and show records began to be recorded, we go first to England. It was in that country that the best records were being kept of the dog's activities. You may remember that the blacks predominated the other colors. Therefore, it is not surprising to see the plate in Colonel Hamilton Smith's *Jardine Naturalist* of "The Original Breed," dated 1840, showing a predominantly black dog even though he has a brown muzzle, cheeks, and feet, and a gray-and-white tip to his tail. Even at this time Colonel Smith was commenting about the better heads of the dogs in England as opposed to those in "our North-eastern Colonies of America." Apparently he felt that somehow the skulls of the English dogs were better domed, the muzzles less snipey.

The earliest record showing activity of the breed in England is of the Birmingham dog show of 1860 which included an entry of six Newfoundlands. A bitch imported from St. Johns and bought by Lieutenant Colonel Inge won first prize. The interest in the breed must have increased rapidly because at another show two years later the entries jumped to 41. In 1864 H.R.H. the Prince of Wales was the owner of Cabot, the winner of the London show. From 1867 through 1879 a fine black dog by the name of Cato, and owned by the Reverend S. Atkinson, appears to have been the big show winner. He was followed by Mr. Mapplebeck's Leo during the period 1875 to 1878. Modern pedigrees can be traced back to both of these fine specimens. (See pedigree chart.) First published by Vero Shaw in 1881, a plate depicting Leo shows the great similarity to our present breeding. Through almost 100 years of controlled breeding we have only deepened the muzzle and enlarged the head a little and increased the angulation of the stifle of our very best specimens.

The first registry of dogs was established in England by The Kennel Club in 1878. From then on their records make it possible to chart the history of the breed with somewhat more authority. We not only can chart pedigrees but can also keep track of show wins, although here the necessary information appears erratic at first and at times contradictory. The fact that The Kennel Club permitted owners to change their dogs' names adds to the confusion as does the fact that more than one dog of the period bears the same name. One must bear in mind also that any record keeping is limited to the integrity of the recorder. One other note on records is worthy of mention. In 1889 Dalziel in his *British Dogs* (page 172) comments on this latter point as follows:

"Although it is a natural inference from the statement 'imported' respecting a Newfoundland dog in the Kennel Club Stud Book that imported from Newfoundland is meant, it by no means follows that it certainly is so. . . . We have many good Newfoundlands from other places and some of them are said to have been 'imported' from St. Bernard kennels at home, the word imported in such instances being used by the owners who catalogue their dogs so in a purely Pickwickian sense."

Although such a comment may appear to be amusing, the action behind it is extremely dangerous to the purity of the breed. Fortunately for us such incidents occurred long ago and their effect on our pedigrees is now approaching insignificance. We must ever be on the lookout to prevent any further such dilution of our present pedigree lines. This reported activity emphasizes the importance of breeder integrity.

In 1876, in addition to the bench shows, the English held water trials both at Maidstone and Portsmouth. Later trials were also held at Alston. The English were simply refining the natural aptitudes of their dogs while making a start toward the eventual standard.

Another equally famous contemporary of Leo was Nelson I, sometimes referred to in old pedigree records simply as Nelson. Bred by Mrs. Cunliffe Lee, December 30, 1878, Nelson was apparently a little on the small size but quite typey. He was bred to innumerable bitches by his owner, Mr. E. Nichols, who apparently experimented with the line-breeding techniques which were later perfected by the owners of the famous Siki. More of Siki later. Nelson was, therefore, not only the progenitor of many present day American champions, but also one of the famous ancestors of a number of the best continental dogs. For instance, we find his name frequently at the beginning of the pedigrees of well-known Swiss dogs.

Next appearing in our pedigrees is a series of Nelson offspring that seem to have been not only excellent prize winners in their day but also did enough breeding to have passed their bloodlines down to our modern dogs. Examples of these dogs are: Ch. Courtier, Ch. Lady Mayoress, and Sybil. A full brother of all of these dogs which does not appear in our pedigrees was Black

Leo bred by Mr. William Coats 1872.

Measurements as given by Vero Shaw

Weight	149 pounds
Nose to stop	5 inches
Stop to occiput bone	7¾ inches
Length of back	34 inches
Girth of muzzle in front of eyes	14½ inches
Girth of skull	26½ inches
Girth of neck	30 inches
Girth of brisket, in front of legs	45 inches
Girth of chest behind front legs	42 inches
Girth around loins	38 inches
Girth around hind legs at stifle	22 inches
Girth of arm, 3 ins. below elbow	11 inches
Girth of pasterns	8 inches
Height at shoulders	32 inches
Height at elbow	17½ inches
Height at loins	32¼ inches
Height at hocks	8½ inches
Length of tail	24 inches
Girth of forearm	9 inches

Ch. The Black Prince

Ch. King Stuart

Nelson I

Prince (K.C.S.B. #16,199). The reader should beware of confusing this dog with his numerous namesakes which appear later in the pedigrees. We are fortunate to have a picture of the Black Prince because it shows the type which exists in the backgrounds of our modern dogs through Courtier, Lady Mayoress, and Sybil.

We are also fortunate to have the following critique which appeared in the *Stock-keeper and Fanciers Chronicle:*

"His grand head, small ears, benevolent expression, and well proportioned powerfully built body are well shown in the sketch which Mr. R. H. Moore took from life. In spite of the great massiveness of his limbs he is very active and moves with the greatest of freedom."

The first of our breed clubs was established in England in 1886. A few years later the club formulated the Standard which remains virtually unchanged even today, although in recent years some of the neophytes among breeders have drawn the erroneous conclusion that there can be many acceptable "types" among the black dogs. Even if the Standard could be interpreted in more than one way, it should certainly be obvious from the study of the pedigrees that the excellent Siki type is the ideal for which we are all striving. All the American champions during the test period came from his line.

Possibly as a result of the breed-club activities and interest, 128 Newfoundland dogs and bitches were entered in ten classes at the Preston, Lancashire, dog show of 1892. That certainly gives our modern breeders a big goal to shoot for!

English Ch. King Stuart (K.C.S.B. #36,708, whelped February 6, 1892, bred by Mr. John Milne) is the next in line of the very famous stud dogs of the breed and held an almost unparalleled record on the show bench. Although we lack his physical dimensions, we are fortunate in still having one of his old photographs taken about 1899 while he was owned by Mrs. Vale Nicolas.

Although many excellent specimens were bred in the intervening years, they all seem overshadowed by the magnificence of a dog named Siki that appeared on the show scene shortly after World War I. Bred by Mr. G. Bland on March 10, 1922, he rose quickly to become not only the most famous Newfoundland show dog in history, but the most famous stud dog of the breed. As shown in the chapter on the significance of pedigrees, every Newfoundland that attained its American championship during the years 1950 through 1954 owes at least part of his excellence to one or more of three Siki sons imported to this country and Canada between 1926 and 1935. These were Canadian Ch. Baron, imported by Mr. D. R. Oliver of St. Mary's, Ontario; Canadian Ch. Shelton Cabin Boy, imported by Montague Wallace in Saskatchewan; and Ch. Harlingen Neptune of Waseeka, imported

Later he adopted the old family farm name Westerland for his kennel. From this kennel have emanated dogs that have traveled to all parts of the globe, dogs that were famous for rescue, guardianship, and others that were best known and loved as being distinguished members of the family or group who owned them. Probably the best-known of all Newfoundland dogs, with photographs reproduced on many stamps, is Westerland Sieger. Mr. Macpherson continued his interest down through the years until his death in 1963. He served as president of the North American Newfoundland Club and also was an officer and member of the Board of Governors of the Newfoundland Club of America. (His last two dogs were sent to the Glenmire Kennels of Hugh Baird and to Dryad Kennels.)

Others who have helped the breed in early years include Miss Ada F. Coombes, whose Willinez Weather Kennels at Little Silver, New Jersey, earned her the presidency and later life membership in the North American Newfoundland Club; Mr. R. A. Gillespie of Abbotsford, Quebec, who between 1914 and 1930 bred many dogs in the ancestry of the modern American and Canadian Newfoundland. The most famous of these which appear in American pedigrees are Joan and Lady Cabot. Mr. Gillespie is also remembered for having sent Queen of Sheba (whose name was changed to Asgard) to Switzerland. There she produced four litters of very fine pups and successfully established her Canadian lines in subsequent Swiss pedigrees. A male dog sent with her went to Mr. E. Burkhard in Reiden. It is Mr. Burkhard who carried on the fine tradition often attributed to Dr. Heim, and it is he who has provided much of the modern Swiss information which is quoted by us. Josiah H. Clark of Paterson and Boonton, New Jersey, is remembered for his breeding of Clark's Prince Haakon and Laessaer Farms Tar Lassie, as well as a series of dogs with Clark's Farm as a prefix. Both Mr. Gillespie and Mr. Clark served as officers of the North American Newfoundland Club. Dr. Fenton is remembered not only as a founder of that club but also as a famous breeder of the early twenties. Still others whose names appear frequently among the early registrations are Bert Carmony of Shelbyville, Indiana; Dr. Aristine Pixley Munn of New Jersey; J. A. Graydon of New York City; Earl Thurston of Hartesville, Indiana; Joel Birkey of Fisher, Illinois; and Fred W. Probst of Linwood, Ontario.

Among the early members of the North American Newfoundland Club was Mr. John Cameron of Ossining, New York. In the early thirties he joined with Mrs. Eleanor Ayers to found the Camayer Kennels primarily to breed and promote the Landseers. Later Mrs. Ayers, then Mrs. Ralph Jameson, as owner of Seaward Kennels became well known for Ch. Oquaga's Sea Pirate, a group

Mrs. Davieson D. Power with some of her early Siki-sired stock.

winner, and her Landseers. Another well-known Landseer kennel of the thirties was the Denobie Kennels of Miss Denise O'Brien (later Mrs Frank Shay).

The name of Mr. D. C. Williams of Jordan, New York, first appears in the breeding records about 1920. After considerable experimentation, he was apparently the first American to recognize the value of Siki on future pedigrees. He imported two Siki-sired bitches, Ch. Princess Sonya and Ch. Naida, and became famous when he bred Ch. Tanya (708422) and Sancho II (489280). He served as an officer of both the North American Newfoundland Club and, when that was dissolved, as an officer of the present Newfoundland Club of America.

In 1928, following similar breeding principles used by Mr. Williams, we find Miss Elizabeth Loring (later Mrs. Davieson Power) importing Siki stock via the Harlingen Kennels to her Waseeka Kennels in Ashland, Massachusetts. Mrs. Power was largely responsible for the revitalizing of the breed in this country. From the start in imported Siki stock (Ch. Harlingen Viking of Waseeka, Ch. Harlingen Neptune of Waseeka, and Ch. Harlingen Jess) came the famous Best in Show dogs, Ch. Waseeka's Sea King, Ch. Waseeka's Sailor Boy, and Ch. Waseeka's Square

Rigger. These winners established a high standard for our breeders to emulate.

In the early 1940s, another young woman began to influence the breed, this time in California, with her Coastwise Kennels. Mrs. Hilton, later Mrs. Major B. Godsol, was training and breeding her first Newfoundlands. To her everlasting credit is the fact that she trained both the first CD and CDX Newfoundland in this country, Ch. Mark Anthony of Waseeka, CDX, was also the first of his breed to win a group on the West Coast. Recognized for her prowess as an all-breed judge not only in this country and in Canada but also in Europe, Mrs. Godsol holds the added distinction of winning the Gaines award as the outstanding judge of 1950. Her husband, Major Godsol, is not only the first judge to be approved by the AKC to judge all breeds, all obedience, and all tracking trials, but served as chairman of the Los Angeles trial board, then as AKC representative on the West Coast from 1950 through 1954. He was delegate from the Newfoundland Club to the AKC from 1947 to 1951. Both have served not only as active members and committee workers, but also as officers of the Newfoundland Club of America. The pedigree records of the

Representation of Newfoundlands in the Gay Nineties, The Golden Era of Newfoundlands.

Mrs. Geraldine Irwin and Ch. Irwindyl's General Ike.

future will demonstrate the value of their having been the breeders of Ch. Coastwise Steamboat Bill, Canadian Ch. Coastwise Shore Leave, and Ch. Coastwise Tugboat Annie.

Other breeders of note were Mr. and Mrs. Clifford Hartz of the Oquaga Kennels at Windsor, New York, known not only for having bred Ch. Oquaga's Queen Mary and Ch. Oquaga's Sea Pirate, but also for having bred some of the basic breeding stock of many of our present kennels. Though not showing to any great extent, Mrs. Barrett of the Moral View Kennels, New Palestine, Indiana, has done much to promote the breed and to make it a popular one in the Midwest.

Among kennels that came into prominence later were the Dryad Kennels of Mr. and Mrs. Drury, best known for having bred Ch. Dryad's Coastwise Showboat, a Best in Show winner; Ch. Dryad's Coastwise Gale, and Ch. Dryad's Lieutenant, probably the most prolific sire of his time. Ch. Dryad's Sea Rover, Ch. Dryad's Trademark O'Golly, and Dryad's Goliath of Gath have all influenced the breed. Another was the Midway Kennels of Mr. and Mrs. Fred Stubbart of Columbia, South Carolina, importing dogs from Newfoundland and other Canadian areas and producing many winning champions. Others getting established at this time include Mr. Alfred Forest and Mr. Bill Hart, owners of the beautiful and well-fitted Harforidge Kennels which they constructed themselves at Millington, New Jersey. Both men have served as officers and committee members for the Newfoundland Club.

About ten years later additions to the breed were begun by the Little Bear Kennels, owned by Mr. and Mrs. V. A. Chern, of Norwalk, Connecticut, and by Mrs. Arthur Irwin's Irwindyl Kennels. Mrs. Irwin has bred many dogs in her kennels and has been active in obedience-training work. Ch. Little Bear's James Thurber, a Group and Best in Show winner, was bred by the Cherns.

Ch. Oquaga's Sea Pirate, owned and shown by Seaward Kennels.

Although there are many kennels raising Newfoundlands, the only ones breeding them in 1956 were Dryad, Glenmire, Harbourbeem, Irwindyl, Little Bear, Moral View, Oquaga, and Seaward. Persons at any time interested in a current list of breeders should inquire of the Corresponding Secretary of the Newfoundland Club of America.

History of the breed clubs in this country follows:

On May 19, 1914, at the quarterly meeting of the delegates we find the American Kennel Club recognizing the first Newfoundland breed club—the Newfoundland Club of America. This organization continued with the same officers during its entire existence in Philadelphia.

President	Mr. E. J. Lame
Vice-president	Mr. R. B. Fritsch
Secretary-treasurer and delegate	Mr. C. R. Wood

There is little of record as to their accomplishments. We have seen a short folder on the breed which they published in 1926 and know that they adhered very closely to the English standard. Although we have found records of some of the dogs owned by these men there is nothing spectacular in them. We can find no surviving membership list nor any record of Specialty Shows. In other words, the organization apparently suffered by being too small or too closely controlled, and at the death of Mr. Wood, the organization was read out of the A.K.C. at the meeting of February 7, 1928, for non-payment of dues.

Another organization that struggled to do something for the breed was the North American Newfoundland Club. Since this group never joined the A.K.C., we have few positive records to rely on. From various articles written by one of its presidents, Mr. Morris, we do know that the organization was established sometime between 1922 and 1924, largely as a result of the fact that only one Newfoundland, Jake, owned by H. W. Palmer of Downsville, New York, was shown at Westminster in 1922. The officers at the time of inception were:

President	Dr. M. J. Fenton
Vice-president	Honorable Harold Macpherson
Vice-president	Mr. D. C. Williams
Secretary-treasurer	Mr. Edwin H. Morris

Mr. T. D. Dillon and Mr. Zabriskie are also mentioned as executives, possibly directors. Honorable Harold Macpherson and Mrs. Coombes later became presidents of the club.

This club not only produced many spectacular prizes and much publicity for the breed, but it also set up a very interesting standard which included among other things a list of "defects" or faults. It was also the first English-language Standard to emphasize the tremendous importance of undercoat.

In 1929 this club staged Newfoundland Water Trials at Mr. Orr's lake near Cornwall, New York. As far as can be ascertained, these are the only water trials on record so far in the United States, although many breeders have privately tested some of their dogs from time to time. Winner of these trials and a silver trophy was Billie, owned by Mrs. Vivian B. Moulton of West Woolwich, Maine.

History fails to record what became of this club. It is known that committees were appointed by both the North American Club and the present Newfoundland Club of America in an effort to consolidate. Apparently such a consolidation was unacceptable to the membership. However, most of the members of the North American Club subsequently joined the Newfoundland Club of America and the North American Club was dissolved.

Our present Newfoundland Club of America began with a meeting on February 21, 1930, at the home of Mr. and Mrs. Homer Loring at 468 Beacon Street in Boston. It was a small club, but made up of members who knew and loved the breed, and also worked hard for its improvement. The following officers were elected that first year:

President	Mr. Quentin Twachman
Vice-president	Mrs. Vivian Moulton
Treasurer	Mr. Harold Ingham
Secretary	Miss Elizabeth Loring

Apparently this organization was welcomed by the A.K.C., for on May 6 of that same year the delegates of the American Kennel Club accepted them as members. In February of the following year Mr. Twachman's credentials were accepted for the position of delegate.

Honorable Harold Macpherson was elected to the Board of Governors at the June meeting in Greenwich. The following year, at which time the Standard was proposed, Mr. D. C. Williams of Jordan, New York, became a vice-president. In those early days the club was a small, closely knit group whose members gave generously of their time, energy, and money to promote the breed. It is interesting to note how this group worked together under Mr. Twachman's direction. Although meetings were held only once or twice a year, a minimum of time was devoted to the problems of ordinary club business. Most of the administrative work was carried out by individuals or small committees. There was, therefore, considerable time in the meetings for illuminating discussions on care, feeding, veterinary problems, and breeding. Guest speakers, such as Dr. Leon Whitney and Mrs. Sherman Hoyt, appeared at the early meetings. In short, the members seemed dedicated to the principle of learning rather than preaching. Two Specialty Shows were organized—at Katonah, New York, in 1940 and 1941, held in conjunction with the North Westchester Kennel Club. As their efforts bore fruit, it became necessary to expand the club. Mr. Twachman continued as president until 1947, when the club's secretary, Mrs. Elizabeth (Loring) Power, succeeded him. During her administration the first postwar Specialty Show was held in May, 1948, at the Ladies' Kennel Association on Long Island. Forty-eight dogs were entered and Mr. Alva Rosenberg judged, giving Best of Breed to Waseeka's Jolly Sailor Boy. Six dogs from two different California kennels flew all the way East to make the show a truly national specialty. Also during her administration Mrs. Power appointed Mr. Maynard Drury to prepare the first revision of the constitution and by-laws. At the Specialty Show meeting held in the Stock Yards Inn at Chicago in March of 1950 the revised constitution and by-laws were accepted. This Chicago Specialty Show was unique in many ways. In the first place, it marks the most western of all of our annual specialty shows to then. Although only 23 dogs were entered, this was a high point in obtaining a representative cross section of Newfoundlands on this continent. Though dogs were sent from California and the East Coast, there were a number from the Midwest also. However, it was Mr. and Mrs. Leroy Page of Hamilton, Ontario, who with their kennel of two dogs won both Best of Breed, with Topsail's Captain Cook, who later became both a Canadian and American Champion, and

Best of Opposite Sex with their Oquaga's Queen Bess.

In 1947, when Mrs. Power became president, Mrs. Godsol was elected to the secretaryship of the club. At that time Mrs. Godsol revived the *Gazette* column and also set up the foundation for the future growth of the club by establishing breeder lists, publicity lists, check lists for Specialty Shows, and other useful features.

Following Mrs. Godsol as secretary was Mrs. Leroy Page of Hamilton, Ontario. During her period in office it is notable that the Newfoundland Club of America more than doubled in membership. It is to her credit that she was able to organize and efficiently administer the additional work occasioned by the sudden growth of the club.

During this period of growth certain members must be recognized for their unstinting efforts for the betterment of the breed: Mr. and Mrs. Glen Butler of Cleveland for their wins in the show ring and for their faithful attendance at every Specialty Show and club meeting, time and distance being no deterrent; Mr. and Mrs. Edgar Bahney for their work as officers of the club, and Mrs. Bahney's fostering of obedience work in the breed. Other members have been outstanding in their loyalty to the breed over the years: Mr. L. R. Lewis, as club officer (and for his Kay of Kingsley, a dog consistently a show winner which became the model for the small iron Newfoundland which Newfoundland lovers throughout the world are proud to possess); Mr. G. Gilson Terriberry served exceptionally well as treasurer of the club, and with Mrs. Terriberry was the proud breeder of the magnificent Far Horizon's Stormalong pictured in the Gallery of American Dogs.

In 1951 when Mrs. Power declared herself unavailable for further service as president, it was logical that Mrs. Godsol should succeed her. To the office she brought the experience gained as a member since 1933 and of having served as a board member, secretary, and vice-president. Additionally she brought with her the prestige of breeder, obedience trainer, and professional all-breed judge.

During her term as president, Mrs. Godsol's primary contribution to the club (in the view of many) was forming acquaintances with Newfoundland lovers in many parts of the world and inspiring many to carry on the work of improving the breed. She traveled to Europe and Hawaii in these activities.

Following Mrs. Godsol as president was Mr. Maynard Kane Drury. Mr. Drury came by his interest in the breed through his marriage to Kitty Fiske, who had joined the club in 1932. Previous to serving in the presidency, Mr. Drury had been a member of the Board of Governors and for three years was a delegate to the American Kennel Club. He had been recognized as an official judge of the breed by the American Kennel Club. During his

Mrs. Major B. Godsol with Ch. Waseeka's Skipper and Ch. Coast-wise Steamboat Bill.

term in office, the club membership grew and it was under his direction that Mrs. Katherine Baldwin was appointed to supervise the preparation for publication of the original edition of this official volume for the Newfoundland Club of America.

Elected to succeed to the office of president in 1956 was Mr. Harry Wiswell of Portland, Maine. He had long been a fancier of the breed and was owner of Cruise, a great Newfoundland ambassador. Mr. Edward Wilson was the next president. Many new committees were formed and more Specialties were held, and during the ensuing six years there was tremendous growth in the breed. Mr. Wilson had owned Newfoundlands for many years and became the proud owner of American and Canadian Champion Dryad's Tambaram of Cayuga, a Specialty Show and Group winner.

Mrs. Maynard Drury became president in 1964. She has continued operations of Dryad Kennels since the death of Maynard Drury in 1956, is a judge of Newfoundlands and several other breeds, and as Chairman of the Standards Committee guided completion of the Standard. Our Secretaries have been the life blood of our organization; we have been fortunate in having devoted ones. Rose Levy, Millie Clarke, and Mary Butler served following Lil Page. When Eleanor Gleason, our present Recording Secretary, found the load of correspondence growing, a Corresponding Secretary was elected. The Rev. Robert Curry has held that post and reports that he answered 45 letters in his first year in office and over 400 during the early part of the next year.

Bob Redwood, Doug Marshall, and Jim Schmoyer have kept our finances on an even keel throughout the years. Charles Webster has been our Delegate to the American Kennel Club. We were honored that he served a term on the Board of Directors of the A.K.C.

The Newfoundland world is indebted to several members of the Club who as Committee Chairmen encouraged the breed by their guidance and enthusiasm: Mrs. E. J. Lyons (novelties Committee), Mrs. William Kurth (Specialty Shows), Christian Cannell (Water Trials), Betty McDonnell (Obedience) and Bob Dibble (West Coast).

In 1968 the Club approved a regional plan, as suggested by Doug Marshall. To date four regional Clubs have been formed. These Clubs will be able to promote the breed through education and "fun" get-togethers on a local scale. The Newfoundland Club of America as the parent Club is encouraging these groups.

It is indeed fortunate that the registered Newfoundland has never been an overly popular dog. By being bred at a steady pace, his future as a breed is assured and yet his popularity is not so large as to lead to indiscriminate breeding just for the sake of any puppies that might only remotely resemble or be called Newfoundlands. Obviously, the steady demand for pups is an incentive to breeders to maintain a steady output of stock of the highest possible quality.

So the present-day Newfoundland stands ready to meet the challenge of the future. Whatever that future may hold in store for him, he will, we feel sure, prove himself to be readily trained to assume his proper place in future history with the same dignity and poise he has shown in the past.

REGISTRATION COMPARISON 1914 THROUGH 1968

	Newfoundlands			
Year	*AKC*	*CKC*	*Total*[3]	*All Breeds*[1]
1914	22	—	22	
15	32	—	32	
16	42	14	56	
17	18	4	22	
18	26	22	48	
19	14	5	19	
1920	36	—	36	
21	47	18	65	
22	54	7	61	
23	127	12	139	
24	138	20	158	
25	182	27	209	
26	200	39	239	59,496
27	163	60	223	57,598
28	156	61	217	52,800
29	175	127	302	48,200

REGISTRATION COMPARISON 1914 THROUGH 1968

Year	Newfoundlands AKC	CKC	Total[3]	All Breeds[1]
1930	117	86	203	48,200
31	134	88	222	46,800
32	96	115	211	47,200
33	123	123	246	59,500
34	179	140	319	60,200
35	193	138	331	72,400
36	245	111	356	84,475
37	244	105	249	84,525
38	179	85	264	82,825
39	176	77	253	80,000
1940	178	53	231	83,375
41	160	32	192	88,000
42	141	24	165	89,100
43	114	23	137	78,200
44	99	16	115	77,400
45	175	25	200	127,599
46	285	19	204	206,978
47	290	28	318	235,720
48	238	32	270	227,647
49	226	49		241,811
1950	175	34		251,813
51	161	42		264,415
52	156	27		294,242
53[2]	161	28		326,234
54	208	0		346,525
55	175	33		359,900
56	251	40		430,900
57	226	35		436,600
58	198	39		446,625
59	219	82		460,300
1960	177	63		442,875
61	209	78		493,300
62	251	71		516,800
63	361	118		568,300
64	490	165		640,300
65	571	139		722,800
66	796	229		804,400
67	850	186		885,800
68	980	271		909,300

[1] No recorded annual total registrations either for individual breeds or for all breeds were tallied by the A.K.C. prior to 1926. To obtain prior Newfoundland data, the registrations for each of the twelve-month periods were counted.

[2] The figures shown for 1953 and 1954 vary somewhat from prior computations showing 192 and 177 respectively. The reason for the change lies in the change of the calendar base for the twelve-month period ending in October to the present base of twelve months ending December 31.

[3] Registrations of dogs on the island of Newfoundland from 1923 to the time of Confederation in 1949 are not included in this table. They are left out not because of any feeling of unimportance, but rather because no reliable data are readily available.

Chapter III

The Newfoundland in Art, Literature, Lore, and Legend

ART

An approach to this subject by one who is a lover of the breed might very well be the familiar, "I don't know much about art, but I know I like Newfoundlands." Yet concession must be made to the connoisseur, not of the Newfoundland dog, but of art, especially since the names of Rubens, Velasquez, Reinagle, Lawrence, Landseer, and Renoir are associated with this part of the story.

May it suffice to say that the dog as friend and companion of man has had ageless appeal to artists of all time, and that the Newfoundland possesses a unique combination of size, conformation, dignity of expression, and legendary fame of heroic traits in his character which has appealed strongly to certain artists who have conveyed him to canvas and plate.

Whether the result belongs in the category of highest art is not in our opinion to be the judgment of this chapter, nor is it considered a requirement in a book devoted solely to a breed of dogs whose admirers consider him to be a work of highest art in his own right.

The Dog in Early Art

Just as the origin and history of the Newfoundland breed are obscured by lack of recorded fact, subject to contemporary account of explorer and traveler, and later interpretation from rcsearch into his origin, so is there a scarcity of early artistic material of that period in the development of the Newfoundland as we know him today.

However, since the chapter on origin and history places the Tibetan Mastiff and the Malossian dog in his ancestry, it seems proper to mention a few examples of art from this early period which included the dog with some characteristics that were later to be seen in the modern Newfoundland.

Early woodcut of the Newfoundland.

In the figures of the Basalt dog from the Roman epoch in France, the eighteenth-dynasty plaster dog from Egypt and the bas-reliefs from the palace of Assurbanipal (668–626) B.C. are characteristics of massive bone structure, pendent set of ear, or heavy ruff of coat on neck and shoulder that suggest the Newfoundland's ancestry and later similar forms of art devoted exclusively to the breed.

Paintings, tapestries, and hand-illuminated manuscripts of the Middle Ages included dogs of the period. For example, "The Kill," fifteenth century, from the Duc de Berry's *Books of the Hours*, or the sixteenth-century "Depart de Foret," a hand illumination for Maximilian's *Les Chasses en Chantilly*, contain dogs in beautiful detail with head outline, sloping stop, set of ear, and massive size which lend credence to the theories of his origins.

"The Country Fair" by Rubens, "Las Meninas" by Velasquez, and Sir Peter Lely's, "Earl of Romney" include large dogs in their groupings of family and country gathering with as careful attention from the artists as their human companions. Of the Velasquez, with the large mastiff-like "house dog" in the lower right foreground, Miss Margaretta Salinger of the Department of Paintings, Metropolitan Museum of Art, New York, states, "Painter and picture, child and dwarfs, dog and courtiers, all are arranged in credible eternal relation." The Newfoundland in later art, as in

"Newfoundland" by Phillip Reinagle (1749–1833).

"Newfoundland" by Orrin Smith; Illustration used by Stonehenge and Youatt.

"Newfoundland Dog," from a lithograph on stone by Thomas Doughty.

life, has maintained this "credible eternal relation," and with children in particular from his first appearance in the world of the dog.

Artists as Illustrators

After his authentication as an original breed from the account of Sir Joseph Banks in 1765, the artists who depicted the Newfoundland may be divided into two categories: those whose work was produced for the illustration of books and periodicals on natural history, or histories of the dog, and those whose works included the Newfoundland in separate works of art.

The first artist and illustrator was the prolific and talented engraver, Sir Thomas Bewick, and his plate used in *Quadrupeds*, 1790, set the style and type which have been followed even to contemporary time.

Although these artists were limited in their knowledge of the breed until 1886, when the first breeding standards were adopted, they employed their talents to give good outline prints or engravings, several of which are reproduced in our illustrations.

Typical, but nevertheless charming, is the engraving, sometimes colored, of the early English sporting artist Philip Reinagle (1749–1833). His plate in *The Sportsman's Cabinet*, London, 1803, has intelligence of expression. The background of mountains against which are the smaller figures of four Newfoundlands hauling timber gives his work a truly artistic as well as educational appeal.

Capable English illustrators, such as Vero Shaw, Vaughan Davies, Orrin Smith, and Harrison Weir were used in the nineteenth-century books on the history of dogdom. The plate of Leo, by Vero Shaw for *The Illustrated Book of the Dog*, in 1881 is a good example of this work.

In America the first expression of this type was from a lithograph on stone by Thomas Doughty for *The Cabinet of Natural History*, Philadelphia, 1830–1834. Doughty was one of our earliest and talented painters of birds and animals, and his plate of the Newfoundland is a milestone in the field of American art of this type.

Louis Agassiz Fuertes and Edwin Herbert Miner lent their capable talents to illustrate two series in *The National Geographic Magazine*, in 1918–1919, and later in 1941. The Fuertes pair, one black, the other black and white (Landseer), are bold prototypes of the modern breed. Miner's group of three in a water retrieving scene conveys the feeling of legendary feats which had become so much a part of the character of the breed. The 1958 Edition's Newfoundlands are done by Robert E. Lougheed.

On the contemporary scene such fine animal painters and illustrators as Edwin Megargee, Marguerite Kirmse, Gladys Emerson Cooke, and Ernest Hart, whose drawings are part of

"Water Retrieving Scene,"
by Edward Herbert Miner.©

Design for Diploma of the Neufundlander-Club für den Kontinent.

this book, are but a few who have contributed much, artistically, for the Newfoundland, much to the enjoyment and appreciation of all owners and lovers of this breed.

Also it must not be overlooked that such artistic expression was not limited to Great Britain and America. The Newfoundland knows no geographic or ethic boundaries. Artists in Germany, as, for example, the design of the diploma for the *Newfundlander Club fur den Kontinent*, the Italian dry point by Amos Nattini, the French etching of the Newfoundland retrieving a mallard duck, the painting by the French artist Alfred De Dreux, the many expressions from the country of his origin, Newfoundland, show the universality of this wide company of artists and illustrators.

Space will not permit mention of all of these talented people, but the selected illustrations and bibliography will, it is hoped, speak more eloquently than words!

Sporting Artists, Animal Painters, and Others:

The Pre-Landseer Period

In the early nineteenth century a British sporting artist, Ben Marshall (1767–1835), who had studied under L. F. Abbott as a portrait painter, was said to be so impressed with Sawrey Gilpin's 1793 Academy picture "The Death of the Fox," that he turned from human to animal portraits. As Mr. Guy Paget (*Sporting Pictures of England*, London, 1945) has commented:

"Strictly speaking, Ben Marshall remained a portrait painter and a very good one too. He is not essentially a sporting artist. The portrait comes first and the sport second. . . . Ben Marshall is a brilliant colorist and a powerful delineator of character."

In his first period (1791–1804) Marshall painted Chestnut Hack, a dark bay pony accompanied by two boys and a dog. The dog in the left-hand corner of this painting is a black-and-white Newfoundland, not yet in Marshall's time to be identified with the name Landseer. (Reproduced from George Stubbs and Ben Marshall by Walter Shaw Sparrow in *Sport of Our Fathers* series, London, Cassell & Co., Ltd.; New York, Charles Scribners Sons, 1929.)

In Marshall's second period (1805–1820) he painted in 1811 "Self Portrait of the Artist with His Newfoundland Dog," an attractive painting with the artist as the central character, his dog a companion piece.

In 1814 *Sporting Magazine* published an engraving *after Marshall* associating painter and subject with a memorable anecdote. The subject is Satan, a large black Newfoundland, and his piebald chestnut-and-white pony friend. According to the legend, when Satan was a puppy, perhaps a leggy six months, owner unknown, lived about the racing stables at Newmarket,

Self-portrait of Ben Marshall with his Newfoundland dog.

England. One day the artist, who was living at Newmarket during this period and painting horses on commission, was walking about with a Mr. Welliman, owner of several racing horses, watching a horse, Mary Andrew, being exercised. The horse broke, throwing the rider, and ran away headed in the direction of Marshall and his friend. Satan is said to have run for the pony, jumping and grasping it firmly by the nose, and holding it until it could be caught. This stirred the artist to paint the incident for posterity. Of Satan's further activities his owner went on to say:

"He would, without tuition, knock at the door of any house he wished to gain admittance, and if one rap with the knocker was not sufficient to obtain admission, he would give a double and treble one, as correctly as any puppy of the biped species."

This is a rare painting of Marshall's that is not often reproduced and present whereabouts is unknown. It is interesting to note that the two Newfoundlands were all black whereas most of the Newfoundlands of the earlier period were portrayed as black and white, brown and white, or russet.

The Newfoundland puppy "Satan" and chestnut-marked pony.

"A Distinguished Member of the Humane Society," by Sir Edwin Landseer, 1837.

Marshall's pupil, Abraham Cooper, R.A. (1787–1863), produced several paintings with Newfoundlands. "Newfoundland Dog with Fox" was reproduced in at least one of the early sporting periodicals. Marshall's work included one very good head of a Newfoundland. Edmund Bristow, painting during the same period, did one of a Newfoundland, Beauty, said to be a favorite of King George III, and the engraver J. Bateman did the very attractive "Prince George's Favorites" or "My Pack."

These artists were younger contemporaries of Philip Reinagle whose Newfoundland dog was reproduced in Taplin's *Sportsman's Cabinet*. Reinagle's acquaintance with the Newfoundland undoubtedly influenced these painters, and we know that they encouraged a young painter of almost precocious talent by the name of Edwin Landseer (1802–1873) to exhibit at shows staged by the Society of Painters in oil and water colors, aware, perhaps, of the genius that was soon to flower.

When in 1837 Sir Edwin Landseer laid aside his palette and the completed "A Distinguished Member of the Humane Society" sat on the easel ready for its first public exhibition at the 1838 Royal Academy show in London, it may be said that the Newfoundland in art had reached his highest point of perfection. Such was the sentiment of the artist for dogs of all breeds and especially for his own Newfoundlands, and such the growing popularity in the English dog world of this comparative new-

"My Pack," by J. Bateman.

This oil painting, estimated to have been made about 1820, was purchased in England in 1968 by a Minneapolis art dealer. The 18″ × 24″ painting is unsigned. The dog's eyes are brown and very expressive.

comer from far-off shores, that Landseer here combined both physical conformation with facial expression of heroic dignity that entranced the public.

Bob, who was the "Distinguished Member," was a well-known character about London. According to legend and recorded fact, he was reported to have twice been shipwrecked with his master, once swimming with him from the wreckage two miles off England to safety, but the second time having to leave his master drowning in the wreckage to swim alone to shore. He then made his way to London and, as a stray, gained public fame along the Thames water front, saving several individuals from drowing. Bob was adopted by the Royal Humane Society and awarded a gold medal, with a special roving commission to save lives. His record stands officially at twenty-three rescues in fourteen years of service before his death. Bob was not available to sit for Landseer but the artist had seen a Newfoundland, Paul Pry, owned by Mrs. Newton Smith, carrying a basket of flowers along the street, and he engaged this model and posed him on a table in his studio at St. John's Wood Road, London, applying his fine technical skill and feeling for his subject to this very important painting insofar as Newfoundlands are concerned. It hangs today in the Tate Art Gallery in London. Soon after a "Distinguished Member" appeared, it was a poor household that did not have a copy on its walls, and indeed what contemporary American does not recall with nostalgia his first acquaintance with the reproduction of this painting which became a favorite with printmakers in America.

The "Distinguished Member," of course, was not the first Newfoundland painted by Sir Edwin. Fifteen years earlier he

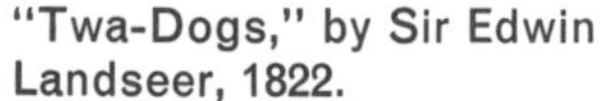

"Twa-Dogs," by Sir Edwin Landseer, 1822.

"The Late Duchess of Teck as a Child," engraved by Thomas Landseer from a painting by Sir Edwin Landseer.

had painted "Twa Dogs," inspired by Robert Burns's poem by that name. The Newfoundland was Mr. Gosling's Neptune in contemplative pose with Luarth, a Scottish sheep dog. It is known that Landseer actually did competent sketches before he was six; by seven he could not only draw but etch, and at the age of thirteen had accepted for exhibition by the Royal Academy a picture of a pointer bitch and puppy. There may have been an earlier Newfoundland in this collection.

Using the black-and-white two years later, he did a head of Neptune, shown herein for comparison with heads of Newfoundlands done in later periods by other artists. Lion, a Newfoundland, was painted in 1824. He did a head of Bob in 1853.

Landseer was socially acceptable to the royal family as well as to the general public, and his painting of the Duchess of Teck, later the mother of Queen Mary, grandmother of the present Queen Elizabeth, belongs to this period.

It is pure speculation to assume that Landseer knew how powerful his influence was, how much he was influencing the Newfoundland breed, or how controversial his black-and-white type had become in the world of dogs. Whether he was conscious of this or not, it was so, and Hugh Dalziel in *British Dogs*, London, 1889, writes:

"Landseer, having immortalized a black-and-white dog, Newfoundland type, in his painting, "A Distinguished Member of the Humane Society," made this variety too popular to be ignored by fashion, which is most arbitrary in those cases, and had determined that all black should be the color of Newfoundland dogs; fashion, therefore, finding itself opposed by genius which was popular, very wisely entered into a compromise by setting up two classes of Newfoundlands, and in honor of genius, calling the black-and-white sort the Landseer Newfoundland. To Dr. Gordon Staples belongs the honor of first naming the black-and-white variety the Landseer Newfoundland."

Also Vero Shaw in the *Illustrated Book of the Dog* (1879) claims "that Sir Edwin had corrupted the public mind" and that he only chose the black and whites because their coloring made a brighter picture. Vero Shaw in his book, uses a black, Leo, that had been referred to in the chapter on origin and history.

This controversy is not entirely behind us. Landseer is in the contemporary official standard. However, present-day controversy is merely one to clarify and not to remove from the black and white his "immortalized" name.

After 1844 Landseer suffered from a mental depression which to some extent influenced his work. His later animals have almost human expressions and attitudes. In the Newfoundlands, two in particular, "Saved" (1856) and, to a lesser degree, a companion picture "He Is Ready," captured the imagination of the enterprising and prolific firm of Currier and Ives of New York. In their voluminous listings no less than four titles were offered for sale:

"He Is Saved"
Currier and Ives, undated, 8.14 x 12.7
"Newfoundland Dog"
Currier and Ives, undated, small
"Newfoundland Dog"
N. Currier, undated, 8.3 x 11.3
"To the Rescue"
Currier and Ives, undated, 7.13 x 12.7

It is significant that these were classed in the great group of sentimentals. Obviously the dog's coat seems scarcely wet and the figure of the child quite dry and her buttoned boots still nicely shined. Mr. John Cameron, noted breeder of the Camayer Kennels, relates the story of a man who came to his kennels to buy his first Landseer Newfoundland and, seeing Mr. Cameron's copy of "Saved," stood for some time in quiet contemplation, then, sighing, said, "Well, no wonder the little kid is exhausted, hauling that great dog out of the water!"

"He is Saved," by Currier and Ives.

"Saved", from a painting by Sir Edwin Landseer as reproduced in The Perry Pictures.

Early Landseer school, about 1840.

Please also note that these reproductions are not exact copies of Landseers. The black-and-white markings are altered somewhat. This probably excused the firm of Currier and Ives from giving direct acknowledgment to the artist!

When the great firm of Currier and Ives passed out of existence, these titles were reproduced by other firms in processes newer than lithographing from stone. Typical is the collection offered by Perry Pictures of Malden, Massachusetts. They, however, offered their works duly copyrighted (1906) and properly accredited to Landseer.

The fact remains that after Landseer's *chef-d'œuvre* of 1837 no other artist has painted such a Newfoundland, and the field is open for the artist who will one day do as much for the all black.

Post-Landseer and Contemporary

The story of the Newfoundland in art might very well have stopped with Landseer except that it must be remembered that

"Madame Charpentier and Her Children," by Renoir (1841–1919). Courtesy of the Metropolitan Museum of Art.

the Newfoundland was endearing himself to more and more owners and has found his special place as companion of man, and artistic expression continued after Landseer and doubtless will go on and on. Therefore, the story of the Newfoundland in painting would not be complete without including "Mme. Charpentier and Family," painted during his impressionistic period by Pierre Auguste Renoir, 1878. The black and white of the Newfoundland dog lying at the feet of the two young daughters not only unites the grouping of the picture in its "eternal relation" as did the earlier Velàsquez, but it furnishes the artist with opportunity to express contrasts in texture with the black and whites of the little girls' dresses and the gown of Mme. Charpentièr. When a copy of this painting was requested from the Publications Shop counter of the Metropolitan Museum of Art, the young lady making the sale exclaimed, "I am so glad you are using this painting. He is my favorite dog in the whole museum!" A detail from this painting, showing only the small girls and dog, has been reproduced in a work on Renoir and his painting.

Although it is true that contemporary painters have not used the Newfoundland to express their art, several contemporary animal painters have done exceedingly fine paintings of Newfoundlands. These are sometimes portraits of favorites commissioned by their owners. Mr. Edwin Megargee's head of Waseeka's Crusoe done in 1941 for the Dryad Kennels is an example. Another is the French crayon drawing of Sue who was owned by Mrs. Lovett Garceau of Woodstock, Vermont. In acquiring permission to use this drawing, we were told that this dog's registered name was Aïda and that her expression, as drawn in 1940 by Howard Proctor, was one she always assumed when listening to her favorite musical piece, *Celeste Aïde*. Just for interest compare

Mr. Gosling's "Neptune," by Sir Edwin Landseer.

Mrs. Garceau's "Sue," by Howard Proctor.

"The President," by H. H. Couldrey; original owned by Mr. and Mrs. M. B. Godsol.

"My Dog," by Sir Edwin Landseer.

Mr. and Mrs. Drury's "Waseeka's Crusoe," by Edwin Megargee.

Captain Samuel Samuels on the deck of *Dreadnought* with his dog Wallace. Painting by Gordon Johnson, courtesy of the Atlantic Companies.

Coke Smyth's *Moose Hunter*, a hand-colored lithograph from the series *Sketches in the Canadas* (1839). Courtesy the Montreal Museum of Fine Arts.

these with the earlier head of Mr. Gosling's Neptune by Sir Edwin Landseer.

Insofar as art is expressed in paintings, and as illustrations and separate works, this completes the story which is in fact only an introduction to the appended reference list of paintings available.

Other Forms of Art or Illustration

Postage Stamps: It is natural to expect that the Canadian homeland of the Newfoundland should have commemorated its famous breed in at least one stamp issue. In point of fact there are several which feature the Newfoundland.

In its native land the Newfoundland dog first appeared on a stamp issued in 1887, when the half-cent rose appeared. This stamp shows the head of a Newfoundland, with white muzzle and narrow white blaze reaching to dome, typical marking of the Landseer-type Newfoundland. The head is circled by a dark band with the word *Newfoundland* in white lettering on the upper part and *half cent* on the lower half. This issue was engraved and printed by the American Bank Note Company, Montreal, P.Q. This design was reissued in 1894, in black, and in 1896, in orange-red.

It is believed the dog used as a model was Watch owned by Mr. Macpherson's grandfather, Henry Duder, who came to Newfoundland in 1833. The kennel name Westerland takes its name from the Macpherson family farm there. Lieutenant-Colonel Cluny Macpherson, famous inventor of the gas mask well remembers calling for Watch and Min, a pair of Newfoundland puppies, in the early eighties.

There is no doubt about the dog in the next design. It is the famous Ch. Westerland Sieger, a fine black whelped in Newfoundland, June 22, 1929, and chosen because of his reputation as the best specimen of his breed in Newfoundland, when Perkins Bacon and Company, the London banknote firm, was requested to produce the 1931 series for Newfoundland and a native dog had to be selected for use of the fourteen-cent denomination. Sieger is shown against a white background with black border, on which appears the words *Newfoundland postage*, and *fourteen cents* in white lettering. This stamp first appeared in the industrial issue 1931–1937 and is known as the fourteen-cent black. The same picture was used on the long Coronation stamp, when the whole set was redesigned to include a portrait of the new British monarch, King George VI, in 1937. Westerland Sieger shares the stamp vignette with King George VI and is the only dog to have been so honored. The fourteen-cent black was reissued in 1941–1944, with some slight change in the perforation and in the printing of the black border.

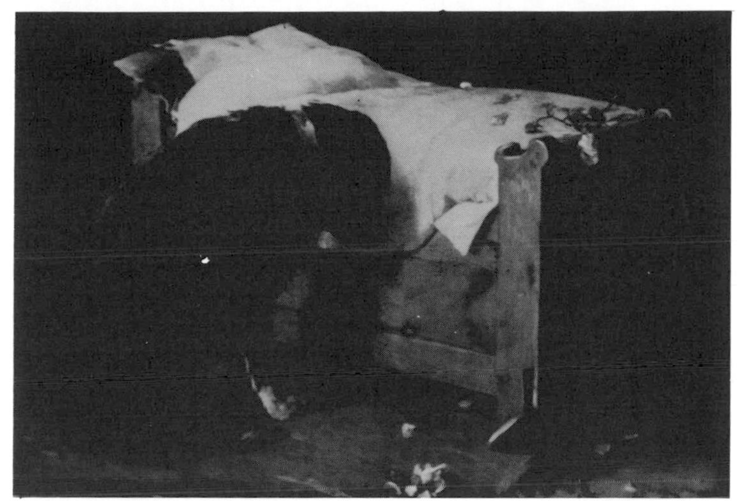

The Lost Playmate, a copperplate by Gustave Henry Mosler. Courtesy A. G. P. van Zijl, Holland.

Robert E. Lougheed's Newfoundlands as they appeared in *The National Geographic* magazine. Copyright 1958 by National Geographic Society.

1. Half-cent reissue of 1894. 2. Half-cent rose. 3. Fourteen-cent Black. 4. Coronation Long. 5. St. Pierre and Miquelon, 1932. 6. St. Pierre and Miquelon, 1941, "Free France" surcharge. 7. St. Pierre and Miquelon, 1938, Dog Team. 8. St. Pierre and Miquelon, 1941, "Free France" surcharge.

St. Pierre and Miquelon has also issued stamps featuring Newfoundland dogs. In 1932 appeared a full-grown black Newfoundland standing on some rocks by the water's edge and looking out toward the open sea. This design is on eleven different stamps valued from five centimes to three francs and was also reissued with surcharge *France Libre* in 1941.

In 1938–1940 a stamp was issued by St. Pierre and Miquelon with a very pleasant design, showing two men in winter dress preparing their sled and team of Newfoundland dogs, with a row of snow-covered houses in the background, the whole scene reminiscent of a northern lumber camp. This design was used in eight different values 2, 3, 4, 5, 10, 15, 20, and 25 centimes. This stamp was also reissued for Free France in 1941.

While other dogs appear on stamps as part of the main design, the Newfoundland was, with one exception until recent years, the only dog to be the main feature of the stamp, chosen because he typifies a breed that has earned wide fame for its characteristic loyalty, utility, and fearlessness. (Certain governments have lately resorted to a revenue producing ploy and issued stamps with such designs as dogs and cats which appeal to children and induce purchase for collection without intention of using the stamps for postage.)

BOOKPLATES, EMBLEMS, ET CETERA: The Newfoundland dog, as one of the few dogs originating in America, has been honored on the bookplate used for the American Kennel Club library and is reproduced herewith by permission. This plate was adopted in 1935 after a design by Edwin Megargee and is a credit and honor to the breed.

In 1942 in *Dogs*, edited and illustrated by Edwin Megargee, the artist designed a canine coat of arms in honor of truly American dogs, and in this figure you will see the Newfoundland in what might be said is the place of honor at the head of the table!

The club insignia, the Newfoundland Club of America figure adopted by the club in 1952, was designed and is used on club stationery and medal awards. It is a composite figure and perhaps as such lacks the personal charm of portraits of a particular dog.

The letterhead and bookplate of The Newfoundland Club, in England, designed by their member Mr. Pettit is also reproduced here with their kind permission.

The club insignia of the Trenton Kennel Club, New Jersey, is that of a Newfoundland head, one of the few show clubs in this country that has adopted this breed for its official emblem.

POTTERY AND PORCELAIN: The authors and collaborators know of no famous statue of the Newfoundland. This somehow does not seem to be right, for surely somewhere there exists a tribute from the hands of sculptor or modeler. However, in the smaller

Bookplate of the
American Kennel Club.

figures, the Staffordshire potters and their predecessors, successors, and imitators reproduced figures of most of the popular breeds of dogs. In this group are many large dogs with heavy coat, black-and-white marking, and Newfoundland-like conformation. Typical perhaps is a pair in the collection of Mrs. Charles D. Webster of Islip, Long Island. She believes them to be late nineteenth century and would definitely fit into the Landseer conception prevalent during that period.

Contemporary figures of dogs are produced in woodcarvings, baked enamel and china. All breeds are usually included. These can be seen in shop windows and are often displayed at dog shows. They are attractive, but as art, we shall say no important work of this nature is known.

This Newfoundland, triumphant over its serpentine enemy, was sculpted in marble in England.

Letterheads of the Newfoundland Club of America and the Newfoundland Club (in England).

NEWFOUNDLAND CLUB OF AMERICA

THE NEWFOUNDLAND CLUB

THE ORIGINAL NEWFOUNDLAND CLUB FOUNDED IN 1886 TO ESTABLISH THE STANDARD AND TYPE FOR THE BREED NOW ACKNOWLEDGED BY NEWFOUNDLAND CLUBS THROUGHOUT THE WORLD.

President:
Mr. D. F. Blyth
Vice-President:
Miss K. I. Herdsman
Hon. Treasurer:
Mrs. C. Handley
26 Vista Ave., Enfield, Middx.
Hon. Secretary:
Mrs. Chas. Roberts
Harlingen, Hendon Wood Lane,
Barnet Gate, N.W.7.

China Cup.

Wedgwood Plate.

Staffordshire Models of Newfoundlands.

Cast Iron Newfoundlands "Sailor" and "Canton" in Baltimore, Maryland.

CAST METAL FIGURES: Reference has been made to the large cast figures of animals including dogs which once were considered a necessary part of the Victorian home landscaping plan. Today, in motoring about the countryside in the United States, Canada, and the British Isles, the traveler may often come upon this figure of a Newfoundland on doorstep, lawn, or tavern stoop.

Most famous perhaps as a pair are Sailor and Canton flanking the entrance to the Koppers Company, Bartlett Hayward Division, at Baltimore, Maryland, commemorating the rescue in 1804 of two Newfoundlands of this name by the ship *Canton* from a sinking English brig. These dogs were cast in the 1850's during the peak of demand for such fashionable curiosities. The animals, which had been ordered by an English gentleman, were rescued from a foundering ship en route to England.

Kay of Kingsley, who served as the model for the small cast iron figures produced for Mr. L. R. Lewis.

Another pair typical of this odd expression of art are blacks, one facing up the street and the other down, at the entrance to the Hawley Manor, a well-known inn at Woodbury, Connecticut. Bearing the name of the J. L. Mott Iron Works on the pedestal, these dogs have been in the Marcus Hawley family for years and acquisition date is unknown.

Gracing the lawn at Little Bear Kennels is a handsome large iron Newfoundland of this period. A pair was recently removed from the Manor at Gardiner's Island to Sherwood Forest, the plantation of John Tyler.

As written by Mr. Alexander C. Brown in a Sunday feature article of the *Daily Press* of Newport News, Virginia: It is a tribute to the character of the Newfoundland dog that the greater part of these iron watchdogs were molded in the line of this noble and gentle breed.

Smaller in size, but with no less sentimental association, is a cast figure of the Newfoundland dog conceived and designed to special order by Mr. L. R. Lewis, longtime member of the Newfoundland Club of America, who has presented castings to a number of members of the club.

The magazine *Antiques*, in a short article in 1929, reports a small glass figure of cast-iron mold of a Newfoundland, which is one of the few instances on record of the use of the Newfoundland in pressed glass.

SAMPLERS, TAPESTRIES, HOOKED RUGS, ET CETERA: Products of the Victorian and early twentieth century era, full of sentiment and sentimentalized figures, quite frequently have as their subject a large dog which the lover of Newfoundlands would be only too glad to swear boldfacedly were in fact true representations, but usually the large and shaggy-tailed creature so lovingly worked in yarn or rag may be described as having most of the faults and few of the correct points of the breed. One such example in the writer's library is done in chocolate brown with lovely cream-colored ears and is dated April, 1883.

Other Victorian expressions in *objets d'art*, were found in rough reproductions of Newfoundlands cast in various shapes, such as the penny banks, nutcrackers, doorstops, and similar objects of the era.

CARTOONS AND COMICS: Prior to the creation of the current crop of death-dealing comics gaited to a nuclear world, there regularly appeared in the old New York *Sun* and other papers a syndicated comic strip created by Clifford McBride, and featuring a delightful pair of characters known as Napoleon and Elby. The original Napoleon was undoubtedly a St. Bernard, but was outlived and succeeded by Flintridge Rollo, a Newfoundland well known in the community and always participating in the annual

Rose Bowl Parade at Pasadena, California. His character and his association throughout his comic-strip-life were in the true Newfoundland tradition.

Creator of a shadowy outline of a very much Newfoundland-like dog was James Thurber in the days before his eyesight had failed, and many an early issue of *The New Yorker* contained at least one of Thurber's dogs. Appropriately, one of the breed's contemporary champions of record, owned by Mr. and Mrs. Robert Dowling of New York, carried with dignity the name of James Thurber.

PHOTOGRAPHY: The first use of photography in illustrating breeds of dogs was in the year 1872 when *Dogs* by Henry Webb was published. It set a precedent for use of more and more photographic reproductions from life to illustrate books of this nature. A few of these are mentioned in the bibliography. However, on the level of art, a fine example of the use of photography is in the Gallery of American Dogs, and the photograph there of Mr. G. Gilson Terriberry's Far Horizons' Stormalong is a classic.

To encourage the Newfoundland owner in his photographic efforts, the following tips have been offered by Miss Evelyn Shafer, well-known dog photographer. It is often difficult to get good results because of the Newfoundland's size, and particularly with the all blacks.

1. Try for a light background, either in the middle of the lawn or driveway.
2. Pose your dog so that full light falls across him from tail to head to minimize any shadows.
3. The ideal light is on a day when the sun is hidden by a light overcast so that there are no sharp shadows.
4. If it is a bright, sunny day with no overcast, use a flash bulb to "wash out" sharp shadows and show up the detail of coat.

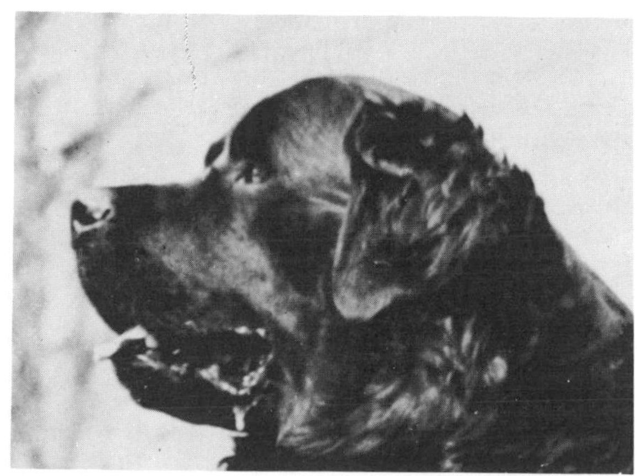

"Stormalong."

5. Don't pose your Newfoundland so that he faces the sun for he will protest; out comes his tongue, and his squint will spoil his usual expression.

6. Use more exposure than for the human skin because he is a dark object.

7. Photographing early in the day, before the dog is fed, will usually result in getting a more alert and lively expression. An occasional tidbit as reward for patience may effectively be offered during the posing session.

8. Success may be more assured if another person can help, perhaps to pose the dog with light lead, or if only to stand beside you to encourage his attention.

LITERATURE

Although his appearance in literature by name was delayed until the late eighteenth century when his breed was first reported by early traveler and naturalist, the Newfoundland dog through his common heritage must, it seems, share in all of the early literature and legendary account of the dog. To deny him this would be to deny that he possess the traits of character which have interested writers from our earliest ages.

Mr. A. Croxton Smith in his delightful chapter on the dog in literature reminds us: "When the goddess Fidelity was lost she was found in a dog kennel. This old legend has inspired incomparable Homer whose Argos stands for what is most endearing in the canine character."

As he recalls it for us, the exiled Ulysses returning home from his travels approaches his palace, accompanied by Eumaeus, the swineherd, and is unrecognized by anyone. As they walk along, Ulysses, ragged and speaking as a stranger, they come upon his dog Argos lying on a dunghill, half starved and tick-ridden, and, as translated by T. E. Shaw (Lawrence of Arabia) in 1932, Homer wrote: "This was Argos whom Odysseus bred but never worked because he left for Ilium too soon . . . yet the instant Odysseus approached, the beast knew him. He thumped his tail and dropped his ears forward but lacked the power to drag himself ever so little toward his master."

However, Odysseus saw him out of the corner of his eye and brushed away a tear which he covered by quickly saying to Eumaeus in an offhand way: "Strange that they let such a hound lie on the dung hill! What a beauty to look at! Though of course he cannot tell if he has speed to match or is merely one of those show dogs men prize for their points."

Eumaeus then tells the stranger that he wouldn't have recognized the dog if he had seen him when his owner had him but that he is not cared for and neglected, and, as they pass him by toward the palace, Homer writes, "But Argos the dog went down

Newfoundland giving spaniel-puppy a swimming lesson.

into the blackness of death that moment he saw Odysseus again after twenty years."

To deny the Newfoundland even the sentimental association with this ancestral and legendary dog possessing the eternal traits which all dogdom have inherited, association with a figure touched by the gods of Olympus, would, it seems to us, be thoroughly unfair.

For from the first mention of him the Newfoundland graces the passages of literature in his own right, swimming with powerful stroke in rescues from the sea, moving with his easy, rolling gait on errands ashore, worker for man, sometimes actor, model of virtue for the young, always a joyous, loyal companion and member of the family, literary and living alike.

IN NATURE STUDIES: "The Bear dog is of very large Size, commonly sluggish in his Looks but he is very watchful. He comes from Newfoundland. His business is to guard the Court or House and has an unendearing Voice when Strangers come near him, and does well to turn a Water Wheel."

So wrote "A Person of Quality" in a book on dogs published in England in 1732. He was writing of the dog that was later (1765) reported by Sir Joseph Banks in his journals as a new breed and a dog that was to be illustrated and described with measurement in *British Quadrupeds*, written and illustrated by Sir Thomas Bewick. Accompanying the illustration and description was an account which was to be repeated, embellished, and retold, which Bewick cited, to demonstrate "the great sagacity" of this newly discovered member of the dog world.

It is the story of a shipwreck off Yarmouth and in Bewick's words: "A Newfoundland dog alone escaped to shore bringing in his mouth the Captain's pocketbook. He landed amidst a number of people, several of whom in vain endeavored to take it from him. He would not give it up at first. The sagacious animal acted as if sensible of the importance of the charge in all probability delivered to him by his perishing master. He at length leapt fawningly on the breast of a man who had attracted his notice and delivered the book to him. The dog immediately returned to the place where he had landed and watched with attention for everything that came from the wrecked vessel, seizing them and endeavoring to bring them to land."

Thus from the first a Newfoundland's great ability to swim, his particular association with the saving of human lives or objects belonging to his master, were traits that singled him out from other breeds as story upon similar story was written.

The naturalist writers from the time of Bewick, when including the Newfoundland dog, repeated the Bewick story. Dog historians, whose first purpose was to instruct and inform, included at least the account of the wreck off Yarmouth and as time went on were able to add additional stories of his exploits. Space permits mention of only a few examples from this group of naturalist writers and dog historians.

In Jardine's *Naturalist*, Edinburgh, 1840, Lieutenant-Colonel Charles Hamilton Smith, mentions not only the Bewick account but a further story of the Newfoundland that is sighted from the masthead of a ship in the middle of the Bay of Biscay. A small boat was lowered and the swimmer taken aboard, said to be showing no sign of fatigue. The dog became a pet of Colonel Smith for a time but was lost again at sea. The inference is that he must have been a wanderer at heart and undoubtedly was picked up again at sea.

About the same period in America the *Cabinet of Natural History* in Philadelphia, 1830–1834, introduces the Newfoundland as follows: "The greater number of naturalists who have written professedly on these or similar subjects have made no mention at all of a dog of this appellation. . . .

"The Newfoundland dog, in a state of purity, uncontaminated by the blood of any inferior race, is one of the most majestic and awefully attractive of all the canine variety."

Captain Brown in 1821 wrote that when he was visiting opposite to Falmouth, at breakfast with a gentleman, a large Newfoundland dripping with water came into the room with a newspaper and laid it on the table. The gentleman informed the captain that the dog swam regularly across the ferry every morning, went to the post office, and obtained the papers of the day.

Further to illustrate what the Newfoundland could learn is a most charming tale of a magistrate of Harbour Grace whose Newfoundland was trained to carry a lighted lantern at night for his master, stopping and proceeding as the master went about his rounds. Furthermore, if the magistrate went visiting and was needed at home, his Newfoundland was sent out with his lantern to fetch his owner. He would stop at each house where he thought the magistrate might be, would put the lantern down, growl, and "beat at the door" until someone came. But if the magistrate was not there, he went on until he was found, and it was said it took only one visit to a house to enable the Newfoundland to remember to stop there again if sent out to fetch his master.

One of the respected English naturalist writers of the nineteenth century, Reverend Thomas Pearce, who wrote under the nom de plume "Idstone," includes in *The Dog* his version of the Bewick anecdote but adds as a fact that this Newfoundland was afterward owned by a Lord Granville who kept him at his estate near Dropmore until his death and then wrote his epitaph in Latin with English translation.

Hugh Dalziel, another of the respected English dog historians, includes the Bewick version but also adds the story of his own Newfoundland that carried the mailbags from the village post office to the Carlisle and Glasgow mail coach.

Contemporary, too, were many definitive articles and publications by *The Field*, an English sporting magazine. In one entitled "Stonehenge," on the dog, Mr. J. H. Walsh includes the story of the Newfoundland, Cato, owned by a Reverend Atkinson who, while strolling along the shore, noticed two young ladies who had gotten out of their depth while bathing. The Reverend attempted their rescue, but when his own swimming strength failed he called for his companion Cato to come to the rescue, which Cato did, saving all three.

In *The American Book of the Dog*, Mr. G. O. Shields adds the example from life of a Newfoundland in New Jersey that met the mail train every day. This Newfoundland knew which was the mail train out of dozens passing daily through but could also, it was said, tell Sunday schedule from weekday.

Edward C. Ash, in *Dogs, Their History and Development in 1923* adds to the lifesaving lore a new trait, telling of a Newfoundland that became so disgusted at a small spaniel that would not swim out to a nearby boat that the Newfoundland seized the spaniel by the scruff of the neck, and proceeded to give him a swimming lesson as shown in the illustration included herein.

In the 1932 series by Freeman Lloyd in the *American Kennel Club Gazette* the earliest Bewick account was repeated along with many more incidents which time had added to the original story.

It must be remembered that the purpose of these naturalist writers and dog historians was primarily to describe the dog according to latest type and breeding standards and to tell something of its nature and personality, and that each borrowed from the others and added their own anecdotes. Such capable works as *The Book of the Dog*, edited by Brian Vesey-Fitzgerald, published in 1948, are examples of contemporary literature about the dog, which include many references to the Newfoundland, bringing him up to date from the earliest Bewick account.

CHILDREN'S BOOKS: While the naturalists and dog historians were including anecdotes with their descriptions of the Newfoundland dog, the people who really appreciated him were the writers of books for children, both natural history and juvenile tale. This was easy to understand because the Newfoundland was a "natural." He was an original breed only recently discovered in a rather wild and mysterious part of America. He was big and brave. He saved lives. He was loyal and he was gentle, especially with children. So from the first he was "adopted" as the ideal dog to demonstrate

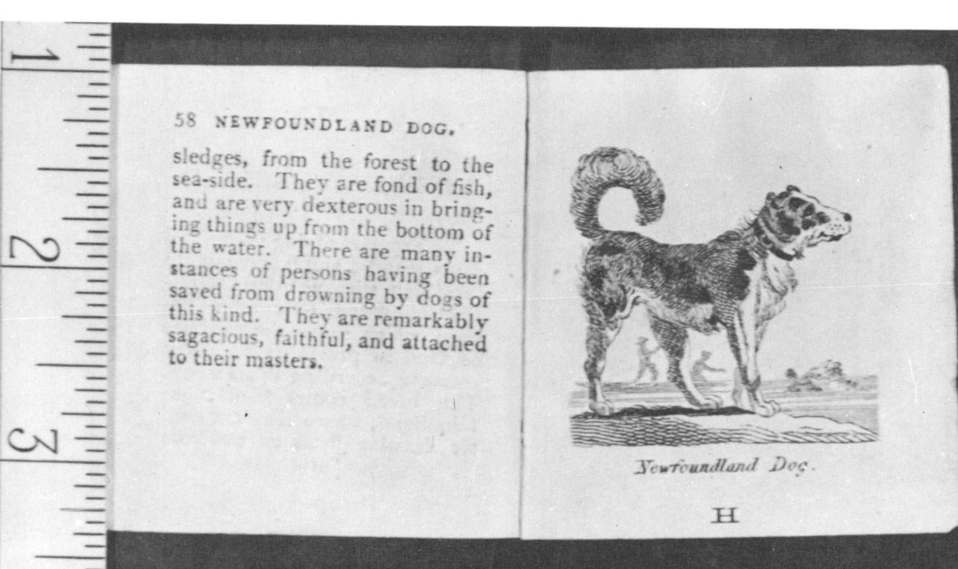

58 NEWFOUNDLAND DOG.

sledges, from the forest to the sea-side. They are fond of fish, and are very dexterous in bringing things up from the bottom of the water. There are many instances of persons having been saved from drowning by dogs of this kind. They are remarkably sagacious, faithful, and attached to their masters.

Newfoundland Dog.

H

"Beasts," 1815.

to the very young, by example after example, how they could find virtues in a dog that they themselves should have.

I am the noble Newfoundland,
  My voice is loud and deep;
I keep a watch all through the night
  While other people sleep.
Late Nineteenth-century children's song—Anonymous.

For this section, Children's Books, we are fortunate to have had access to the great Osborne collection of children's books in the Public Library at Toronto and we find there one of the earliest of the child's naturalist books which includes an extraordinary number of the early children's books about animals. Many of these, as you will see from the Appendix attached, of the late nineteenth century were illustrated with engravings by Thomas or John Bewick or possibly one of their apprentices. A charming example is the natural history of forty-eight quadrupeds published in London in 1815 under the binder's title of *Beasts*. Note particularly the text.

These works often included the Bewick account but were also likely to include some additional fact which endeared the Newfoundland to the writers as, for example, in 1813 in *The Natural History of Quadrupeds for Children*, Anthony of the Decoy tells of Newfoundlands being used to pull sledges in Kamchatka.

Illustrations from children's books of the 1880's.

"Dandie Counting His Money."

One of the classic stories and oft repeated was that of Dandie who had been trained by his family to fetch each day from the baker a small loaf of bread which was his ration. For this he was usually given a penny which he carried to the shop to lay on the counter in payment for his bread. He was well known along the way, and often a neighbor might give him another penny. One day he was given a bad penny, and when the baker refused him the bread and, shaking his head, handed back the bad penny, Dandie carried it back to the house of the man who had given it to him and dropped it at the feet of the servant who came to the door; and, furthermore, Dandie's expression was such that the trick was never repeated! On some days Dandie got no penny. Or along the way he might collect more than one, but he never failed to get his loaf of bread, and his owner wondered until one day she discovered Dandie digging at the foot of the tree, counting his pennies undoubtedly for a rainy day. Harrison Weir's charming illustration appeared in *Animal Sagacity*, London, 1867.

Another early favorite, first published in 1850, *Bingley's Stories for Children*, with plates by Thomas Landseer, was in the classic tradition. The illustration shows that the great dog has saved a child without harm and to the evident relief of two distressed figures on the bridge in the background. Irish travelers will recognize this as typical of one of the bridges over the Liffey River in Dublin, where on this occasion a young nursemaid was playing on the bridge with the child in her care when over he went. Colonel

"Sancho Rescuing a Child."

Wynne was passing by with his Newfoundland and sent him to the rescue. A passing spectator rushes up to admire the noble dog and discovers that it is his child who has been saved. Thereupon he offered the colonel five hundred guineas for the dog Sancho, but naturally the offer was refused.

The *Peter Parley Annuals*, which were published as a Christmas and New Year's present in America by Samuel G. Goodrich, one of the most prolific of the early nature writers for children, often included stories of Newfoundlands. The *Annual for 1866* tells of George Melville, a rich man's son, who carried Christmas presents to the poor in the heaviest of snowstorms. He would have been unable to carry out his charitable endeavors but for Cicero, his Newfoundland. Cicero's collar was marked in the tradition of Alexander Pope:

Bow-wow-wow
Whose dog art thou?
I am Melville's dog,
Bow-wow-wow.

Among other helpful things, Cicero held the pony for George while he dealt out his parcels.

Through it all the moral of each anecdote is hammered home in traditional Victorian manner. The Newfoundland has survived unperturbed and unruffled by the moralists.

Newfoundland as Central Hero

French history records the Newfoundland belonging to Napoleon I, as mentioned earlier. At the same period there are records of the heroism of Lord Nelson's Newfoundland at Trafalgar in the battle between the *Cleopatra* and the *Nymph.* Both of these are described in more detail in the chapter on working dogs.

Space prohibits the recital of all the heroic exploits of the animal. Certainly we know that in our own country's history he has played his part and we have many cast-iron models of the venerable creature giving us an idea of just how popular he has been here.

Justifiably he has been named the hero dog.

It was to be expected that the naturalist writers and their expanding collections of anecdotes should inspire someone to write a book wholly devoted to a Newfoundland dog. The Honorable Harold Macpherson's book on the Newfoundland dog in 1937, that of Johann Pieterse of The Netherlands of the same year, and currently this book, are included in this category and listed in the bibliography.

However, less well known to the public perhaps than Ollivant's *Bob, Son of Battle*, and Richard Harding Davis's *The Bar Sinister,* the Newfoundland back in 1860 was the central figure or hero in *The Dog Crusoe* and his master, R. M. Ballantine, a story of adventure on the Western prairies. Judging from the well-worn copy at hand, it, too, had its great popularity. We shall not spoil the story for you but recommend you read it. In part, the tale relates that Crusoe, when but a puppy, was rescued by his owner-to-be from an Indian squaw who was singeing him and about to drop him in the pot. He survived this and many other episodes of the West, even to rescuing an Indian papoose from the swirling whirlpool while his anxious squaw-mother paddles precariously in a birchbark canoe attempting a rescue. This book lacks nothing of Western excitement: buffalo hunts, stampedes of wild horses, Indian ambuscades, but Dick Varley with Crusoe by his side, except on two memorable occasions, survives with glory.

Although *Dogs*, by George Frederick Pardon, published in London, in 1857, illustrated by Harrison E. Weir, was not devoted entirely to the Newfoundland, Chapter VII is devoted to the Newfoundland "whose sagacity is greater than all other kinds of dogs." This book is dedicated by the author to his Royal Highness Prince Alfred, "the most distinguished of the children of England," and the introduction starts as follows:

"Down, Rover, down. And as little Charley, a curly-headed boy about six years old, says the word the great Newfoundland dog crouches at his feet and looks imploringly up to his laughing face."

Chapter VII relates a true story of Rover, of his attachment to little Charley Smithers, and how Rover influenced and improved Charley's character, teaching him not to lose his temper which he did once with Rover, striking him with a red-hot poker. Through prayer and solitude and the help of his mother Charley was made to see the error of his ways and was forgiven by the Almighty as well as Rover, who carried the scar through life as a reminder to Charley of the evil of losing his temper. Rover went to sea with Charley and his father, a sea captain, and rescued his young master when he fell into the waves one day while aloft in the masts.

Storm, A Dog of Newfoundland, was the only book whose setting was laid in Newfoundland.

Neptune or The Autobiography of a Newfoundland, London, 1839, is quite probably the Neptune belonging to Mr. Gosling, whose head Sir Edwin Landseer painted and is reproduced in the art section.

In 1953 Mr. Keith Robinson wrote *Mascot of the Melroy*, attractively illustrated in black and white by Jack Weaver. It is a nice story of the Newfoundland, Bosun, befriended on the docks in Newfoundland during World War II by Slim Teague, coxswain of a United States destroyer, *Melroy*. The fine traits of the Newfoundland are splendidly incorporated by Mr. Robertson, well within the realm of probability, in a series of episodes which include action in the Mediterranean, Bosun's experiences ashore in Norfolk, Virginia, Honolulu, and with Moroccans in Algeria.

Our Newfoundland often seems perhaps not as a hero but frequently made a leading character in the time-honored "shaggy dog" stories. In a privately printed little book published in England there were assembled many of these stories by the author, Eric Partridge. One, in particular, involved a man calling on a friend one evening and surprised to see a Newfoundland sitting at the poker table with the other guests. No one seemed to think it unusual but the visitor couldn't wait to get his friend aside and ask him about this. His friend was rather offhand about it, stating that the Newfy wasn't much of a poker player anyway because, as he said, "whenever he gets a good hand, he wags his tail."

Newfoundlands in the Background

That the Newfoundland was definitely a part of the contemporary scene is shown by many surprising instances where he is introduced by writers of the period.

"Crusoe Proves a Friend in Need."

One of the earliest was Sir Walter Scott, who was a great lover of all dogs. His Maida, the Scottish deerhound, was perhaps his favorite, but we know he had Newfoundlands soon after they were introduced to Great Britain. For this reason the figure from Madame Tussaud's Museum of Wax Works in London is reproduced, even at the risk that our Labrador friends may wish to claim the author's dog more nearly their type, but then they both come from Newfoundland. In *Red Gauntlet*, 1832, Scott introduces two Newfoundlands in the house of Darsie Latimer's reluctant host. They were at the door to greet them and later reappeared at the supper table. "I never saw finer animals or which seemed more influenced by a sense of decorum, except that they slobbered a little as the rich scent from the chimney was wafted past their noses!" And who could blame them?

Charles Dickens, who loved dogs as much as Scott, wrote in 1886 of his Don and Bumble, Son of Don: "The other day Bumble got into difficulty among some floating timber and got frightened. Don was standing by, etc."

The dog in *The Idiot*, by Dostoevski, is a Newfoundland.

In America James Fenimore Cooper in *The Headsman*, 1891, includes Nettuno "having a dusky brownish, shaggy dress with shades of black." Nettuno was the beloved companion of Masso and his lifesaving exploits took place in the Italian setting of the Lake of Limon.

Nathaniel Hawthorne did not include Newfoundlands in his writings so far as we know, but his granddaughter, Rose Hawthorne Lathrop, in memories of Hawthorne and Julian, Nathaniel's son, in *Hawthorne and His Circle* tells of the Newfoundland owned by Herman Melville. As Julian wrote: "We did not keep a dog but Herman Melville, who often came over from Pittsfield, had a large Newfoundland which he sometimes brought with him and Mr. G. P. R. James, a novelist of the Walter Scott school, had another and I was permitted to bestride both of them; they were safe enough but they would turn their heads and lay their cold noses on my leg."

Henry David Thoreau wrote (1839) in *Walden*: "A man is not a good man to me because he will feed me if I should be starving, or warm me if I should be freezing or pull me out of a ditch if I should ever fall into one. I can find you a Newfoundland dog that will do as much."

William Stanley Braithwaite pleases in describing his character, a Mr. Sedgwick, in *The Bewitched Parsonage*, 1839: "As he strolled through his fields with his magnificent Newfoundland at his side he looked very like what a frank, wealthy, conservative gentleman ought to be."

Effigy of Sir Walter Scott and his Newfoundland in Madame Tussaud's Wax Exhibition in London.

Perhaps *The Call of the Wild* should have been included in the previous section. I doubt if many casual readers realize that it was the savage attack and killing of Curley, the friendly female Newfoundland, that taught Buck a lesson that ruthlessness paid off in a battle to the death.

Newfoundlands were imported into France in 1844 and at one time used to patrol the banks of the Seine River. The great American writer on dogs, Alfred Payson Terhune, relates the story of the Newfoundland, Malakoff, that repaid an attempt to drown him by a jeweler's apprentice, Jacques, by saving his life in the Seine.

The Poets

The poets of the early nineteenth century also knew and appreciated Newfoundlands. The *Twa Dogs*, written by Robert Burns during a period of disillusion with persons in high society, is to the point. Caesar was perhaps not the finest physical specimen of his breed, but Burns knew that he was from Newfoundland.

> His hair, his size, his mouth, his lugs,
> Showed he was nane o' Scotland's dogs;
> But whalpit some place far abroad,
> Where sailors gang to fish for cod.
> His locked lettered braw brass collar
> Showed him the gentleman and scholar;
> But though he was o' high degree
> The fient a pride, nae pride had he.

To those familiar with the dialect used by Burns, "lugs", and "whalpit," and "fient" are recognized as *ears, was whelped*, and *evil.*

As Mae Trovillion Smith wrote in 1943: "Perhaps no dog in all history ever slumbered and dreamed in an atmosphere fraught with so many ghosts and family skeletons as did Boatswain, the huge Newfoundland owned by the famous English poet, George Gordon, Lord Byron."

In his earliest formative years so full of disillusion and bitterness, when Byron knew he was not to have Mary Chaworth, Boatswain bore the brunt of his grief. It was a brief and stormy career for Boatswain, whelped in Newfoundland May, 1803, and died Newstead Abbey, November 18, 1808. Deep in grief and disillusionment over the loss of Boatswain, Byron wrote a memorable inscription for the monument of his Newfoundland dog.

Most references are to excerpts. It seems to us that the poem, in full, gives more genuine expression to the depth of Byron's grief, for with Boatswain went much of the innocence and hope for enjoyment from life symbolized in all the happy association of the great dog and his young, aristocratic and talented owner.

"The Inundation," by Kiorhoe, typical Victorian dramatic episode-type picture.

INSCRIPTION ON THE MONUMENT OF A NEWFOUNDLAND DOG

By LORD BYRON

When some proud son of man returns to earth
Unknown to glory, but upheld by birth,
The sculptur'd art exhausts the art of woe,
And stoned urns record who rest below;
When all is done, upon the tomb is seen,
Not what he was, but what he should have been;
But the poor Dog, in life the firmest friend,
The first to welcome, foremost to defend;
Whose honest heart is still his master's own,
Who labours, fights, lives, breathes, for him alone
Unhonour'd falls, unnoticed all his worth,
Denied in Heaven the soul he held on earth;
While man, vain insect! hopes to be forgiven,
And claims himself a sole exclusive Heaven!
Oh, man! thou feeble tenant of an hour,
Debas'd by slavery, or corrupt by power,
Who knows thee well, must quit thee with disgust,
Degraded mass of animated dust!
Thy love is lust, thy friendship all a cheat,
Thy smiles hypocrisy, thy words deceit!
By nature vile, ennobled but by name,
Each kindred brute might bid thee blush for shame.
Ye! who, perchance, behold this single Urn
Pass on—it none you wish to mourn:
To mark a Friend's remains these stones arise,
I never knew but one, and here he lies.

Newstead Abbey November 30, 1808.

The above, interestingly enough, was reproduced in *The Cabinet of Natural History*, Philadelphia, 1830, at the end of the chapter on the Newfoundland dog. Writing at twenty, Byron was soon to celebrate his majority, a sad sort of celebration separated from his close friends of school days and this unexpected separation of Boatswain. In André Maurois's biography, *Byron*, he writes of this as follows: "When he was dead, Byron said: 'I have now lost everything except old Murray.' " (his manservant, Joe Murray). He had long kept saying that he wished to be buried with his dog, and he turned his attention to the construction of a vault. With a strange and characteristic gesture of defiance he had this monument raised on the site of the altar in the ruined chapel of the monks. A foundation of large circular steps led to a finely chiseled pedestal with an engraved inscription supporting an antique urn, the beautiful outline of which stood out against the ogive windows. On one side of the pedestal he had inscribed:

NEAR THIS SPOT
ARE DEPOSITED THE REMAINS OF ONE
WHO POSSESSED BEAUTY WITHOUT VANITY
STRENGTH WITHOUT INSOLENCE
COURAGE WITHOUT FEROCITY
AND ALL THE VIRTUES OF MAN WITHOUT HIS VICES
THIS PRAISE WHICH WOULD BE
UNMEANING FLATTERY
IF INSCRIBED OVER HUMAN ASHES
IS BUT A JUST TRIBUTE TO THE MEMORY OF
BOATSWAIN, A DOG
WHO WAS BORN AT NEWFOUNDLAND, MAY 1803,
AND DIED AT NEWSTEAD ABBEY,
NOVEMBER 18, 1808.

Byron told Joe Murray that he would have him buried in the same vault. But Murray showed scant enthusiasm. "If I was sure his lordship would come here too," he said, "I should like it well enough; but I should not like it to lie along with the dog."

It must have been more than coincidence, then, that in another tragic period in Byron's life, 1811–1812, soon after the death of his mother and his close friend Matthews he drew up what Maurois calls "a curious testament," wherein he bequeathed Newstead, other properties, his library, and with provisions to pay off personal debts. To his document he added, "The body of Lord Byron to be buried in the vault of the garden at Newstead, without any ceremony or burial-service whatever, or any inscription, save his name and age. His dog not to be removed from the said vault."

Nor was it coincidence when Boatswain's collar was found among his personal effects returned after his death.

"Ho! Carlo!"

Aside from the dramatic and tragic life of the poet and his contribution to the poetry of the world's literature there remains this bright and sincere tribute to the ageless character of the Newfoundland. Nowhere yet has it been so well inscribed.

Dr. Edwin J. Pratt of Canada, has endeared himself to students of the Newfoundland by several poems about it. Our Canadian members of the Newfoundland Club of America write that the poem "Carlo" is well known and considered quite good, but that even Dr. Pratt admits that "The Reverie" is dull in spots. In his *Collected Poems*, published by The Macmillan Company, Canada, 1946, with whose kind permission these few lines from "Carlo" are quoted, Dr. Pratt writes:

I'll not believe it Carlo; I
Will fetch you with me when I die
And standing up at Peter's wicket,
Will urge sound reasons for your ticket;
I'll show him your lifesaving label
And tell him all about that cable,
The storm along the shore, the wreck,
The ninety souls upon the deck.

In 1888 Eleanor C. Donnelly included in her poems *Pleasant Hours* one "to our Trusty":

Seven months old and black as night
Of the true Newfoundland breed and race,
Up on your hind legs, Trusty dog,
And let our young folks see your face.

The following verse appeared with the Newfoundland illustration in the *St. Nicholas Magazine* for August, 1896:

Bingo is thirty inches high
And Buster thirty-two
While Beau, who isn't quite so big,
Is their loving friend and true.

Beau, the children's joy and pride,
Is a black Newfoundland dog,
Bingo and Buster ponies are
From the land of rain and fog.

No whip nor spur the little chaps
Need when the children ride;
They prance and caper on the road,
While Beau runs by their side.

Two little steeds and one big dog
Make a fine sight to see,
Two little girls in a yellow cart
And they all belong to me.

I think nobody has more fun
Or makes a braver show
Than the little girls who ride behind
Bingo, Buster, and Beau.

From *Bingo, Buster, and Beau*
James Harvey Smith

There are many other verses which can be quoted about the breed. However, it seems appropriate that this section be closed with the following, for which we are indebted to Mrs. Florence Pretty, Limington, Maine:

Dictionary of Dogs
by
Aletha Bonnea

When featuring a dog review
Much laudatory praise is due
The Newfoundland—a dog world famed,
That came from the small isle, as named.
A massive body, square-set thighs,
A noble head and kindly eyes;
A Coast Guard dog, it knows no fear
And oft saves life when death is near.

The Newfoundland on the Stage

It's a pity that William Shakespeare predated the Newfoundland, for it seems to us he might more appropriately have been in *A Midsummer Night's Dream* than the hounds of Sparta. However, lesser playwrights of later years recognized the dramatic qualities of his lifesaving feats.

Sometime in 1804 there appeared in a performance at the Drury Lane Theatre a Newfoundland, Carlo. The verse reproduced by an unknown author starts as follows:

> No actor great in histrionic name
> Than Carlo boasts a prouder, nobler fame:
> E'en Garrick, Nature's favorite child, must yield
> Nature *herself* with Carlo takes the field.

In this performance a huge tank was placed on the stage and nightly Carlo plunged therein and saved the lass in Elizabethan costume with drooping plume.

In 1856 the English poet, Charles Machey, commemorated the event in the following lines:

> Ho! Carlo! Newfoundland! go, follow his cry,
> As it graspingly answers the sea-moaner's sigh;
> The boat shall be lowered, the men shall belay—
> Life-saver! Wave-stemmer! Deep-diver! Away!

In Jesse's *Anecdotes* appears an account of a performance on January 28, 1858, of Jessie Vere at a Woolwich theater. Just as the kidnaping scene was well under way, it was interupted by a large Newfoundland dog who leaped upon the stage, unable to stand the suspense. This dog belonged to the chief engineer of H.M.S. *Buffalo* who had been watching intently by her master's side.

But the accolades must go to Nana, Newfoundland nurse for the Darling family and for more than half a century favorite of "children who never grow up." It is true that the J. M. Barries had owned Porthos, a St. Bernard whose loss at an early age was mourned by them. In *The Story of J. M. Barrie*, by Denis Mackail, he relates: "It was Mrs. Barrie who first discovered as dog lovers do that mourning for Porthos was no protection against the risks and responsibilities again. A new dog there had to be. She found it, bought it and Barrie again named it."

This was in 1902, and in November of 1903 James Barrie began his play *Peter Pan*, a manuscript which he gave later to Maude Adams, who was to appear in the American premiere at the Empire Theater on November 6, 1905. From the start, the Newfoundland dog, Nana, was included as nursemaid. In the world premiere at London in the Duke of York's Theatre, Nana

Nana meets another Newfoundland: Boris Karloff as Captain Hook and Norman Shelly as Nana.

was played by Arthur Lupino, a dancer, Nana has always been played by a man except on one occasion; while the actor was serving in World War I, the part was played by his wife.

Mary Ansell, who was the author's first wife, wrote the story of Nana in *Dogs and Men*, Charles Scribner's Sons, 1924. Nana's name in real life was Luath and she says in associating it with Porthos, "Porthos could never have made a Nana whilst Luath was born one." She tells how the actor who played the part came to the Barrie house to be instructed by Luath on how to do it. In a quite delightful account she relates this and many other instances in the life of Luath, who died in 1917.

In *Peter Pan* or *Peter and Wendy* will be found the following paragraph: "Mrs. Darling loves to have everything just so, and Mr. Darling had a passion for being exactly like his neighbors; so of course they had a nurse. As they were poor, owing to the amount of milk the children drank, this nurse was a prim Newfoundland dog called Nana, who had belonged to no one in particular until the Darlings engaged her."

For more than half a century Nana has shared the footlights from the very first Peter Pan of Dion Boucicault with Maude Adams, Eva Le Gallienne, Marilyn Miller, Jean Arthur, and Mary Martin. In the superb television production with Mary Martin (with Norman Shelley playing Nana), she reached the largest audience of all time. James Barrie did for the Newfoundland in literature what Landseer did for him in art.

Newfoundlands and Famous Persons

It is probably no coincidence that the Newfoundland has always attracted many interesting and famous owners even from the very first day he became known. On preceding pages, mention has been made of artists and writers who owned Newfoundlands and wrote of them, and of Samuel Adams and his dog QueQue.

In Germany, Richard Wagner owned two Newfoundlands and is responsible for the familiar anecdote that after a dinner with friends he announced, "We will now be entertained by two of Nature's gentlemen," whereat his two large dogs were shown into the dining room.

It is related that General Tom Thumb wanted very much to own a particular Newfoundland whose owner would not sell him because he didn't think the general would be able to manage the dog which would likely not consider the general an adult and probably butt him about and treat him as a child. P. T. Barnum must not have known of this or he surely would have brought a Newfoundland into the act.

Bessy deserves special mention as she was the companion of the famous Anna of *The King and I*. In *The English Governess at the Siamese Court*, Mrs. Leonowens wrote, "And there was our own true Bessy,—A Newfoundland, great and good,—discreet, reposeful, dignified, fastidious, not to be cajoled into confidences and familiarities with strange dogs, whether official or professional. Very human was her gentle countenance, and very loyal, I doubt not, her sense of responsibility, as she followed anxiously my boy and me, interpreting with the heart the thoughts she read in our faces, and responding with her sympathetic eyes."

In contemporary life may of our actors and actresses have owned Newfoundlands—among them: Bing Crosby, Gene Raymond, Jeanette MacDonald, and Humphrey Bogart. Bing Crosby presented the Newfoundland, Snowball, to the children at the Warm Springs Foundation for infantile paralysis because the Newfoundland, after due consideration, was considered the best dog to be with the children there. Former New York Governor Dewey was fond of the breed and owned at least one. The poet, Robert Frost, and Stephen Leacock, the Canadian humorist and economist, also owned Newfoundlands.

The late Senators Edward Kefauver and Robert Kennedy owned Newfoundlands. And there are several Newfoundlands in the glamorous Court of the Prince of Morocco.

Dogs by George and Helen Papashvily has already been mentioned and *Famous Dogs of Famous People* by Mae Trovillion Smith, 1943, includes the story of Lord Byron with several other references to famous people who owned Newfoundlands.

Mungo Meets Charlie McCarthy and Edgar Bergen.

One contemporary literary figure, Mr. Hendrik Van Loon, owned a Newfoundland that became famous in its own right. He was Mungo, bred in Newfoundland from the Westerland Kennels of the Honorable Harold Macpherson. Mungo became a member of the crew and mascot of the Air Force bomber *Subconscious*. Lieutenant Nick Robeson saw Mungo in St. Johns, Newfoundland, and adopted him as part of the crew. He was fitted out with his own oxygen mask and parachute and went on many missions. When the crew was shifted to Great Britain, Mungo was barred because of canine quarantine regulations, so Mungo lived aboard the bomber except for exercise at night. He was lost, however, in a blackout in London and picked up by the authorities and placed in quarantine. Strangely enough, on the next mission the bomber was shot down over Bremen, November, 1943. Lieutenant Robeson wrote to Mr. Macpherson from a German prison camp, imploring him to intercede on behalf of Mungo, which he did, although it seemed red tape might hopelessly prevent it. However, Mungo arrived at Newfoundland on the paper-carrying boat *Cornerbrook*, eventually being sent to Lieutenant Robeson's farm near Sabrina, Kansas, where he was on the day that Lieutenant Robeson returned from war.

Trivia, maybe lore, but in any event legendary, is an account by Hans Fantel in the Montreal (Canada) *Gazette*, April 1967, on the "Blue Danube" waltz (later condensed by *Reader's Digest*) in which he describes the fantastic, spectacular staging for a concert in Boston in 1872 when Johann Strauss himself, by special invitation of the promoter, conducted the "Blue Danube," before an audience of 100,000, an orchestra of 2000 players, and a chorus of 20,000, plus sound effects!

Strauss deplored the event but the audience loved it, and Fantel says that for the remainder of his visit Strauss was a hero: "Women besieged him for locks of his hair, and Strauss' valet obligingly handed out scented envelopes—each containing a black curl snipped from the shaggy pelt of a Newfoundland dog."

Fame has come to Newfoundlands and to their owners. The question might be asked as to whether dogs or owners have earned the most. Doubtless the owners would bow out delightedly in favor of their dogs. And so long as there is a Newfoundland dog, the literature about him will never end.

MAGAZINE SECTION

The New York Times.

SUNDAY, JUNE 5, 1910.

FIRST ACCOUNT OF CONQUERING MT. McKINLE

Thomas Lloyd, Leader of the Successful Expedition, Tells How He and His Comrades Planted the Stars and Stripes on the Heretofore Baffling Peak, the Highest Point on the American Continent.

DRAMATIC STORY OF THOMAS LL

He Reinforces His Simple Narrative of the Remarkable C with His Diary of Each Day's Journey.

Chapter IV

Companion and Guardian

"Now we have a Newfoundland!" This acquisition is usually the result of a great deal of thought and consideration and the beginning of a delightful and rewarding experience—the finding of a loyal friend, companion, and guardian.

Basically, most people want a dog for companionship. For adults and children alike, the Newfoundland is ideal in this respect. Throughout history he has been known for his sweet disposition, even temperament, great dignity, and devotion to his master and family. When with children he will take their mauling and teasing without snapping or growling. Many small children have ridden horseback on a Newfoundland, pulled his ears, and hitched him up to a cart. He sweetly bears these indignities with patience and love for his charges.

Disposition is of primary importance. Most kennels breed for disposition and feel that it ranks higher than show points. As far back as 1869 this has been an important factor. We find that in the Standard of those days that 20 points were included for "temper."

As a rule a Newfoundland will not provoke a fight and gets along well with all dogs. In fact, Newfoundlands enjoy the companionship of a smaller dog, and many families that own Newfoundlands also keep a smaller dog as a playmate and an added companion in the household. However, this does not mean that a Newfoundland will not stand up to another dog if he is attacked.

The guardian instinct of Newfoundlands is shown in many ways. It has often been observed that a Newfoundland will stand between his owners and an approaching stranger. There is no malice is such a stance, but this massive dog, standing near his charges, serves as a warning to strangers. He has an intuitive ability to recognize danger to others in circumstances completely alien to his own experience. Many stories are told of

Mrs. Albert Fellows with "Grenny" and Ch. Bounty of Quaker Acres, owned by Mrs. Raymond Gunnison.

warnings given. Mrs. E. W. Baldwin tells of Hilda who allowed workmen to climb a ladder and work on the roof but sensed the danger for the daughter of the household and warned her by barking and jumping at the ladder, knowing that the roof was no place for a little girl. Mr. and Mrs. Joseph Laderoute have told us of Senta that, like Nana in Peter Pan, kept a close watch on their five children. She would push them off the roadway, and in one instance pulled a child off the road just as the milkman came by in his truck. Viking, the family pet of the Fiskes, received a medal for twice giving the alarm when fires broke out, at the Fiske home in one instance and at the local school in another.

The Newfoundland's guardian instinct is shown, too, in the many cases of rescue from danger. Mrs. Albert Fellows of Willow, New York, owes her life to Grenny. Mrs. Fellows was taking a walk through the woods with Grenny. The dog was investigating some of the intriguing smells of the forest when she heard her mistress cry out and came running back. A man had attacked Mrs. Fellows, but as Grenny rushed at him he hastily released her and retreated, with the dog in full pursuit. Mrs. Fellows had been badly mauled and fell unconscious. As she regained consciousness she saw Grenny bouncing back through the woods to her side.

Mr. Alfred Forest's Linda is the heroine of another rescue. Mr. Forest worked at night and upon returning home at 6 A.M. would usually sit in the kitchen and have a cup of coffee before retiring. One morning he dozed off and a little while later felt a tugging at his leg. As he drowsily roused himself, he smelled gas. He stumbled to the door, opened it, and collapsed. When he woke he found his trouser leg torn to shreds and teeth marks on his ankle. Linda had finally resorted to taking hold of his ankle when his trousers had failed to hold.

Champion Coastwise Steamboat Bill, familiarly called Barry, is another hero of recent years. His mistress, Mrs. Major Godsol of California, was driving with him for companionship through a snowy mountain pass when they met another car head on. Their car was overturned and Mrs. Godsol was thrown out into the snow. For several hours Barry lay in the snow next to her with his head on her chest keeping her warm until help arrived. He would not leave her side and sat next to her on the long ride to the hospital in the ambulance. At the hospital Barry wanted to go in, too. Here the hours of obedience training given him proved valuable. When Mrs. Godsol told him to guard her coat until Mr. Godsol arrived, he did so for several hours.

Captain Henri Rice wrote, "I would not be here now to write this article!" The story that brought forth this comment he relates as follows: "At 2:30 A.M., on Saturday morning, the twelfth of June, 1954, we were awakened out of a sound sleep in the front third-floor bedroom of our little city house—423 South Carlisle St., Philadelphia, Pennsylvania—by the roaring of our Newfoundlands—Ch. Irwindyl's Lady Beale Isoude (fourteen months of age) and Sir Tristam of Irwindyl (three years). Tristi, as we call him, had my right shoulder in his mouth and was gently pulling me out of bed. Muffie, as we call our bitch, was jumping on my stomach with her front paws. The room was a mass of flame and smoke. Needless to say, we rushed to call the fire department, but the dogs would not leave the third floor until we left—including a Landseer puppy, Panda Bear, who added her voice to the general clamor in a sincere effort to be helpful. We owe our lives to these dogs. The lieutenant in charge of the firemen remarked that in another ten minutes we would have been overcome by the smoke. Without making our dogs members of our family and allowing them the run of the house this could never have happened."

For those who live near the water, the Newfoundland will be particularly valued for his swimming ability. Nature has equipped him with a powerful frame, webbed feet, great strength, and an instinct for lifesaving. He can easily pull an adult from the water. His fame as a lifesaver is incomparable, and the picture of Sir Edwin Landseer's "Saved" is more expressive than words.

Charcoal, owned by Mr. Gerald Kendall, is credited with having saved two children from drowning off the beaches of Southampton, New York, during the summer of 1951. Charcoal was a regular visitor to the local beach and was tolerated but not loved by all. Some were frightened by his size, others dismayed by his desire to stay close to swimmers. These facts combined with the village ruling "No Dogs Are Allowed On the Beach" resulted in many trips by Mr. Kendall to bring his

Captain Henri Rice and Sir Tristan of Irwindyl and Ch. Irwindyl's Lady Beale Isoud.

"Barry," Ch. Coastwise Steamboat Bill.

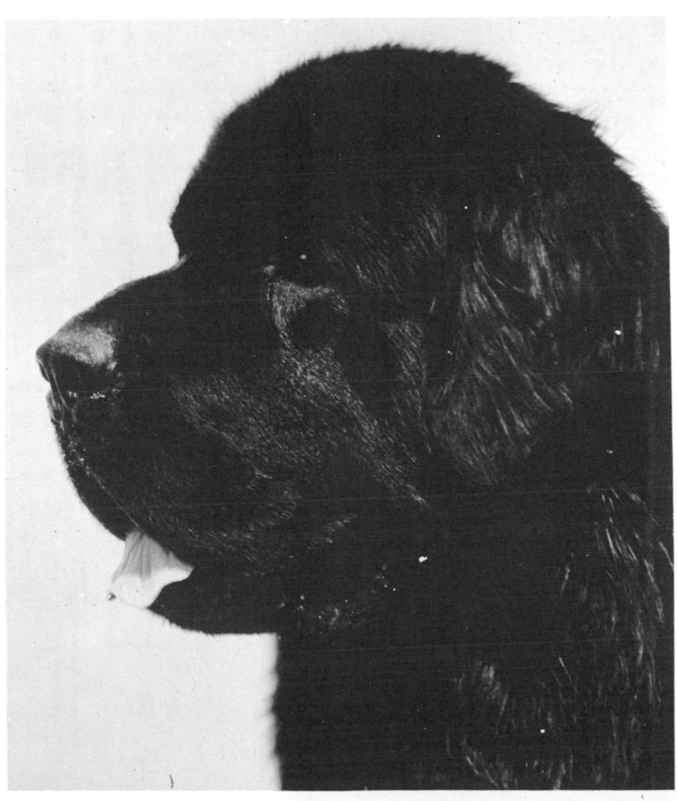

dog home. However, one day, before Charcoal was sent home, he saw a twelve-year-old child in distress in water over his head. He swam out and grasping the child's shoulder pulled it ashore. Several days later he again saved a child in like manner. Because of these rescues Charcoal was allowed and encouraged to stay at the beach. He is the only dog ever to be allowed on the beaches of Southampton.

A newspaper clipping from the scrapbook of Mr. Macpherson tells this story: "June 28, 1928—Special to the Daily News, St. Johns, Newfoundland. John Walter Gibbons, son of J. Gibbons postal operator of Proweston, had a narrow escape from drowning today. Whilst the boy was fishing for Tom Cods he tripped and fell head first into the deep water. A large Newfoundland dog named Jumbo, owned by Patrick Hickey, saw the boy, jumped overboard, and swam to him. The boy caught the dog and held fast, and the noble animal took him to land. The little fellow was in an exhausted condition but after a short while was none the worse for his experience. The dog is a hero and deserves a medal."

The Newfoundland does not confine his rescues to members of the human race. In Natick, Massachusetts, a few years ago a little Cocker Spaniel fell through the ice in Lake Cochituate. Before the summoned firemen arrived, a large Newfoundland plunged through the water and ice, picked the spaniel up in his teeth, and carried it to safety.

Captain Bob Bartlett, belonging to Mr. Macpherson, saved his playmate, a terrier puppy, from the stream that flows through Westerland. The puppy had fallen into the stream and was being rapidly carried down by the current when Captain Bob heard his yelps of fright. He jumped into the water below the terrier and swam out through the rushing water, grasped the pup, and pulled it to shore.

Dr. Coburn of Kansas City writes: "The late Champion Midway Sea Raider, known to all of us as Salty, was an excellent example of the fine instinctive protective qualities that make the Newfoundland such an exceptional breed. We had long known that he was an excellent watchdog, but had no occasion to be aware of his great instinct for guarding and saving human lives until we took him to Lake Crane of the North country for the first time. Our children, Shari and Frank, who at that time were ten and seven years of age respectively, were fond of taking a small rowboat out into the bay at the front of the house and would at times spend hours on end rowing about the bay. The first time they took the boat out, Salty, without a word of command from anyone, leaped into the water and followed them. He swam up to a distance of two feet or so behind the boat, and there he stayed the whole time the children were on the

Elinor Ayers exercising her dogs, Winnie the Pooh and Prince of Ayers II.

"Salty," Ch. Midway Sea Raider, owned by Dr. Donald F. Coburn at Staten Island, 1953.

Canadian Ch. Oquaga's Queen Bess and "Larry."

Dryad's Coastwise Sailor Boy and friend (copyright DEopaul Photo).

Ch. Waseeka's Hesperus, Waseeka's Crusoe, and Ch. Dryad's Fan with their charges.

Seaward's Ocean Echo, C.D., with Crystal and Loren Latimer.

"Member of the Wedding," Carol Fenlin Heinel and Carol's Queen Ann.

water. We attempted to distract him in various ways by calling him on the dog whistle, a command he never ignored, and by calling his name and throwing cans for him to retrieve, one of his favorite sports. He not only could not be distracted, but not once did he even take his eyes from the boat and the children. Every day that the weather permitted the children would be on the lake, and Salty would be right behind them, patiently swimming and watching them for any length of time. We did not have to worry about their safety or stand and watch them as we knew that Salty was doing it for us, wisely and well."

Another instance of their instinct for protection comes from Mrs. Arthur Irwin as related in the Buck's County Training Club Bulletin: "Gerry Irwin tells of an experience which happened to her in New York during this last Garden show. She was exercising her Newfoundland, Lorelei, at about 1:30 A.M., Tuesday, and as she crossed the street to go into Central Park, she thought she noticed someone following her. As she entered the Park, a man spoke to her and asked her what in the world she had there, was it a bear. Gerry realized that the man had had a few too many, and said that it wasn't a bear but a dog. The man asked Gerry if she didn't think it unsafe for her to be on the street at that hour alone. She said No, I have my dog and am very safe. With that the man said, The h— you say, and struck her on the shoulder. In less time than it takes to write it, Lorelei had the man by the throat. This was the first time that

Butch of Camayer receiving the John P. Haines medal for saving the lives of two people in Westchester County in 1947. Mr. Sydney H. Coleman of the A.S.P.C.A. is making the award to Butch, who is held by Mr. John S. Cameron.

Lorelei had been in a position to protect her mistress, but she knew what to do. Lorelei was 11 months old at that time."

These accomplishments, only a few of the many, may fade with time and distance, but those of us who live with dogs can never forget the things they have done nor what they will do whenever called upon to act for those they love.

Ch. Dory-O's Bonny Venbrun and friends.

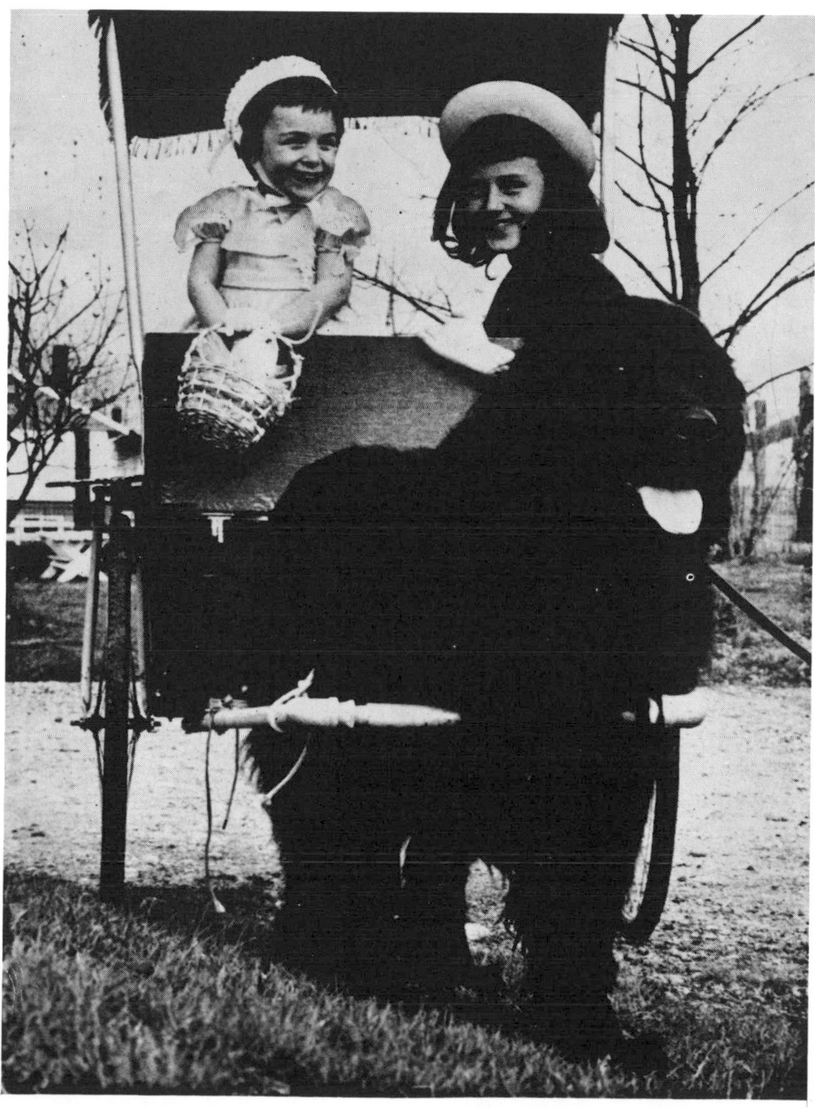

Chapter V

The Newfoundland as a Working Dog

In all canine history there are few breeds that can compare with the Newfoundland's contribution to the welfare of the human race. In addition to the animal's instinctive impulse for lifesaving tactics, his pliability of temperament and his devotion to mankind have made him amenable to training for useful work in many fields.

The written records of the Newfoundland's share in man's labor do not go back much beyond the nineteenth century, but the engraving by Philip Reinagle (1749–1833) depicts a large black-and-white Newfoundland in the foreground, with a team of a number of dogs of the same breed drawing a load on a sledge in the background. From this picture we may conclude that it was not at all an unusual occurrence for these dogs to be used for overland transportation of goods in the British Isles at the turn of the century. In 1808 Lord Byron wrote in his diary of the training of Boatswain, and other literary and artistic references show that the working characteristics and ability were known and appreciated in Europe at that time. Dogs pulling carts were prohibited around Metropolitan London in 1837, but a letter to *The Times* in 1836 mentions fish taken from Southampton to London in carts drawn by two or four dogs. In Old West Surrey Miss Gertrude Jekell mentioned that the dogs were usually Newfoundlands, of which a team of four would pull three or four hundredweight of fish.

However, it is from the island of Newfoundland that most of the statistics on the transportation work of the breed may be gathered, for in his native land he was kept more for use than ornament. As early as 1824 it was estimated that there were 2,000 Newfoundland dogs in the town of St. Johns and that they were constantly employed. They drew cut wood from the

Sledging in Norway.

Daguerreotype of Honorable Harold Macpherson's father and uncle and their favorite Newfoundland about 1850.

Newfoundlands hauling wood in their native land.

forests for fuel and building purposes, drew loads of fish from the shore and helped to pull in the heavy nets, and they transported all kinds of merchandise from one part of the town to another as well as delivering milk. It has been estimated that during one month of the year 1815 these dogs furnished the town of St. Johns with labor valued at from $4,500 to $5,000 per day, and that a single dog would, by his labor, support his owner throughout the long winter. They were used singly and in teams. Three to five dogs harnessed to a sledge or other vehicle containing a load of firewood, lumber, or fish (280 to 450 pounds) would draw it steadily for miles with ease. This they would do without the aid of a driver, if they knew the road, and having delivered their burden, would return to the home of their master for a reward of dried fish, their staple food. In addition to their less glamorous tasks the dogs were also used to transport His Majesty's mail from the outposts north of the railway to the railway junctions and from one outpost to another through a chain of settlements. Teams averaging about seven pulled these sledges over frozen marshes, through thick woods, and over trails impossible for even a hardy pony. For this service to the King the Newfoundland dog was honored by having his head made the subject of a postage stamp for his native country.

The useful work of the Newfoundland for man at sea was so internationally recognized during the era of the sailing ship that reports of their enterprises come from many countries on both sides of the Altantic Ocean as well as the Mediterranean Sea. His powerful swimming ability plus his docility and intelligence were great assets to any ship's company, and it became customary to take at least one web-footed Newfoundland on all voyages as "ship dog." The specific service he rendered was to swim ashore with a line, thus establishing communication with help on land. Untold numbers of lives were saved because of the swimming help of the "ship dog" and his ability to find a footing on rough rocks in a heavy sea where the best of watermen might not survive. In less rough water he could also haul a small boat ashore by its painter.

In Holland, France, Italy, England, and the United States are early records of the Newfoundland in his role of ship dog. One of the most famous stories centers about the Battle of Trafalgar (1805). The English frigate, *The Nymph,* joined battle with the French ship, *The Cleopatra.* On board *The Nymph* was a Newfoundland ship dog which had never before seen naval action. Although the crew attempted to keep the dog below decks during the encounter, he resisted their efforts and remained on deck during the entire engagement. He was undismayed by the firing of the frigate's guns and "barked and exhibited violent

Illustrations of harness types.

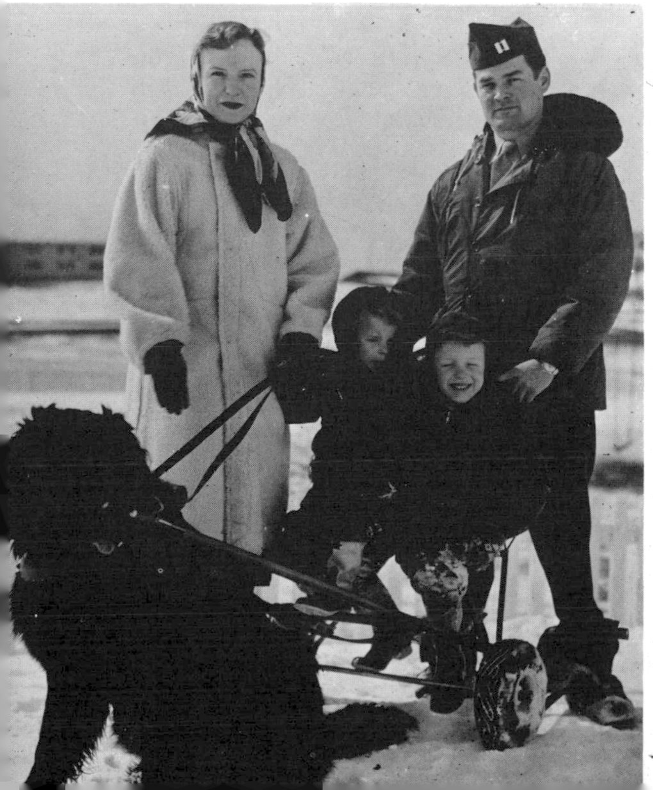

Capt. and Mrs. Ray Clark and children with Carbonear.

rage throughout the battle." When *The Cleopatra* finally struck, and an English boarding party went over the side, the dog was the first on the French deck. The Newfoundland, for all his gentleness, can display an astonishing amount of courage and will defend his friends even to the point of risking his life.

Because of the prompt action of another Newfoundland ship dog the life of Napoleon Bonaparte was saved. The Emperor was being secretly returned from Elba on a suitably dark night and in the course of boarding the boat which was to return him to France, he slipped and fell into the water. He was unable to swim, and his friends could not locate him in the darkness. The large Newfoundland dog on the ship's deck dived into the black water and towed the drowning Emperor to the boat.

As late as 1919 comes the account of the rescue of all hands aboard the coastal steamer *Ethie* which was breaking up on the rocks in a blinding snowstorm at Bonne Bay on the coast of Nova Scotia. The ship was listing heavily and the lifeboats had all been washed away. Rockets were fired and rescue parties came to the shore, but though they tried again and again they could not launch their boats through the pounding surf. One man from the ship had already been drowned in an attempt to swim ashore with a line, and the last hope of passengers and crew lay in the ability of the Newfoundland ship dog, Tang, to make the shore where the sailor had failed. With the end of the line in his mouth, the captain ordered him overboard with the command, "The shore, Tang." He leaped into the water only to be spun over and over in the swirl among the rocks. It seemed to those on deck that he, too, would be lost, but he steadied, straightened out, and, nothing more than a tiny speck in the turmoil of foam, he headed for the shore.

As he reached it, willing hands drew him through the surf. The line was taken from his mouth, a hawser was drawn from ship to shore, and a boatswain's chair was rigged. Passengers and crew were all saved, including a small baby who made the trip in a mailbag! Tang later received the medal for Meritorious Service from Lloyd's of London which he wore on a collar around his neck until he died of old age at St. Johns.

The working ability of the Newfoundland dog has also contributed to Arctic exploration and to army maneuvers in the frozen North, where he was used as a pack animal during World War II. In a recent book, *The History of Dogs for Defense*, the breeds classed as war dogs in the *Army Technical Manual*, July, 1943, were listed. At that time thirty-two breeds were accepted and the Newfoundland was described as "a massive, powerful dog. Water-resistant coat equips him for cold and wet weather. An excellent pack dog, he possesses also talent for rescuing

Società Italiana del Terranova (S. I. T.)

NOTIZIARIO

Italian dry-point by Amos Nattini illustrating the Newfoundland as a ship dog.

drowning persons." A year later, 1944, the list of breeds preferred by the Armed Forces had been reduced to five for scout duty, three for sledge dogs, and Newfoundlands and St. Bernards were favored under pack dogs. Careful training was required, as pack dogs must respond promptly to the command, "Back," so that they do not crown up behind their handler and step on his snowshoes. Instant obedience to "Down" and "Stay" avoided trail accidents and stopped chases after game. The dogs were taught not only to obey voice commands but hand signals as well. The author Fairfax Downey says, "A memorable spectacle against a snowy background at Camp Rimini was a string of laden pack dogs faithfully following a soldier master up a mountain. One man handled up to eight. Usually big, sturdy Newfoundlands or St. Bernards, the dogs were unleashed as soon as they had left the camp area."

NEWFOUNDLANDS AND GREAT PYRENEES IN WORLD WAR II

(Recorded in an article by John E. Shaw.
Reproduced by permission of *Popular Dogs*.)

"When I walk by the benches at some of our larger dog shows and see a well-groomed, well-pampered Malamute, Huskie, Great Pyrenees, and the massive black-coated Newfoundland, it is hard for me to realize that only a few short years ago members of these same breeds were performing arduous duties for our Armed Forces under the most severe and exacting conditions which any dog on our earth today can work under. Stranger yet, the majority of those dogs which worked so gallantly were probably sitting on some of these same show benches, well groomed and conditioned, or lying in front of a fireplace at their masters' feet prior to their call to war duty.

"The majority of the Newfoundlands and Pyrenees underwent training at Fort Robinson, Nebraska, and Fort Remic, Montana. They were trained primarily for harness work, both pulling and packing. The training at Fort Robinson lasted three months and the raw winters of the Nebraska plains with freezing winds that swept down from the Dakotas, driving the mercury to lows of forty and fifty below, roughened them for the ordeal they were destined to endure in the Aleutian Islands and Alaska. In weather that would freeze leather leashes as hard as rock they underwent their basic and advanced training, which consisted of packing heavy weights through deep snowdrifts against strong, freezing winds; along with the usual heeling, sitting, and stay exercises. This training proved its real value in the many instances in the Aleutians when patrols were often caught in the midst of a blinding Aleutian "Willi-Way" (Aleutian blizzard), where snow and ice drive parallel to the ground with force enough to pin an unsupported man to the ground; they depended on their dogs to guide them safely back to base. Without their dogs they would have been hopelessly lost and risked being frozen to death.

"People often associate fierceness of a dog with his size, and yet I remember that the easy-going temperament, the never-flagging strength of the Newfoundland allowed him to keep a steady pace when other breeds of lesser strength and less serene temperament were ready to quit. In my opinion, the Newfoundlands, along with your Great Pyrenees, are the greatest dogs for heavy weight pulling. Any soldier who endured the forsaken islands of the Aleutian chain can vouch for the tenacity of Aleutian mud and yet there stands out in my mind the day a Newfoundland and a Great Pyrenees astonished a group of soliders by pulling their jeep out of a mud hole. At the time I was serving overseas I worked with several Newfoundlands and it was there that my admiration for these dogs began.

"On one occasion my four black Newfoundlands hauled sacks of coal in loads up to 1,200 pounds from the beaches of Adak Island in the Aleutians to inland bivouac areas—a distance of approximately five miles. They kept this up for about ten hours, steady and uncomplaining. At the end of the day the dogs acted as if they had been out for a leisurely stroll in Central Park. Dogs doing harness work were used for rescue work whenever necessary. A three-hundred-mile trip to pick up survivors of a plane crash on the Alaska mainland was another assignment where four Newfoundlands teamed with Huskies and Malamutes, worked together. A long, hard, and tedious journey—but the dogs were dependable—keeping a steady run about twelve hours a day for five days. Thousands of stories of the heroic duties which these dogs performed will remain untold because we human beings forget so easily.

"Packs carried by the dogs were similar to saddlebags on the old-time Pony Express saddles and were used primarily for the carrying of thirty- and fifty-caliber ammunition. Offhand I can't remember the weight of two cases of "ammo," but I was always happy to delegate this task to two Newfoundlands to whom I gave the improbable names of Moe and Blow.

"Housing with these dogs presented no problem. During heavy snowstorms they lay out in front of their kennels, allowing the snow to cover them completely. It was a strange sight to get up in the morning and look down a row of kennels and see only the chain leading down into the snow and not a dog in sight. Their heavy coats afforded them all the necessary protection. The only man-made protection the Newfoundlands needed was rawhide boots for their feet. Being water dogs with great renown as swimmers, their web feet had to be protected from the sharp cutting edges of the ice; however, their web feet were of great advantage to them in soft snow.

"I could go on and on telling of the feats of strength, endurance, companionship, and tractability of these great dogs. Because I lived, slept, and ate with them for two years in a country where a good dog often means the difference between living or dying, I know the value of dependability and temperament. Don't let that soft-eyed look fool you—the Newfoundlands are rough, tough customers—as far as courage is concerned, and they will work their hearts out for you."

The dogs' participation in exploration is recorded in the book *Arctic Explorations* by Dr. Elisha Kent Kane. On May 30, 1853, the doctor set out on an Arctic expedition with the purpose of searching for the missing English explorer, Sir John Franklin. With him he took ten Newfoundlands as well as the usual Esquimaux dogs, and he speaks of his island dogs in very endearing terms: "My dogs were both Esquimaux and Newfoundlanders. Of these last I had ten. They had been carefully broken to travel by voice without the whip and were expected to be very useful for heavy draught as their tractability would enable the driver to regulate their pace. They had been trained to draw a light sledge two abreast, unlike the Esquimaux, with a regular harness, a breast collar of flat leather, and a pair of traces. Six of them made a powerful traveling team; and four of them could carry me and my instruments for short journeys with ease."

By October 10 some of the members of Dr. Kane's party had been absent from camp overly long and he decided to go out with supplies to rescue them. About this trip he writes: "I took four of our best Newfoundlanders, now well broken, and our lightest sledge, and Blake will accompany us with his skates. We have not enough hands to equip a large sledge party and the ice is too unsound for us to attempt to ride with a large team."

The missing members of the party were located and the account of the rescue, with pictures of the dogs, appears in the book. Of the journey back to camp the author says: "On this return I had much less difficulty with the ice cracks; my team of Newfoundlanders leaping them in almost every instance and the impulse of the sledge carrying it across."

No account of the Newfoundland as a working dog would be complete without mentioning his great ability as a game retriever. This comes so naturally to the dog that it is more play than work to him. The amphibious Newfoundland has a good nose, a soft mouth, and an understanding brain which make him superb in bringing in all varieties of killed and wounded waterfowl. He may also be trained to retrieve woodcock and pheasants without inter-

"Newfoundland and Wood Duck," by Alfred DeDreux.

fering with the work of the pointer in the field. Owing to his size and his heavy protective coat, he is also valuable for the fearless manner with which he will penetrate the thickest cover.

He requires very little training, as is illustrated by the following incident. An ardent sportsman relates how one morning at daybreak he and a friend took their guns, gaff, and their Newfoundland and proceeded below the hill to the salt-water creek frequented by ducks. Just as they arrived, their nine-month-old pup, which they had barred in, escaped and joined them. They tied the pup to the older dog's collar. The two double-barreled volleys (in the days before reduced waterfowl numbers required bag limits) killed and wounded some twenty-two ducks. Both dogs were released, and the pup followed his leader into the water. The tide was out and a barrier of ice was along the shore about eighteen inches above the water level, so that it was impossible for a dog to get back. By the aid of the gaff which they hooked into the dog's collars they pulled them up sufficiently to take the birds retrieved, then let them drop back. The pup took to the work instinctively, and of the twenty-two birds he retrieved ten. They then pulled both dogs over the ice barrier, none the worse for their long immersion in the icy sea and their repeated hangings.

Unlike many other water dogs, the Newfoundland will frequently dive deeply and bring up sunken objects. In deep water fishing on the southwest coast of Canada it is no uncommon thing to see a dog at the gunwale of a boat ready to grasp the fish which so often slips off the hook when it reaches the surface. One man kept a record of his dog's help and found he accounted for one third of his summer's catch. The dog, to retrieve the fish that broke from the hook, would sometimes find it necessary to dive deeply under the water.

As has been shown in this chapter the strength, ardor, webbed feet, and swimming ability of the Newfoundland dog made him particularly useful to inhabitants along seacoasts, rivers, and lakes, and even today he remains the ideal dog in these locations. However, in his pliable fashion, he can acclimatize himself to any section of the world his adored master chooses and, in this mechanized age when his services are less necessary than in the past, he still takes a singular pride in being employed. If not guarding a small child, or a smaller dog, his habitual inclination to industrious employment will lead him to carrying a stick or a basket or bundle for miles.

This inclination was well illustrated by a story that comes from Cornwall, England, during the severe winter of 1955. Mr. and Mrs. M. E. Aberdeen wrote: "During the recent and unprecedented heavy snowfall which brought all road transport to a standstill in the usually mild, sub-tropical county of Cornwall

Newfoundland cart exhibit at Kanadasaga Kennel Club. Left to right: Douglas Marshall, Carol Drury, Maynard Drury, Pearl Garnsey, Hub Garnsey, Phil Haust, Janice Bellows, Helena Linn.

we were cut off entirely by deep snowdrifts. Being short of food for both the dogs and ourselves, we constructed a light sledge and, optimistically, made improvised harnesses for our two stud dogs. Although they had never previously ever worn a harness or pulled anything, as dogs are not permitted to work in this country, the two dogs immediately started hauling the sledge, and finding tracks where the snow was most firm, took the sledge to the village, more than a mile away, and returned with it laden with necessities. During the weeks that followed they hauled in all supplies and enjoyed every minute of their labors. Even now that spring is once again with us, whenever we handle either the sledge or harnesses both dogs become excited. It is wonderful to know that although bred purely for companionship and show for so many generations, the instincts of their ancestors came to the rescue when so urgently needed."

Many years ago the Newfoundland earned his keep by hauling cart-loads of fish for his master. Today his work has changed to play and many Newfoundland owners have acquired carts and sleds of various types for their dogs to pull. It has become a special event at many Dog Shows to see the Newfoundland Cart Exhibit. The Working Trials also now include a class for cart pulling.

More people are enjoying the companionship of their dogs on hiking and camping trips. They are following the tradition of

Frederick H. Holt and family hitch up "Sylvester" to homemade cart.

"Buster," the first dog to climb Mt. McKinley. For these trips, a Newfoundland carries a "back-pack." Alan and Joanne Riley are the pioneers in this field. They have developed packs that are particularly suited to a Newfoundland and spend many hours hiking and camping. Their dogs carry their own food, quite a help on a long hike.

Newfoundlands like to fish. Major General Hutchinson writes in *Dog Breaking*. "At certain seasons of the year the streams in some parts of North America, not far from the coast, are filled with fish to an extent you could scarcely believe, unless you had witnessed it—and now comes the Munchausen story. A real Newfoundland, belonging to a farmer who lived near one of those streams, used, at such times, to keep the house well supplied with fish. He thus managed it:— He was perfectly black, with the exception of a white fore-foot, and for hours together he would remain almost immovable on a small rock which projected into the stream, keeping his white foot hanging over the ledge as a

Newfoundlands fishing at Eden Glen.

lure to the fish. He remained so stationary that it acted as a very attractive bait; and whenever curiosity or hunger tempted any unwary fish to approach too close, the dog plunged in, seized his victim, and carried him off to the foot of a neighboring tree; and, on a successful day, he would catch a great number."

Bringing this fish story up to date is the following story told by Mrs. Willis Linn of Edenglen Kennels. "Rock Stream Creek runs through our property emptying into Seneca Lake. Each spring a type of white fish come up the stream to spawn in the pool under our waterfall. These fish weigh from 2 to 3 pounds and are 16 to 20 inches long.

"Chrissy (Ch. Dryad's Christine of Glenora) and Nanny (Ch. Dryad's Nancy of Glenora), litter sisters, came to us in early May when they were eight weeks old, and the fish were running at their best. Even at this tender age the puppies were very interested in the activity in the creek.

"The next year they figured it all out for themselves. They would start fishing at the mouth of the creek and drive the fish into shallow water, making their catch there. Then, if there were young puppies about they were treated to this delicacy. Other times the fish were piled on the bank, and on a good day, each dog would catch from eight to ten fish.

Edenglen's Jib in action.

"As the puppies grew up the mothers seemed to teach them the method involved.

"It has been interesting to watch most of the dogs develop into fine fishermen, but there were always one or two dogs sitting on the bank just observing."

As one great Newfoundland lover says, "They are capable of being trained for any purpose . . . and if properly cared for, and associated with, they seem to lack only the faculty of speech." Yet the truth of the matter remains evident today, as it has held true over the years, that the Newfoundland, with all his sagacity, energy, and other physical attributes, would lack value to man as a working dog and as a pet without his amiable character. . . . "Strength without insolence, courage without ferocity, and all the virtues of man without his vices."

Chapter VI

Care

This chapter is intended as a guide and not as "the be all and the end all" of Newfoundland care, training, and breeding. It is written with the hope that it will give some helpful hints to those who are just starting to raise Newfoundlands. The care of a big, long-coated dog is somewhat different from the care of other breeds. Anyone who has had experience raising dogs will have variations of methods which are better suited to their available time, temperament, and personal preferences.

SELECTING A PUPPY

Do you want a small (six or eight weeks old) puppy, a six-month-old, or a grown dog? You must first realize that a puppy will cost less than a grown dog. The older dog has been fed and cared for longer and thus his cost rises proportionately.

There is nothing that appeals more to most people than the round fluffiness of a little puppy. The fact that he is at an age that enables him to grow into a family appeals to many. Most buyers, therefore, will want a puppy. However, the younger he is the more care and watching he will require. Three or four meals a day, a safe place to play (and one that is escape proof), all add to the problems at this age.

On the other hand, a six-month-old pup is fed only twice a day, he is large enough not to get out of protected areas, and furthermore is sufficiently developed so you can get a better idea how he will turn out as a grown dog. He will be at the "awkward age," that is, all legs, and will probably have lost his puppy coat that looked so attractive when he was younger.

With the year-old dog you will have a still better idea of what he will look like at maturity. He will be on one meal a day and need much less care. The disadvantages are that he will take longer to get acclimated to the new environment and the new family, you will miss the fun of watching him grow through his puppy stages and, if he has not been trained, you will find him

Typical puppies.

Children's Handling Class at the Specialty Show, Greenwich, Conn., 1955. Left to right: Harry Hartz, Mark Levy, Mrs. John Thomson, Mary Drury, and Ray Clark III.

strong and harder to handle. The whole question is personal. Which age is going to provide you with the most pleasure?

Do you want a male or a female? This, too, is a matter of personal preference. The disposition of a male and a female are much the same as are the other pleasant attributes of the Newfoundland, such as loyalty, docility, and protective tendencies. They vary most in physical aspects. The female is usually smaller, being about 26 inches high at the shoulder as compared to the 28 inches for the males. The female also weighs 20 to 25 pounds less, and of course is more feminine or less massive throughout. The female has the disadvantage of her two periods of estrus each year. If you are prepared for this with an adequate, enclosed area that will keep her in and keep all other dogs out, you will have no concern although you may have a number of visitors around the fence. You may want to breed her; on the other hand, if her seasons prove a nuisance, you can have her spayed. Your veterinarian will tell you the best time to have this operation performed. Contrary to popular belief, such an operation does not necessarily change her disposition nor does it make her gain weight excessively. The decision to have this operation must be considered carefully, as we sometimes hear of a family that suddenly decides they want to breed their bitch and this would, of course, be impossible since spaying is an irreversible operation.

Will you ever want to show your dog or will your children wish to show it? Answering "yes" to this question involves purchasing a dog of good enough quality and type to win an occasional ribbon.

Do you want breeding stock? If you intend to raise a litter or start a kennel, you will want to study and know the breeding lines and what breeding produces each type.

How much must you pay for a Newfoundland? Price is usually dependent upon the cost of raising the puppies, the popularity of the breed, and the reputation of the establishment where you purchase your dog. This subject is discussed later in further detail under the heading "How much does it cost to raise a Newfoundland puppy?"

There are many useful things you can do to insure that the individual dog you choose will be satisfactory. Although it may inconvenience you slightly at the time, you will be better satisfied with your dog if you check as many of the following items as you can.

1. Study the standard until you can visualize the type dog it calls for. Then you can compare the adult dogs in any kennel or at any show with your visualization, and the dogs that most closely resemble it should be the best for you.

2. It is wise to write a number of breeders to find out what is available and the general range of prices. You can obtain the name and address of the secretary of the Newfoundland Club of America from the American Kennel Club at 51 Madison Ave., New York, N.Y. 10010. The secretary of the Newfoundland Club will be glad to provide you with an up-to-date list of breeders to whom you can write. Your letters will receive a more informative answer if you will give the breeder an idea of the age, sex, and quality in which you are interested.

3. Go to the local shows and watch the judging. Look at the dogs in the ring and pick out the ones which appeal most to you. Locate their owners and talk with them. Ask them such questions as:

a. How long have they been raising, showing, and selling Newfoundlands? This will give an indication of whether they have been doing it long enough to have a reputation. Ask and expect the breeders to fault the dogs. Use your own judgment or refrain from deciding which is best until you know the good and bad points of conformation in the breed.

b. What is the range of their prices? Remember that no kennel with a good reputation can price according to your pocketbook. Rather, they scale their prices from a low price for a mediocre specimen, breeding and showwise, up to their top price for animals which they feel show great promise. Any extra training which a kennel has had to do for a purchaser will also go into the price.

c. Do they have any dogs for sale now? If not, when do they expect to have more puppies for sale?

d. Question the other exhibitors, too. If they are not breeders and you particularly like their dogs, find out if they ever intend to do any breeding, and, if not, where they obtained their stock. Bear in mind that some people who own Newfoundlands cannot possibly exhibit all their dogs at every show. Find out what they may have at home.

e. Visit as many breeders as you possibly can, until you find the one that offers you what you want. Study the people and the adult dogs as well as the individual dog you are considering purchasing. If the people seem honest, have a good reputation, and have the type of dog you want, then you are wise in buying your puppy there.

KENNEL TO HOME

There are several preparations you can make before you bring your dog home. They are important if you want your first days with your dog to be pleasant for both of you.

Probably the most important consideration is to decide where the dog is going to sleep, particularly if it is to be in the house.

Don't be surprised, though, if the dog chooses some other place after the first few days. If you are going to give the dog a bed, be sure it is large enough to accommodate the dog when it is full grown. It is tragic when a pup gets attached to its bed and suddenly the dog is too large to use it any more. However, you may find that your Newfoundland does not need a bed. He may prefer a large, airy corner, and if so you will prefer one where he can be tied or boxed in for the first few days away from the unusual noise and confusion of a strange household. Put a *large* container of water near where he is going to sleep. It may be more convenient if you feed him there, too. This spot should be home to the dog for the first few weeks and it will help him to adjust more quickly if he can use it as a retreat when things start to overwhelm him.

Ask the previous owner for a feeding schedule from the age when you purchase him until he is on the ultimate one meal a day. If you purchase a small supply of the same brands of food before you bring him home, it will make the transition a little easier for both of you. The same food that he is accustomed to will help to make the new house seem less strange. However, do not expect him to eat heartily right away, as some dogs do not eat well for a while after they leave the kennel. Homesickness sometimes causes them to run a slight temperature. A fever combined with listlessness is serious and you should call your veterinarian. The technique of taking your dog's temperature is described in the chapter on diseases and first aid.

It is wise to build an outside yard for the dog before he comes home. The run should be as large as your property will permit. Twenty by forty feet is a good size for one or two dogs, but if space permits it, a longer run is preferable. If you are building a kennel of several runs remember that the length is more important than the width. There are many different surfaces which you may wish to consider for your runs. The most frequently considered are sand, cinders, gravel, cement, and black top (asphalt) or grass. You will have to choose the one that suits your requirements of cleanliness and availability and cost. In fencing your run, build it strong enough to stand the strain of a full-grown 150-pound animal jumping up on it. It should be at least four feet and preferably five feet high. If you expect to keep a bitch in season safely inside, it should be at least six feet high and covered for absolute safety. The ideal fencing is chain link with metal supporting posts set in concrete and erected by experts.

If the expenditure for such a structure staggers you, you can do your own fencing, buying the wire fencing which suits your needs and pocketbook, using cedar posts for supports, and providing your own labor. Dig postholes, using horizontally stretched

Oquaga's Sea Diver II, owned and bred by Mr. and Mrs. Clifford Hartz's Oquaga Kennels, shown at eight weeks old (top) and three years old.

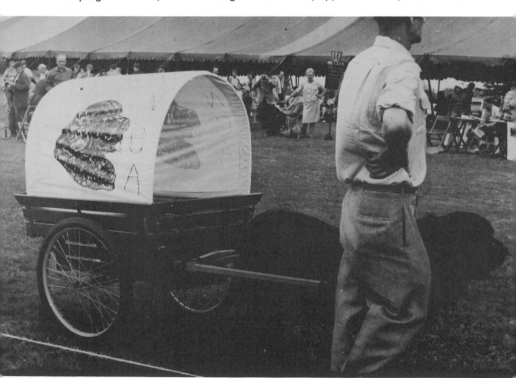

string as a guide to keep them in line, and dig them deeply enough to hold the post securely. Space the posts at six- to ten-foot intervals. Paint the section of the post which is to be buried in the hole with creosote or some other good wood preservative and set the posts in the holes. Concrete and rock poured into the hole around the post will provide a firm base. A horizontal top rail strengthens the run and will make a better, neater job. Brace all corner posts well. When your posts are set, borrow a wire stretcher to place the wire on the posts in a neat, taut manner. Be sure the fencing extends well below the ground level.

Neighbors naturally object to dogs, particularly large dogs, digging or lying in their flower gardens and they often take their resentment out on the dog. A yard provides a place for your pet when you go away for the day or are out shopping. It should include some simple type of shade and windbreak and fresh water. If it rains, you need not stand outside with icy water trickling down inside your collar waiting for your dog. Just put him into the yard for a reasonable time. Most important, no car or truck can run over your dog when he is safely in the yard.

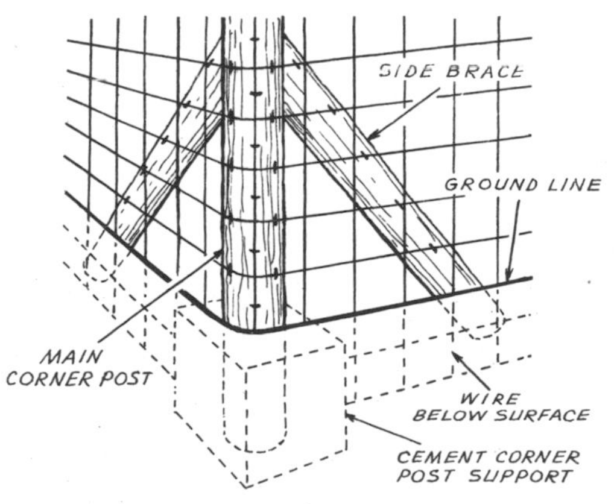

Cedar post run corner.

The last requirement is a good collar and two leads. A choke collar of the proper size is best because it releases as soon as the dog stops pulling. Leads often recommended are a web or leather lead. Dó not use a chain lead. If it is wound around hand (as is often done) and the dog starts running, crushed bones or a badly bruised hand is likely to result. A chain lead is also more easily broken than a good leather or web one.

Just one word of caution. Try to bring the pup home during the quietest part of the day. Instead of overwhelming him with attention, leave him alone to adjust casually to his new surroundings. Let him make friends his own way at his own speed and he will become your dog twice as quickly as when you force your attention upon him.

IF YOU HAVE CHILDREN

The Newfoundland dog is famous for his kindly disposition and great love for children. He will accept all kinds of abuse from a child with patience and tolerance long after a dog of most other breeds would snap or walk away. Perhaps this is because the Newfoundland is such a child at heart that he can understand a youngster and forgive it for its thoughtlessness. However, every dog must have his rights protected by the adults. Perhaps the Newfoundland deserves to be protected from abuse more than other dogs because he will not chastise a child himself.

HOUSING FOR ONE OR ONE HUNDRED

Housing for a Newfoundland can be very simple. He can live in the home, or, if you prefer, in his yard, a windproof house filled with cedar ribbon or clean straw in the winter and lots of fresh water will keep him happy. If he has a cool, breezy spot in the shade during hot weather, he will stay healthy and happy all the year. Unless you plan to raise puppies (which need heat in cold weather), the same housing applies to a kennel of many dogs.

An ideal kennel should have running water and electricity for your convenience. A room for storing and mixing food with sufficient space for your grooming equipment will also save you many steps. A heated whelping stall will be necessary if you expect to raise puppies (as described in the chapter "The Brood Bitch and the Stud"). You will also need an indoor stall with direct access to a large fenced yard for all the grown dogs, a smaller stall and yard for bitches in season, another for visiting bitches, and a stall and yard for puppies until they are old enough to roughhouse with the mature dogs. Ideally, no more than three adult dogs should share a stall 7 by 10 feet which opens into a shaded yard at least 70 square yards in area, preferably facing south. In laying out your kennel remember that the more compact your arrangement the easier it will be for you in its maintenance. Your dogs and your customers will appreciate clean and neat accommodations far more than the most palatial housing that is dirty. It is difficult to give specific directions for a kennel as each situation has its own demands and each individual has personal preferences. So long as the kennel is light and airy, comfortable for the dogs (not drafty in winter or suffocating in summer), and easy to keep clean and neat, it is well worth constructing or remodeling according to your own ideas.

DOG HOUSES

EXERCISE

You might as well face it right now. If your dog is average, your adult Newfoundland is a rather inactive fellow and he won't exercise much unless you make him. Except for an occasional slow and very dignified stroll around your place or about the neighborhood, he would rather observe the world from some cool, soft spot on the lawn. If he is just a pet, that is probably all the exercise he will ever get and he will remain quite healthy. If you are planning to show your dog, to raise a litter, or to start some new and intensive training program, it is wise to start with some slow and easy exercise, gradually increasing as you both can "take it." Ten minutes' trotting on a leash will do more good in less time than any other form of exercise. And if it is alternated with a few moments of walking it can be increased gradually to half an hour at a time. It is often easier to exercise the dog from the back of a station wagon, if it is driven slowly by some friend while you sit on the tail gate holding the lead. A show dog should be hardened until the muscles above the hock are solid and firm as a rock to the touch. A well-muscled dog will move more evenly than one that is soft and wobbly, and this is one reason why such a dog is more likely to win in shows. So give your dog the advantage of good conditioning before you show him.

Exercise is good for every dog and your dog will benefit from it even though you do not intend to use him for any specific program. Just start slowly and stop if the dog shows signs of fatigue. No work after that point will do as much good as that which went before. It is better to give your dog a little exercise regularly than a lot infrequently. The combination of love, exercise, and good food can't be beaten if you want your dog to look and act his best.

GROOMING

Brushing. Why groom your dog? Most people keep their dog groomed for good looks and don't realize that grooming has other advantages. Possibly the most important is that grooming cleans the dog's coat and skin. Dirt, matted hair, and loose undercoat are often the cause of skin trouble and wet eczema, which are very difficult to clear up. Such skin troubles often cause the coat to fall out. Regular grooming will keep a Newfoundland's coat healthy, as it stimulates the skin, and dogs that receive regular grooming usually carry full coats most of the year. Good grooming makes frequent baths unnecessary. A Newfoundland should not need a bath more than two to four times each year. Bathing removes the protective oils from his coat. It takes from five to eight days to replace enough oil for the coat to lie down properly. It is, therefore, wise to bathe your dog a full week before you take him to a show or his coat will not fall into place properly and the judge might penalize him for it. Newfoundlands love the attention they

Correct way to put on a choke collar.

Grooming tools: left to right: nail clippers, tooth cleaner, stripper, trimming scissors, three types of combs, and towel.

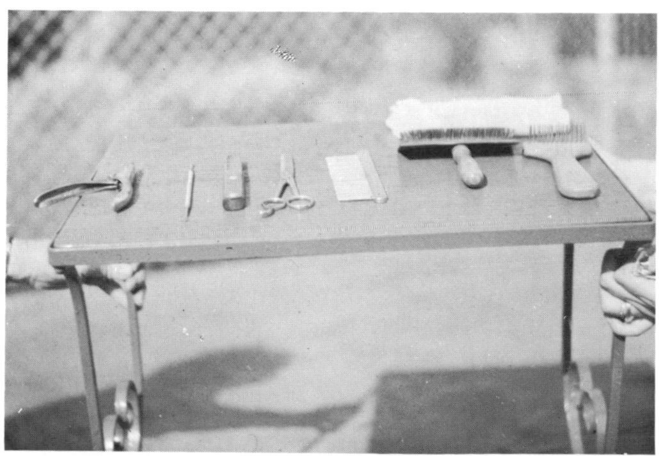

receive when they are groomed and your dog will look forward to his regular grooming. Neither of you will enjoy the tug of war which results if you have neglected it until he is covered with mats. Under such conditions, pleasure and companionship will be quickly spoiled.

The coat of a Newfoundland consists of long, coarse (but not harsh) guard hairs called the top coat and the very dense, soft, and almost woolly undercoat. This combination keeps water, extreme cold, or extreme heat from penetrating to his skin and it also protects him from injury of brush, thorns, and dog bite. The first time you try to give your dog a bath and cannot get his skin wet will prove to you how very adequate this protection is. Although it means that he can endure and even enjoy cold weather and an icy swim, it means also that grooming him will be harder than grooming a dog with a short, sleek coat. If you wait until your dog is shedding out his undercoat and is covered with mats from head to tail, you will have an exhausting all-day job when you groom him. However, if you groom him for about ten minutes each day when he is not shedding and for perhaps twice as long for the two or three weeks when he *is* shedding, you will find it is no problem to keep his coat glossy and unsnarled.

The Newfoundland's coat will be slightly oily to the touch, unless he has had a recent bath. Then it will be lighter, with less "body" to it. The coat will lie flat against his body and will probably have a slight wave in it. This type of coat takes considerable practice to groom quickly and thoroughly. Do not run a comb or brush from nose to tail and then down the sides of the dog. Grooming in this way is a waste of your time, as the snarls and mats are in the undercoat. No implement has yet been devised which will penetrate a Newfoundland's coat if it is used in this manner. The only satisfactory way to groom a Newfoundland is to do it backward. Start at the bottom rear of the body coat and work upward. A right-handed person will press his left arm against the dog's body and, while holding the coat in the left hand so that the skin is visible, will brush or comb a thin layer of coat downward until it lies in the proper position unsnarled. The skin should be visible again above the patch that is finished. Take the next layer above it and do the same. Be sure that you take only as much hair for each stroke as the comb or brush can handle and that you reach the skin each time. Work up to the top of the dog and then start at the next ungroomed section in front of the strip which has just been finished. Work forward to the chest on one side and then start at the rear and work forward in the same manner on the other side.

If your dog will pose as if at a dog show on a two-foot-high table with a surface at least three by four feet (an old door works well) it will be easier for you and it is good practice for the dog. Starting at the base of the tail, brush the hair against the grain until you reach the tip. Then brush it back in place. Brush the legs and chest from the bottom to the top. If your dog will lie down, it will be easier to groom his belly and particularly inside his legs. It is easy to miss the mats that form there and behind his ears. After all the snarls are out and every hair has been groomed you can put a good shine on his coat. Take a stiff brush in each hand and brush briskly in long, smooth strokes in the directions the hair lies normally. A final rubdown with a damp (not wet) towel will add extra highlights. When you finish, your dog should look ready to walk into the show ring.

Bathing. Your Newfoundland will be kept fairly clean simply by brushing, but several times each year you may want to give him a bath. Bathing does not pose the problem that you might expect. Kennels may have a bathtub installed that is waist high with steps leading up and into it. For the individual owner we suggest giving the bath outdoors. If possible, have warm water available. After the dog has been well brushed, tie him to a post and fill a pail with warm, sudsy water. Then wet the dog down with a hose. Apply the suds with a scrubbing brush and work it into the coat as much as possible. Rinse off the suds with a hose. If no warm water is available, get a pail of warm water and use this as another rinse. Any liquid hair soap or soap flakes can be used to provide the suds. Do not worry about his catching cold. The Newfoundland should be accustomed to swimming in the wintertime and will probably enjoy the bath regardless of outdoor temperature.

Trimming. The Newfoundland needs no other trimming or grooming unless he is going to a show. Even then, trimming

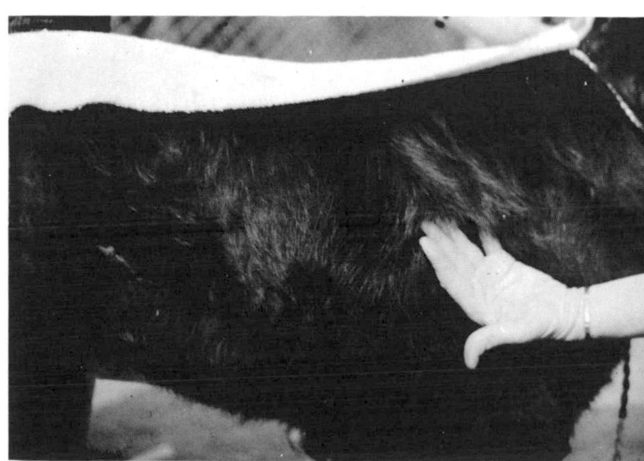

Guard hairs well brushed.

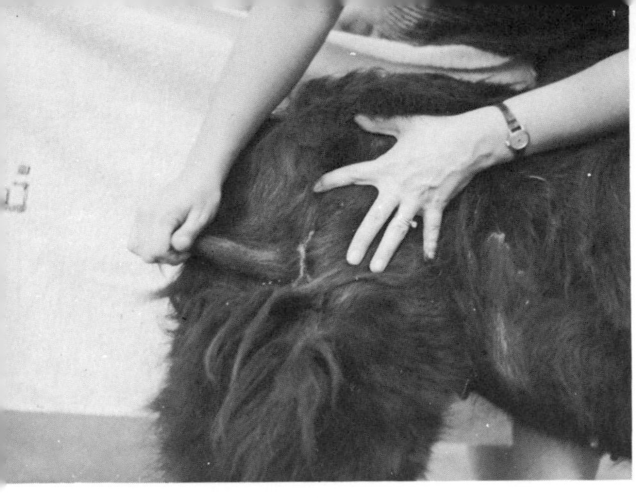

Each one of these mats must be worked apart with your fingers and a comb.

is confined to tidying up his whiskers and otherwise making him neat. Most kennels, therefore, confine trimming to feet, ears, and muzzle whiskers.

(a) *Feet.* In trimming feet, clean the dead hair out from between the toes by pulling the hair upward and using thinning scissors to thin it. Cut away excess hair from around the pads. On the forelegs, trim away the feather from the base of the paw up the back of the legs to the heel button. On the rear legs, trim the feather off about one inch above the back of the paws.

(b) *Ears.* If the ears look shaggy, trim away the excess with thinning scissors. Do not use a straight scissor as this will give too much of a cut appearance.

(c) *Whiskers.* Use a blunt-nosed pair of scissors to cut off the whiskers around the muzzle and long hairs over the eyes. This work tickles him and you will soon see the reason for the necessity of the blunt-nosed scissors. However, the effort should soon prove fruitful and even your Newfoundland will be proud to present himself at the show ring.

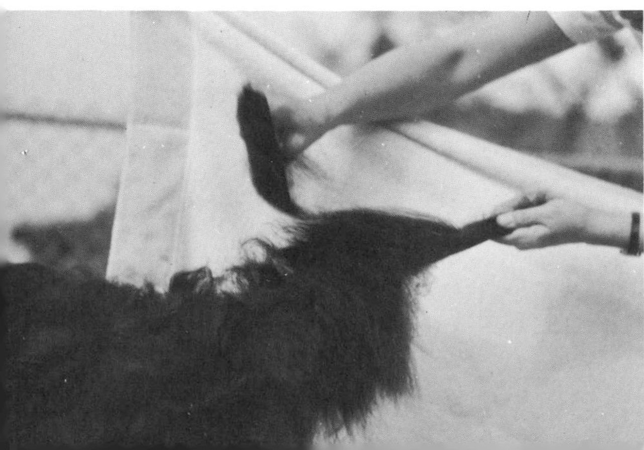

Combing tail.

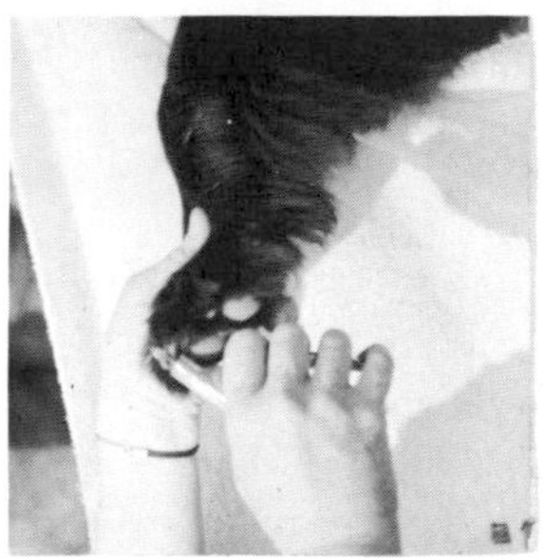

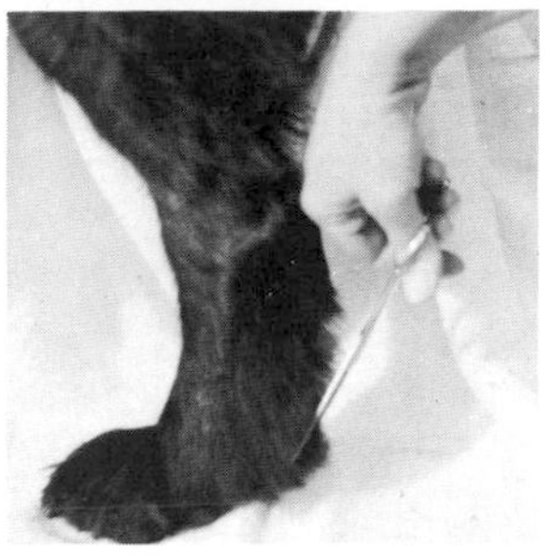

Clipping toenails. Trimming rear leg.

(d) *Toenails.* An active dog rarely needs his toenails trimmed. They are naturally worn down by walking on stones and other hard surfaces. Check the nails, and if they seem long clip ends off with a nail clipper. Be careful not to cut the quick. A simple, safe method is to file the nails with a coarse file. Broken in half, the five-inch end without the tang is easy to handle. Frequent filing will round off the nails without the danger of cutting the quick. The nail should just touch the floor when the dog stands naturally.

Cleaning Ears. Nothing smaller than your finger should be used to clean a Newfoundland's ears. Dip cotton in rubbing alcohol or ether and then gently wipe out each ear. It should be done as often as the ear appears dirty or smelly. Never use any kind of oil (except as a medication) as it will not dry out, and will cause collection of dirt in the ears.

TRAVEL

Half the fun of having a dog is taking him with you when you travel. If you go by car and have a station wagon or other model with washable upholstery, there is no problem. For the nicely upholstered family car, a canvas cover with snaps can be made by an awning maker or washable terry-cloth slipcovers can be purchased ready made.

Ear—untrimmed.

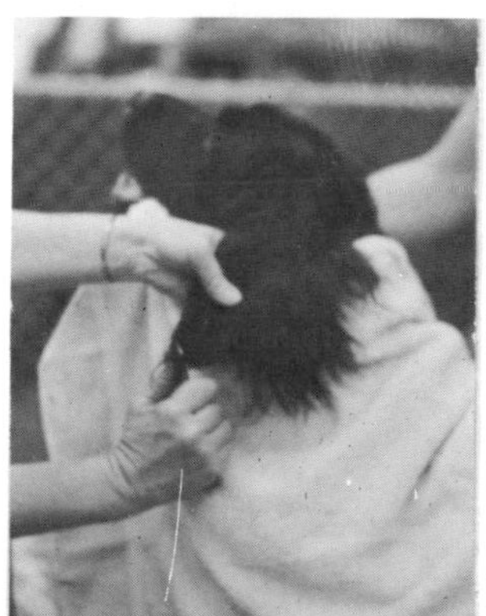

Ear—trimmed.

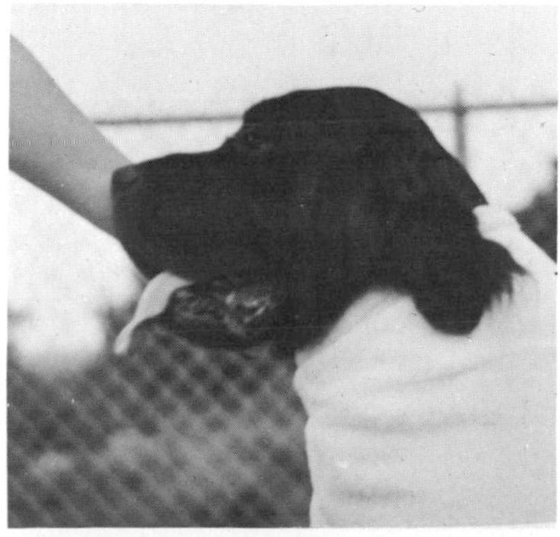

When traveling by car with your dog in hot weather, never leave him in a car with the windows closed. Carry his food dish and water pail with you. A pail of ice or ice cubes will provide your dog with water and prevent messiness in the car. If you intend to change his diet to one more portable, it is wise to begin the change a few days before the start of your trip.

Fifteen minutes before you start on your trip give your dog an adult glycerin suppository and let him air until he relieves himself. This will make him more comfortable and will keep your car clean. Always do this before going to a dog show as it is unpleasant and embarassing to have a dog make a mistake in the ring. Before you send a dog on an air trip it is also wise to do this. It can also be used in training a dog to use the part of your lot you designate for this purpose.

If you find it necessary to ship your Newfoundland to another section of the country, make sure that the crate you use is large enough in all dimensions to keep him from being cramped during his journey. The minimum dimensions of a crate for an adult Newfoundland are 36 inches long by 24 inches wide by 32 inches high. Check to see that there are no large openings or weak sections which might break in transit and allow the dog's limbs to project out of the crate. Consult your veterinarian or your local express agency for data on state health certificates. Supply the dog with a pan, rigidly attached to the crate, for water, and throw a few dog biscuits on the floor of the crate for the dog to gnaw to alleviate boredom during the journey. Be sure there are air holes in strategic locations to provide adequate ventilation. If possible the top surface of the crate should be rounded rather than flat, to discourage the placing of other crates on top of your Newfoundland crate. Strips of wood, nailed horizontally along the outside of the crate and projecting out from the surface, will prevent adjacent crates, or boxes, from being jammed tightly against your crate to thus block and defeat the purpose of the ventilation holes.

To minimize the length of time your Newfoundland is in transit and confined, keep in touch with the person at the other end of the trip so that the dog may be picked up on arrival.

CLUBS AND DOG SHOW ORGANIZATIONS

From time to time you have seen references in this book to the American Kennel Club (sometimes abbreviated to AKC), The Kennel Club (in England), or the Canadian Kennel Club, and it might be well for you to know something about them.

These clubs have been formed in their respective countries for the protection and advancement of purebred dogs. Similar clubs in The Netherlands, Switzerland, and Italy have been formed with the same objectives, but probably the ones you as individual owners and breeders will be most concerned with are those first mentioned.

The Kennel Club of England has recorded pedigrees of dogs in England since 1874, and it is these records that have made possible the completion of the pedigrees used in this book. In Canada, such records and registrations are kept on file at the Canadian Kennel Club (see Appendix for addresses). The Canadian National Live Stock Record Bureau, under the direction of Mr. Theodore Gundersen, kept the records until 1969, when they were turned over to the CKC.

Newfoundland registration in the United States is with the American Kennel Club, which not only maintains a register of dogs but formulates rules of registration, rules and regulations for dog shows, approves judges and handlers, keeps dog-show records, and publishes in the *American Kennel Gazette* all official data. It also publishes the *Stud Book Register*.

The AKC maintains a reference library of more than 7,500 books and periodicals, which are available to the public. If a dog breeder wishes to register a name for his kennel and for his own exclusive use in the naming of registered dogs which he has bred, he may also do this through the AKC. There are many other functions which the American Kennel Club performs in behalf of dog owners and breeders and for the general protection and advancement in the breeding of purebred dogs.

There are dog clubs in most communities. These are generally divided into two types: one is known as an all-breed club, formed for the purpose of staging dog shows in the community; the other is a breed specialty club formed by the owners of some particular breed of dogs, for social purposes, and for the advancement of the breed. The Newfoundland Club of America is a specialty club. When a specialty club is formed, it usually applies for admission to the American Kennel Club and, if it is admitted, becomes known as the parent club of the breed. In this way the parent club is then authorized to give permission for shows known as "Specialties." This means that all the club members are notified and will make every endeavor to show their dogs at these "Specialty Shows," as it is a fine chance to get together and meet other members, as well as to get good competition in the show ring. Each specialty club that is a member elects to the American Kennel Club a delegate who attends at least four of each year's meetings at which delegates from all clubs are present. He may bring before these meetings any matters which his club may request and report to the Newfoundland Club matters of special interest from these meetings. The Newfoundland Club

AKC delegate (who has been serving for sixteen years) is Mr. Charles D. Webster.

Clubs formed to put on dog shows are usually called "show-giving clubs" and run all the details of the shows in their community. The rules and regulations for conducting shows are established by the American Kennel Club, and the show-giving club is responsible for conforming to such regulations. The physical arrangements, such as tents, benches, equipment required, catalogues, etc., are generally handled by professional organizations that send out the entry blanks and take care of many of the details.

Although a dog show may serve as a social event, the real reason for the gathering is to put your dog into organized competition under an accredited judge in a show governed by official rules and regulations, where your dog can compete with others to determine which dog, in the opinion of the judge, most closely represents the ideal of that breed, as advanced in the Breed Standard.

One might look at it this way: if you have gone to the expense of acquiring a purebred dog with a long ancestry of champions in his family tree it seems only fair that you give him the opportunity to go on and prove himself also to be a champion, and recognized for all time in the official records. And the winning of a blue ribbon is an exciting event.

The more informal type of show and one good for puppies is called a "Sanctioned Match Show." Sanctioned Match Shows are small shows, usually held under the auspices of the local club or association, who obtain official sanction for the show from the AKC. Even though champion points are not awarded, your dog will be judged not only against others of his own breed, but against all breeds. It is also a fine place for a young dog and a novice handler to get acquainted with the routine of the dog show and to meet other dog owners in the community. "Fun" matches are informal get-togethers of dogs and owners. They are practice for more formal shows. Usually they include a family picnic.

As has been suggested previously, you might get in touch with your local club if you know of it, or write to the show secretary or superintendent (their names may be found in the *American Kennel Gazette*), and get from them a premium list which will also have the rules and regulations giving the qualifications and requirements for the class in which your dog can be shown. These are the rules and regulations laid down by the AKC which govern all shows. At first reading they may be difficult to understand, but as you show, you will become more familiar with them. For example, you will find in these rules the proper age and requirements for showing a puppy and will learn when he graduates

Winning team owned by Seaward Kennels (Westminster Show, 1954.)

Mr. Major B. Godsol judging a Newfoundland.

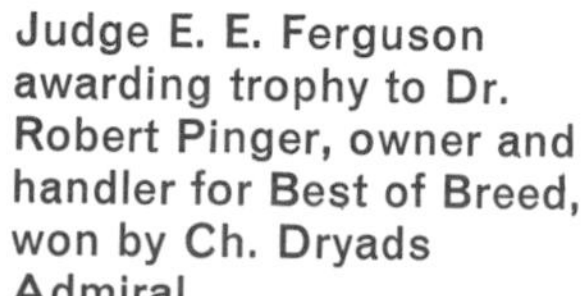

Judge E. E. Ferguson awarding trophy to Dr. Robert Pinger, owner and handler for Best of Breed, won by Ch. Dryads Admiral.

from the puppy to the novice dog class. Other such important matters are explained in these rules.

Other forms of competition for your Newfoundland might be to teach him obedience and show him in competition at obedience trials, which may be held separately, but more often are in connection with a dog show. There have been many Newfoundlands that have won their C.D.X. degrees at these trials.

Because of his great ability to swim and his known ability to rescue people from drowning, there has been considerable discussion among Newfoundland owners in favor of a water trial for the Newfoundland. In 1929 such a trial was held at a lake in New York State. Competition was based on the Newfoundland's retrieving his owner's objects under water, distance swimming, and other interesting forms of competition. Various efforts have been made throughout the following years to encourage further competition of the sort.

In 1969 two events occurred that showed what could be accomplished. First was publication by the Water Trials Committee under the guidance of Christian Cannell of a booklet titled *Newfoundland Dog Trials*. This first manual on Newfoundland training includes training for both land and water work. Secondly,

Ch. Dryad's Brown Betty, owned by Seaward Kennels, shown by Betty Cummings.

Ch. Little Bear's Black Thunder, owned by Charles Visich, shown by Bob Sharp; judge is J. Trullinger.

Am. and Can. Ch. Newfield's Nelson, CDTD, owned, trained, and handled by Mr. and Mrs. Allen Wolman.

under the direction of Mrs. Allen Wolman and Joseph Reinisch, a Land and Water Trial exhibit was held in conjunction with the National Specialty Show in June 1969. This occurred at the edge of the ocean at Paradise Cove, California, and also drew many spectators primarily interested in other breeds.

At this event, it was a thrill to watch Mrs. Arsenault's Barbara-Allen's Poseidon, C.D., T. and the Wolmans' Ch. Newfield's Nelson, C.D., T. Track, and truly an inspiration to Newfoundland owners. There were many entries in the cart pulling class, which is a favorite with spectators, and it was interesting to note that some of the entries worked with natural pulling instinct though never having been hitched before.

There was also a weight pulling class and then the Water Trials. Despite the ebb tide and the chilly weather, the dogs performed well. Winner as outstanding dog in the Trials was Nelson. This dog, trained and handled by Mr. and Mrs. Allen Wolman, was first in the Water Trials and second in the Land Trials, accumu-

Can. and Am. Ch. Eskimo's Grey Mug, owned and shown by Veronica Payne. Judge is Mrs. Maynard K. Drury.

Ch. Sarja's Sir Lionel of Irwindyl, top-winning Newfoundland of 1960. Owned by Geraldine Y. Irwin, Irwindyl Kennels.

Ch. Jewel of Verduron and Irwindyl, top-winning bitch of 1960. Owned by Geraldine Y. Irwin, Irwindyl Kennels.

Margie Richardson and "Joe," Can. and Am. Ch. Dryad's Joe Batt's Arm.

lating a total of 128 points. It is hoped that the success of this event will lead to holding of similar trials at frequent occasions in the future.

In the following pages are given a few simple "Do" and "Don't" rules of conduct to help you enjoy the showing of your dog in competition with others. Showing and raising dogs go further than good manners; they are a true sport, and a principal requisite for participating is to be a "good sport." Your enjoyment of this sport will mean much to you and your friends if you take to heart the words of a famous sportswoman, the late Mrs. R. Ambrose Clark, who said: "Win as if you were used to it, and lose as if you liked it."

WHEN YOU DECIDE TO SHOW

Taking your Newfoundland to a dog show can be a lot of fun. The people who show Newfoundlands are as friendly and easy-going as their dogs and you will make many new friends at your first show. You are sure to enjoy yourself even though the ribbons may not be awarded to the dogs that you may feel deserve them.

If you attend a few shows before you enter your dog you will have a better understanding of what is expected of you and your dog. Watch the Newfoundland judging and observe where and how the people stand and move with their dogs. Every judge has his own variations of the basic procedure but the idea is to show your dog to the judge to the best advantage. Try to show him so he looks as the Standard says he should look and do not try to show him the way you have seen Pointers or Boxers or some other breed handled. Go to shows until you are sure you know what will be expected of you both. Then go home and prepare to show your dog.

When your dog is in proper condition and properly trained, take him to two or three of the better handlers or judges and get an honest opinion of him. No matter how much you love him, or how handsome he appears to you, he may be a poor specimen of his breed. Ask these qualified people if he is good enough to win an occasional ribbon at a recognized show or if you will be wasting

Can. and Am. Ch. Dryad's Tambaram of Cayuga with his owners, Mr. and Mrs. Edward S. Wilson. Mr. Wilson is a former President of the Newfoundland Club of America.

your time and the money paid for entry fees. It is better to know now than it is to realize ten shows and many disappointments later that you should have kept your dog at home. However, if they suggest that you show him, do not expect to win all the ribbons at your first few shows.

It is rather bad manners to ask a judge where you should show your dog, but a professional handler will be glad to give you the information. Or write to your dog or livestock registration organization for the names of the show superintendents who put on shows in your locality. Write to these superintendents for the entry blanks of the shows which will be held in your vicinity. You must file your entry several weeks before the show will be held. Most exhibitors in the United States enter their dogs in one class only, although it is permissible to enter them in several.

Your first dog show may be confusing. You will certainly be nervous and excited and as you step inside the ring with your dog you may wish that you had never come. After one trip around the ring with your dog, you and your Newfoundland will probably be addicts for life, as there is no suspense or fun like it.

Can. and Am. Ch. Captain Morgan's Prince, owned by Mr. and Mrs. Fred Kearsey; a Newfoundland Club of America specialty show winner.

A scene from the National Specialty, 1959: Best of Breed Ch. Harobed's Hamish, owned and shown by Mrs. Rose Levy, and Ch. Dryad's Lighthouse Beam, owned by Dryad Kennels, shown by Maynard K. Drury. Judge is Mrs. D. D. Power.

Here are a few simple "Do and Don't" rules of ring procedure which should help you to enjoy dog showing.

Do:

1. Be courteous to judge and exhibitors.
2. Listen to and watch the judge and do what he asks.
3. Answer all questions briefly and accurately.
4. Have your dog trained and accustomed to crowds before you enter him.
5. Be at the ring with your dog when his class is called.
6. Thank the judge when you receive a ribbon.

Do Not:

1. Speak to the judge except to answer questions.
2. Talk to the people around the ring while you are being judged.
3. Get between the judge and your dog.
4. Get in the way of the other exhibitors and their dogs.

If you wish to ask the judge about the reasons for his placements, do it after all your breed judging has been completed and he is not busy. Do not argue with him, just ask him why he did so and so. His reasons may be very illuminating. Remember he was giving his opinion and it will not always coincide with your own. If you knew before the show which dog would win, showing dogs would not be the sport or fun that it is.

WHEN YOU WANT TO RAISE A LITTER

Perhaps you've shown your dog and you've won a little or maybe you have lost, but you think you would like to raise some dogs that will win. Or more likely, you just think it will be fun to raise a litter. Bringing a litter from conception to weaning successfully is a very rewarding experience. To be successful requires much planning and a lot of work.

If you will read the chapter that deals with pedigrees, study the pedigrees of the best dogs in the shows, and breed your dog to the bloodlines that produce the true type, you will start out with puppies which have a good potential. This subject is discussed more fully under the chapter "The Brood Bitch and the Stud."

REGISTRATION

Every dog eligible for registration with a central organization should be registered shortly after birth. An unregistered dog is no more valuable than a mongrel even though he does have the advantage of being eligible for registration. The object of registration is to keep a record of the breeding of purebred dogs in a central place where it will be available to everyone and where questions of authenticity are easily verified.

To register your litter you should write to your national dog or livestock organization (See Appendix for addresses) and ask them to send you the necessary papers and instructions. You fill out these papers and return them to the registration office. Usually there is a small charge to cover the bookkeeping costs. Some breeders register the litter and let the puppy purchaser send in the individual registration. If you have a kennel name prefix registered with the organization you will probably wish to do the individual registering so that the dog's name will include your prefix. A prefix which cannot be used by anyone but you is a very convenient and lasting means of advertising when every dog you raise carries it in his name. Usually it costs less to register your dogs before a certain age, so it is wise to get your information in time to take advantage of the lower fees.

Your puppies will command a higher price if they are registered, so it is good business as much as a proper conclusion to your planning and care to register them.

WHAT TO KEEP AND WHAT TO SELL

Now that your litter is weaned, wormed, and inoculated it is the time to sell any puppies in the litter you do not want to keep. You have two choices. You can put the same price on each puppy or you can price them according to the promise they show. No

Ch. Tranquilus Betty of Subira, Best of Breed at National Specialty at Beverly Hills, California in 1969. Owned by Peppertree Kennels, shown by William Buell, Jr. Judge is Alva Rosenberg.

matter how even in type the litter appears to be, the puppies will vary in size and quality. Experience with several litters is the only way to tell accurately and it is still easy to make a mistake after years of studying litters. Many stories are told of the promising pup that turned out to be mediocre and the rejected pup that became the champion. The best advice that we can give today is that given in *British Dogs* back in 1903:

"In selecting a young puppy, say one at six months old, a most useful age to commence with, the head properties should be the chief criterion. If there is not abundant promise of a massive head at this age, it may be taken for granted that such a puppy is not likely to finish well. A Newfoundland should also show straight forelegs and dense flat coat. . . . Tail carriage in any puppy must not be too seriously regarded until after the period of dentition is complete. Many puppies carry both tail and ears irregularly while teething."

In other words, you apply the Standard to him almost as well as to an adult dog. Look for the deep muzzle, biggest bone, a dark eye with no trace of yellow, small ears, a deep, square body, an even bite, and straight legs. Usually the best puppy will stand out from the rest and so will the poorest puppy. The only thing to guide you with the others is to balance their faults against their good points and then grade them accordingly. When you have compared pups of your litter, it is wise to compare the outstanding one with the best Newfoundland puppy of the same age that you have ever seen or against your idea of the overall quality of your litter. Remember that females are usually smaller than males, so if you have a small female which is a better type than a large, possibly leggy and long-backed male, she is worth more than he is. Size is not the only yardstick in Newfoundlands because over-all

Irwindyl's Smokey Lady, CD, winner of the "Dog of Distinction" award presented by *Dog World* magazine. Owned and trained by James Schmoyer.

Can. and Am. Ch. Perivale's Admiral Sir Timothy, owned and shown by Bill Cochrane.

Ch. Sea Captain, owned and shown by Ellis Anderson. Judge is Maynard K. Drury. 1957 Newfoundland Club of America Specialty winner.

balance and symmetry (proper proportions) are more important than height and weight.

If you plan to keep a puppy for breeding or showing, keep the best one, as it will do your reputation and program more good than the money from its sale. The puppy you plan to keep often has a magnetism for your customers and they will not buy if they cannot have him. It may be easier for all to put the puppy out of sight of customers than it is to try to persuade them to buy another. You may rather establish the high price at which you evaluate that puppy and sell him only if that price is forthcoming.

HOW MUCH DOES IT COST TO RAISE A LITTER?

Of course there are many factors governing the cost of producing puppies. The number of litters a bitch raises, the number of puppies in each litter, the amount of work you do yourself, the extent of your veterinarian bill, all play a part, as does the size and location of your kennel. Some kennels distribute their costs differently between male and female puppies, charging more for the male than the female. To illustrate how these costs may all be calculated, we have taken a hypothetical case of raising a litter of six puppies to an age of eight weeks.

Stud Fee		$250.00
(If the owner owns the stud this price would be higher, as the amortization of the purchase price and annual cost of maintenance amounts to more than is normally returned in stud fees)		
Transportation (bitch to stud)		50.00
Extra food and minerals and vitamins for bitch and pups		25.00
Veterinarian fees for bitch (assuming no delivery or after whelping problems)		20.00
Food for pups from weaning to eight weeks		150.00
Distemper shots by veterinarian		40.00
Worming pups by veterinarian		30.00
AKC registrations and transfers		23.00
Labor with pups (for eight weeks at two hours per day)		167.00
This is the bare out-of-pocket cost. It does not include the amortization of the bitch nor the cost of maintaining her during her non-productive years. During the average life of a bitch she will produce five litters of six pups each. Therefore the following costs should be added:		
Original cost of bitch	$300 ÷ 5	60.00
Cost of bitch for eight years at $200.00 per year	$1,600 ÷ 5	320.00
	Total cost of litter	1,135.00
	Minimum cost per pup ($1,135 ÷ 6)	189.00

From this you can readily see that even if a kennel owner "just wants to break even" he will have to average at least $200.00 per pup in selling his dogs. These are only stripped expenses and do not include the inevitable extras such as advertising, show competition, and the like that accrue in successful operation of a kennel.

Ch. Edenglen's Miss Muffet, owned by Guy Campbell, shown by Frank Ashby. Judge is Alva Rosenberg.

Ch. Little Bear's Tippo, owned by Dr. and Mrs. John Thompson, shown by Robert Forsyth. Judge is K. Given.

Canadian, American, Bermudian, Bahamian Ch. Newton, bred by Westerlands Kennels of Harold Macpherson, owned by Melvin Sokolsky. The winning Newfoundland of his era.

SELLER TO BUYER AND WHY

Your customers will expect more service than just being handed a puppy in return for cash and you will have a better reputation if you are prepared to satisfy them. They expect registration papers, and if you do not have them back from your registration bureau you must send them to the new owner as soon as they arrive. Your customers will want a list of the inoculations which the dog has received and the dates he received them. They will want to know when their dog was wormed, its registered name, date of birth and written instructions on feeding. It is well to have these all prepared before the buyer comes for his puppy so that you can hand him the list and instructions together with the pedigree and the pup.

If you make any special promises, either about the way their dog will turn out or that you will give them any unusual service, write it out so both of you will have a copy and you keep your word. Your eventual reputation depends upon satisfied customers, and it is good business to keep them as happy as you reasonably can. However, they can become unreasonable if they think you will take it, so decide just what you can afford to do for every customer and treat them all the same way.

STARTING A KENNEL

Many dog owners wake up one day and are surprised to realize that they have so many dogs that they already have a kennel. If you keep one puppy from each litter you will be overrun with dogs before you are aware of it. If you are at this state, you will do well to consider your dogs and decide just how deeply you want to enter this business. If you do not wish to have a full-scale kennel, stop where you are or sell or give away the dogs that you do not wish to pension.

However, if you've been having as much fun collecting dogs as it appears, you will do well to look for "holes" in your kennel. You may possibly have too many bitches and no dogs, or vice

Mrs. Maynard K. Drury with Dryad's Sultana and Ch. Dryad's Harborlight Lookout.

Ch. Little Bear's Black Baron, owned by Jill Carpenter, shown by Bob Carpenter.

versa. Almost every kennel has too much of one thing and not enough of another, and it helps to take inventory at regular intervals, then you can sell what you do not need and raise or buy what you have not got. We hope that you do have a kennel, because it's that much more fun than having one Newfoundland.

CONCLUSION

Any large, long-coated dog will need more attention than the smaller, close-coated breeds. However, a Newfoundland is so quick to learn, so obliging, and so affectionate that he repays a thousandfold for any extra care given him. Despite his size, he is so gentle that he is welcome everywhere and except for a boyish fondness for mud puddles, he is a gentleman from his nose to the tip of his tail. It is worth any price to be owned by a Newfoundland.

Chapter VII

Feeding

What, when, and how you feed your Newfoundland during his first year determines his disease resistance as well as his ultimate growth. Although feeding will not make him grow larger than destiny intends, improper feeding can both stunt his growth and make him grow improperly. A Newfoundland grows from approximately one pound at birth to about 120 pounds at the end of twelve months. Such rapid growth uses a lot of food. Although a mature Newfoundland of two or three years does not need so much food as his size and frame indicate, an active and fast-growing puppy needs a great deal, particularly meat, calcium, and minerals.

Although the bitch usually nurses the puppies until the end of the fifth or sixth week, it is wise to start milk or a formula during the third week. One breeder has found a successful formula to consist of $\frac{1}{4}$ evaporated milk, $\frac{3}{4}$ cows' milk, and 1 tablespoon lime water for each can of evaporated milk. Pelargon and Esbilac are nutritive commercial products which are usually available. You or your veterinarian may have a different one. If you remove the bitch for an hour before you offer the formula, the puppies will have a better appetite for it. Just warm part of it to about 100° F., pour it into a large shallow pan, and offer it to the puppies. Teach them to drink by splashing it gently on their noses or by dipping your finger into it and letting them suck on the wet finger. As you gradually draw the finger down into the pan, the puppies will follow it until they are lapping directly out of the pan. Only offer it to the puppies once the first day but increase to twice the second day, and by the fifth week they should be getting the formula three times a day. Turn the bitch back in with them after they have finished and, if there is any left, let her have it—do not store it after it has been warmed. However, the unwarmed balance of the formula should be stored in the refrigerator.

The traditional method of feeding is to start the puppies on 1 tablespoon of ground raw beef each sometime during the fourth

Feeding time at Edenglen Kennels.

week. Gradually increase it until each dog receives $\frac{1}{4}$ to $\frac{1}{2}$ pound of ground raw meat three times each day. If you remove the bitch for increasingly long periods while you feed the puppies more frequently, you will find they gradually demand less milk from her and she will not only dry up sooner, but will not be dragged down so badly by having to feed the larger puppies. At six weeks the puppies are on six or eight meals each day. Calcium, mineral, and vitamin products may be mixed with the meat during the weaning process and they are very necessary after the puppies are taken away from the bitch. Many breeders add pablum or a small amount of meal or well-soaked kibble, increasing the amount from porridge to mush consistency as the pups grow older. The true secret of raising extra-quality Newfoundland puppies is to feed them small amounts of food frequently. Small meals do not overload their stomachs and they keep extra weight off the puppies' legs. Too much food at a meal is more often the cause of weak pasterns than any inherited weakness.

Very gradually reduce the number and increase the bulk of each meal until they are on three meals a day at twelve weeks.

Nattanin Ralli, Desiree and Mrs. Pieterse, from the Netherlands.

The three meals should be one of milk and meal or kibble and two of meat and meal or kibble. Just be careful to keep the total amount of food during the day adequate without overfeeding them. When the puppies are six months old, combine the two meat meals into one meal and stop feeding the milk after the first year.

In recent years there have been many changes in feeding dogs. Commercial producers of dog foods have spent millions of dollars in research on the nutritional requirements and have developed biscuits, meals, and canned foods that include the required minerals and vitamins to keep a dog in good health. For this reason it is now unnecessary to add calcium and vitamins to the diet unless specifically suggested by a veterinarian, and it has been shown that there is more danger today of overfeeding these elements than of underfeeding. Table scraps (with the exception of bones) are good and should be mixed with the regular meal in moderate quantities.

Meat biscuit (or meal) and milk are considered the basic foods in a good diet for a dog. The quantities supplied vary with the age and with the size of the dog. Feeding methods also vary. It is acceptable practice to feed cafeteria style, with dry food always available in a self-feeder or the mixed food in a dish.

Puppy feeding is no longer considered to be different from feeding a grown dog. Both eat the same foods, and puppies can be fed several times daily as in the past, or the cafeteria style may be adopted. It is basically true that a puppy should eat small portions at frequent intervals, but puppies will regulate their feedings if the food is offered cafeteria style. If a dog has a healthy, glossy coat, bright eyes, and a good covering of flesh so that its backbone cannot be felt, yet is not soft and fat, it may be reasonably assumed that it is being fed correctly.

Sometimes a dog that is lean and hard may appear thin in the show ring. If it is felt that increased weight is desirable, more fat may be added to the diet. This may effect an increase in appetite. A diet of chicken necks and rice boiled together will also increase weight. But one should be wary of over-gaining; a dog that is too fat is as unhealthy as an obese person.

There is no cause for alarm if a dog skips eating for a day or two. If it were in the wild, eating would depend upon the success of the hunt and a meal or two each week would likely be normal. The reason for longer fasting should be determined by a veterinarian. The average grown Newfoundland eats approximately two to two and a half pounds of food daily; a growing pup over six months of age may eat three or four pounds.

Cafeteria style feeding is usually found to be the easiest and most practical in a kennel with six or more dogs. Since the food must be kept dry, a feeder with a cover is important. It need not

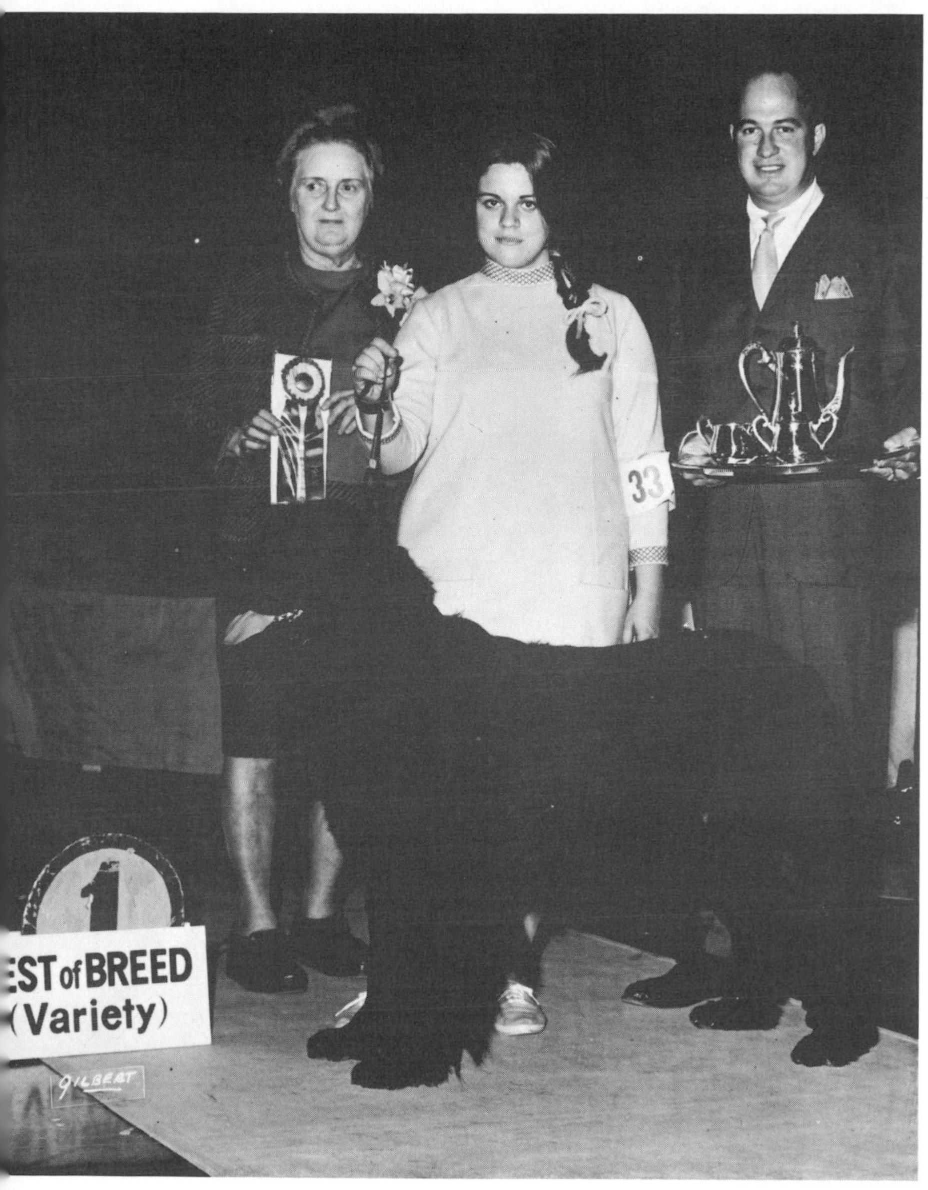

Ch. Little Bear's Commander Tucker, co-owned and shown by Elaine J. Misko. Judge is Mrs. M. Chern.

Ch. Edenglen's Sovereign of the Sea, owned by Mrs. William Kurth, shown by Joanne Lancaster; judge is Mr. Willis Linn.

be a large one as all the dogs do not eat at the same time. Moist food offered in a dish will spoil if left for long and should be removed if it is not eaten within a half hour.

Water is one of the elementary nutritional essentials. It is a major source of requisite minerals. It aids digestion and during hot weather (and to a lesser degree in winter) helps to regulate temperature. Water should be kept in shade in the summer. Poultry water heaters will prevent freezing in winter. Bucket-size vessels are about the right size.

Keep feeding utensils clean to eliminate the danger of bacterial formation, especially in warm weather. Food pans can be of any solid metal. Agate, porcelain, and the various types of enamelware have a tendency to chip and are therefore not desirable.

There are as many feeding techniques as there are kennels. The suggestions made here are offered as guides. Many of the firms distributing dog foods have excellent literature on feeding and these are available free of charge.

Ch. Perivale Sea Ranger, owned by Seaward Kennels, shown by John Davies, Judge is Major Godsol.

Can. and Am. Ch. Little Bear's Thunder, UD, owned by Roger Richards, shown by E. J. Carver. Judge is William H. Ackland.

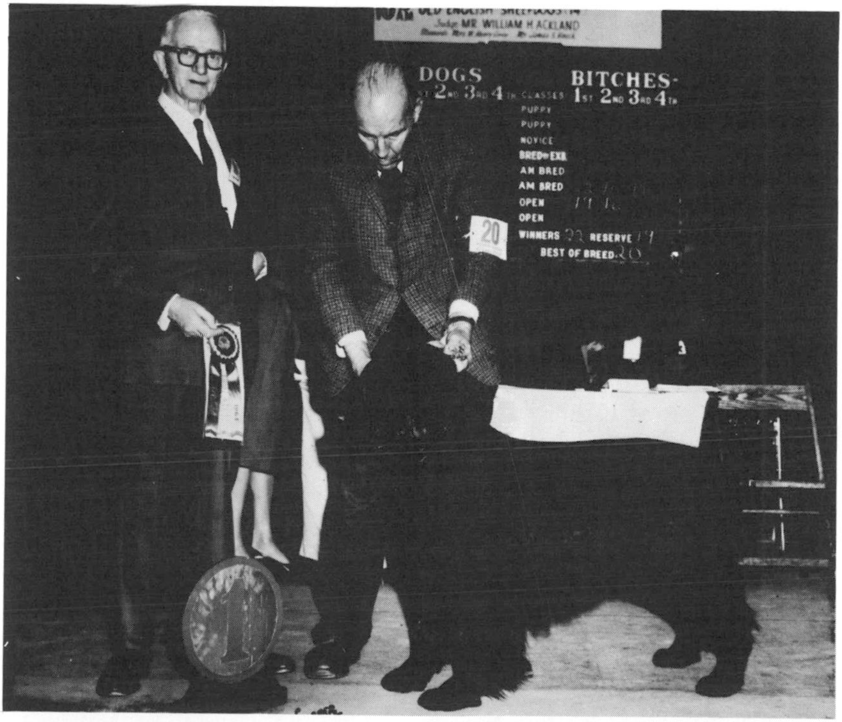

Chapter VIII

Medicine and First Aid

The Newfoundland that is well cared for is usually a well dog. This presumes cleanliness, adequate diet, proper immunization, and annual checkups with your veterinarian. It is both dangerous and ignorant to care for a diseased dog without proper advice and thus, although we can give you here a brief outline of some of the more prevalent disorders, it is wise always to leave the dog's care in the hands of a veterinarian who likes your Newfoundland and in whom you have confidence.

There are certain symptoms you should look for that will indicate that your dog is not well. Some of the symptoms are refusal of food for more than a day or two, diarrhea, constipation, difficulty in urinating, fever, running eyes, listlessness, fits, and a running nose. Should you notice any of these symptoms in your dog, take his temperature. This is done by laying him on his side and inserting a rectal thermometer into his rectum for two full minutes. Do not let go of it, as it is liable to be drawn into the dog. The average temperature of a Newfoundland is 101.5° F. A young puppy may run a temperature of 102° with no illness present. Should your dog's temperature be 102.5° or more or under 101° (excepting bitches about to whelp), call your veterinarian.

There are internal and external parasites to which all dogs are susceptible. Among the internal parasites are roundworms, hookworms, whipworms, tapeworms, and heartworms. Although most of these are rarely fatal, they will lower the resistance of your dog to disease and will inhibit his proper growth. Do not worm him because you "think" he needs worming. Too-frequent worming can be very harmful. Procure a fecal specimen and take it to your veterinarian for examination. If worms are present, he will prescribe treatment. Heartworm requires a bloodcheck. It is more prevalent in the southern states than elsewhere on the continent and its treatment requires expert care.

Coccidia are insidious internal parasites that greatly lower the resistance of their hosts. Adult dogs usually develop a tolerance to them, but a heavily infested puppy may not survive if attacked during its first few days. It is wise to have a bitch in whelp checked for coccidiosis, and treated should she be found to be infested. If this is not done, the puppies may be treated with antibiotics, but very often it is too late for your veterinarian to treat them successfully.

External parasites include fleas, lice, ticks, and mites. They are all disease carriers and are irritating and debilitating. Fleas and lice can usually be controlled by dusting the dog with a rotenone-based powder or an oil suspension of rotenone. Be sure to treat the area where the dog has been living with a good insecticide also or your dog will get reinfestations of these parasites. Repeat the disinfecting (both of dog and area) in ten days in order to kill the bugs that have hatched from the eggs.

There are new solutions on the market that will help keep ticks off your dog. If you do find a tick, remove it with care. If you use eyebrow tweezers, be sure the head is not left in the skin. A drop of ether or nail-polish remover put on the tick will soon make him lose hold. Then kill the tick with a lighted match.

Mites are the cause of mange, a skin ailment indicated by skin irritation and falling hair. There are several types of mange and they are all curable with prompt and proper treatment. Mites may also lodge in the ear and cause irritation. Treatment should be in the hands of your veterinarian. Among other skin diseases that afflict dogs are eczema, ringworm, and acne. Ringworm is contagious to humans and should be promptly attended to. Acne is a condition often found in young puppies. Their stomachs will be covered with small pimples that break and form scabs. This is not serious and requires only a good washing with alcohol or witch hazel and then application of a healing powder.

Eczema is of interest to Newfoundland owners because it is a very common ailment to all dogs and in our long-haired breed it is liable to get a headstart before we notice it. The cause of eczema is not yet known, but many experts believe it to be originated by various fungi and aggravated by allergic conditions. There are two forms which it may take—wet or dry. In wet eczema the skin exudes moisture and then scabs over. In the dry form there are patches of skin that look dry and scaly. Both forms cause great irritation and itching, spread rapidly, and the hair falls out. The spread may be so rapid that one night you may see a piece of wet eczema the size of a fifty-cent piece and by morning it will cover an area ten times the size. One more good reason for brushing your dog frequently and keeping him free of dead hair is the possibility of finding these spots.

There are many remedies that will help bring it under control, and if one doesn't seem to help, try another. Your veterinarian will have the latest knowledge on new medicines. Suggested remedies by kennel owners include Malucidin, Seleen, Led-O-San, 5 per cent salicytic acid and 5 per cent tannic acid in alcohol solution, calomine lotion with phenol and dilute clorox. In many cases a dog that does not have adequate fat in his diet so that his skin is too dry will have more tendency toward eczema. The addition of two tablespoons a day of bacon drippings, lard, or salad oil to his food may reduce the dryness and the likelihood of infection.

The diagnosis and treatment of bacterial diseases such as leptospirosis, tetanus, strep throat, tonsillitis, etc., are not for the novice or breeder to handle. We mention these diseases here only because you should recognize that if your veterinarian says your dog is suffering from one of them it is or may be a very sick dog. They are often fatal.

As in man, the small but deadly virus can invade our dogs and cause diseases such as distemper, hepatitis, rabies, and many others as yet unidentified. Dogs that are weakened by such diseases are susceptible to secondary infections that may leave them with debilities even though their lives may be saved.

Ch. Edenglen's Heidi Bear, owned by Mr. and Mrs. Robert Carpenter, scoring a group win.

Ch. Black Mischief's Christopher, owned by G. Witt. Judge is Mrs. F. Crane.

Immunity. To many of these diseases a dog is usually able to build a resistance to combat the invader with more or less success and survive. When these resistances are acquired as a result of a natural or "street" infection, there are certain risks involved. The dog may die. He may recover, but not without the loss of certain of his faculties. In any case, the dog must suffer and the owner expends time and money, and the dog may be the cause of infection of others in the kennel or neighborhood.

Means have been devised by which a dog's system is encouraged to build resistance to certain diseases without suffering a loss. This is true in the case of distemper, against which a lifetime immunity is usually established by use of modern vaccines. Immunity against infectious hepatitis and leptospirosis can be successfully established in most cases for a period of about a year by vaccination.

When a bitch possesses an established immunity acquired either through vaccination or natural infection, it is passed on to her puppies in greater or lesser degree through her milk. Thus, while they are nursing, puppies usually have some protection. Before they leave the mother's breast, they should be supported by serums, often called "booster shots," which are designed to prevent viruses of distemper or infectious hepatitis from entering the bloodstream. Such boosters are thought to afford appreciable assistance for about ten days, after which they should be repeated until the immunity is established by the puppy itself as a result of vaccination. Vaccination (often called "permanent shots") presently is thought advisable at about eight to ten weeks of age. Field experience may change advice on this subject. Keep abreast of the latest research through your veterinarian.

Although we have mentioned diarrhea and constipation as symptoms of other diseases it must be considered that, as in

Am. and Can. Ch. Newfman's Prince John, owned by Guy Campbell, shown by E. H. Carver. Judge is Mrs. Maynard K. Drury.

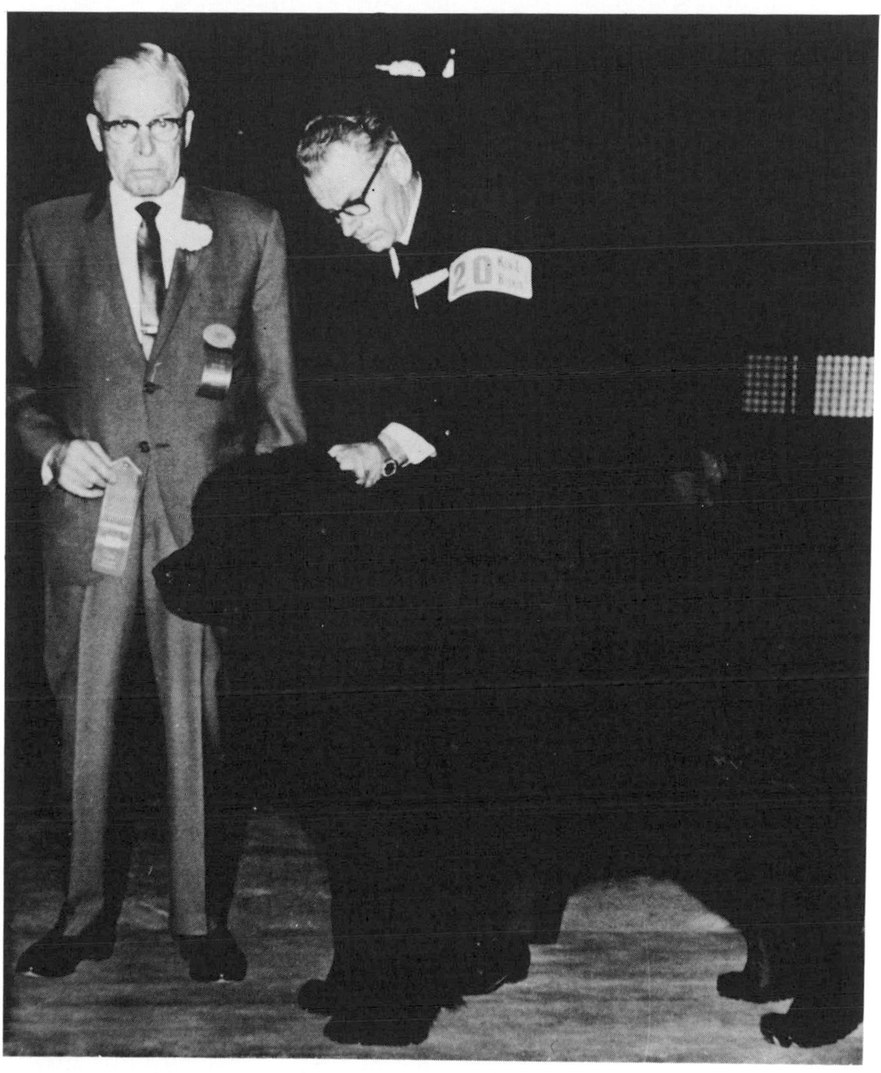

Ch. Carr's Black Sam of Bethward, owned by Paul and Betty Ramey.

humans, a change in diet or water or a slight stomach upset can cause such a disturbance. Check the temperature first. If it is normal and the dog seems to be active and hungry, treat it as follows. Diarrhea will often respond to kaopectate. Boiled milk and kibbled biscuit may also help. Constipation calls for laxative foods, such as fruits and bran, and a mild laxative such as milk of magnesia. If either of these conditions persists, consult your veterinarian.

Ear and eye irritations should always be referred to your veterinarian. If left untended, they can become chronic or may be a symptom of a more serious trouble.

Of invaluable aid to the kennel owner are the hanging strips that repel flies and other flying insects which may carry disease and be a source of annoyance. They are particularly useful in a puppy room.

There is a condition occasionally noted, generally among the larger breeds of dogs, which is variously called congenital hip disease, coxa plana, subluxation, or dysplasia. Usually involved is a hip condition wherein the rounded head of the femur (upper bone, rear leg) can slip in and out on an incompletely formed socket. As this continues, the head of the femur becomes flattened. Deposits of lime may form in time and cause an arthritic condition which can be crippling. The condition is usually manifested when the dog is between six months and a year old. The dog becomes weak in the rear legs and they do not develop properly.

The best means of diagnosing the condition is by X-ray. Veterinarians are not in agreement as to whether or not diagnosis can be determinative at an early age but are of the opinion that X-ray examination should be made as soon as lameness is noticed. Bones of a very young puppy may not be fully developed at the time; a slight movement of the puppy may go unnoticed and result in undetectable distortion of the X-ray, but the picture may, on the other hand, positively reveal the malformation.

Several theories have been advanced as to the cause of the condition. Some suggest heredity, others environmental influence, and general opinion seems to be that both factors may be involved. Recent studies indicate that the amount of muscle mass in the hip region may be of influence. It must also be taken into consideration that many cases of hip dysplasia are the result of accidents. Injury to the hip bones or supporting ligaments can occur as puppies indulge in rough and tumble play or when a very young one is stepped upon in the whelping box. Injury or disease of the spinal column can be a causative factor. Recently research has shown that there may be a relationship between hip-disease and metabolic imbalance.

Although this has not been a major problem with Newfoundlands, the subject has generated much discussion and confusion. To clarify the matter regarding correct formation and function of the hips of Newfoundlands, the Newfoundland Club of America (through the generosity of one of its members) sponsored a research project begun in 1967 under the direction of Dr. Wayne Riser of the University of Pennsylvania. Some thirty dogs over two years of age, sound, and of correct type are being observed and X-rayed. It is hoped that publication of the conclusions reached will serve as a guide to veterinarians and breeders.

In giving medication to your dog, do not be hesitant. A firm and confident manner will make it easier for you and the dog. If you are giving liquid medicine, tip the dog's head up, slip two fingers between the corners of his lips and thus form an opening in which you can pour the liquid. Keep his head up until all the liquid is swallowed. In administering pills, grasp the upper jaw, pushing your fingers against his teeth. In this manner his lips will be between your fingers and his teeth and he will not close his mouth. Push the pills back in his throat as far as you can. Close and hold his mouth and rub his throat until you are sure the pill is gone.

Following is a chart that will be of help in an emergency, before you can get to a veterinarian. Any dog that is injured is likely to become excited and frenzied. In this case it may be wise to muzzle him. If you have no muzzle, fashion one out of gauze, a necktie, or a strip of cloth. Loop it around the dog's muzzle, cross it under the jaws, and tie it up over the head. Try to calm him by talking to him and get aid as soon as possible.

FIRST-AID CHART

Emergency	*Treatment*	*Remarks*
Accidents	Automobile. Treat for shock. If gums are white, indicate probable internal injury. Wrap bandage tightly around body until it forms a sheath. Keep very quiet until veterinarian comes.	Call veterinarian immediately.
Bee stings	Give paregoric, 2 teaspoonfuls for grown Newfoundland, or aspirin to ease pain. If in state of shock, treat for same.	Call veterinarian for advice.
Bites (animal)	Tooth wounds. Area should be shaved and antiseptic solution flowed into punctures with eyedropper. Iodine, merthiolate, etc., can be used. If badly bitten or ripped, take dog to your veterinarian for treatment.	If superficial wounds become infected after first aid, consult veterinarian.
Burns	Apply strong, strained tea to burned area, followed by covering of vaseline.	Unless burn is very minor, consult veterinarian immediately.
Broken bones	If break involves a limb, fashion splint to keep immobile. If ribs, pelvis, shoulder, or back involved, keep dog from moving until professional help comes.	Call veterinarian immediately.
Choking	If bone, wood, or any foreign object can be seen at back of mouth or throat, remove with fingers. If object can't be removed or is too deeply imbedded or too far back in throat, rush to veterinarian immediately.	

FIRST-AID CHART

Emergency	*Treatment*	*Remarks*
Cuts	Minor cuts. Allow dog to lick and cleanse. If not within his reach, clean cut with peroxide, then apply merthiolate. Severe cuts. Apply pressure bandage to stop bleeding—a wad of bandage over wound and bandage wrapped tightly over it. Take to veterinarian.	If cut becomes infected or needs suturing, consult veterinarian.
Dislocations	Keep dog quiet and take to veterinarian at once.	
Drowning	Artificial respiration. Lay dog on his side, push with hands on his ribs, release quickly. Repeat every 2 seconds. Treat for shock.	New method of artificial respiration as employed by fire department useful here.
Electric shock	Artificial respiration. Treat for shock.	Call veterinarian immediately.
Heat stroke	Quickly immerse the dog in cold water until relief is given. Give cold-water enema. Or lay dog flat and pour cold water over him, turn electric fan on him, and continue pouring cold water as it evaporates.	Cold towel pressed against abdomen aids in reducing temperature quickly if quantity of water not available.
Poison	Give an emetic immediately. Hydrogen peroxide and water in equal parts —about 12 tablespoonfuls for the grown dog.	Call veterinarian immediately.
Porcupine quills	Tie dog up, hold him between knees, and pull all quills out with pliers. Don't forget tongue and inside of mouth.	See veterinarian to remove quills too deeply imbedded.
Shock	Cover dog with blanket. Administer stimulant (coffee with sugar). Allow him to rest, and soothe with voice and hand.	Alcoholic beverages are *not* a stimulant.
Snakebite	Cut deep X over fang marks. Drop potassium-permanganate into cut. Apply tourniquet above bite if on foot or leg.	Apply first aid only if a veterinarian or a doctor can't be reached.

A dog that has injudiciously confronted a skunk cannot keep it secret. The tell-tale odor of the skunk's retaliation will be dissipated in five to seven days if untreated. A thorough washing with soap and water can be immediately followed by massaging with stewed tomatoes and another bath to rid the dog of the offensive odor. Fumes from the discharge of the skunk are not harmful to the eyes of the dog but will cause a burning sensation and some inflammation. If the liquid was squirted into the eyes, however, a veterinarian should be consulted.

Chapter IX

Training and Obedience Work

Every dog needs a certain amount of training and exercise. An untrained dog is a liability, particularly when he is large and heavy, and such a dog cannot be very happy as no one wants a wild, undisciplined animal around and their feelings will be conveyed to the dog by their actions. It is not a dog's nature to be pleased when he is rebuffed for making friendly advances just because he unintentionally hurts or frightens people. The reasons for training a dog and the methods used to train him will vary according to the use to which you plan to put him.

There are excellent books which will help you to train your dog for specialized use and there are equally good books which tell you how to teach your dog to be an obedient and mannerly member of your family. The real key to training a dog is to be consistent, firm, and kind. Consistency is the key to all training. If you do not want your dog to jump on people when he is fully grown, do not allow him to jump on anyone as a small puppy. Do not let him do one thing today and then punish him for the same action tomorrow. If you do so, you will lose all authority, for the dog rightly feels he has been punished unfairly, nor can the dog learn to know what you really wish.

A Newfoundland is quick to learn and eager to please. He would rather be good and be loved than to do wrong and be scolded. Simple training by the owner can start as soon as you get your puppy. Housebreaking, wearing a collar, and learning to walk on a leash comprise the early training routine and can soon be followed by simple commands such as "sit" and "down." House training can usually be accomplished the first week by eternal vigilance. Take the puppy out *as soon as* he wakes from a nap and *immediately* after he has eaten. He will need papers on the floor wherever he is confined for the night until he is about six months of age. Walking the boundaries of the property on which you wish him to stay twice a day for a week, with a gentle

Ch. Mark Anthony of Waseeka, the first Newfoundland to have earned his C.D. and C.D.X. degrees in the United States, together with his four-month-old son, Coastwise Anthony Adverse, owned by Coastwise Kennels.

spank administered for wandering beyond them, will usually suffice in teaching him to stay at home. Your puppy will grow rapidly and soon reach the awkward age. It is recommended that he not be exposed to highly waxed surfaces inside the house. He instinctively fears these and being a big dog they present a real danger to him, as he is apt to slip and injure himself.

Formal obedience training in a class or otherwise should be deferred until at least six months of age. Obedience-training classes are available today in many of our towns and cities and are often presented through the Adult Education Program. For a directory of training clubs in your area you may write to The American Kennel Club, 51 Madison Avenue, New York, N.Y. 10010, or Gaines Dog Research Center, 250 Park Avenue, New York, N.Y. The most authoritative book on the subject is *Training You to Train Your Dog*, by Blanche Saunders.

The only training necessary when you plan to show your dog before a judge is very simple to teach and to practice. A show dog must be accustomed to standing in position, with his legs and feet where you have placed them, for several minutes, while a stranger opens his mouth, pushes down on his hindquarters, ruffles his coat, and moves his tail. He should not sit down, wiggle, or move out of position. It takes practice for a dog to get used to standing stationary, but even a small puppy can learn quite quickly with only a few minutes of practice each day.

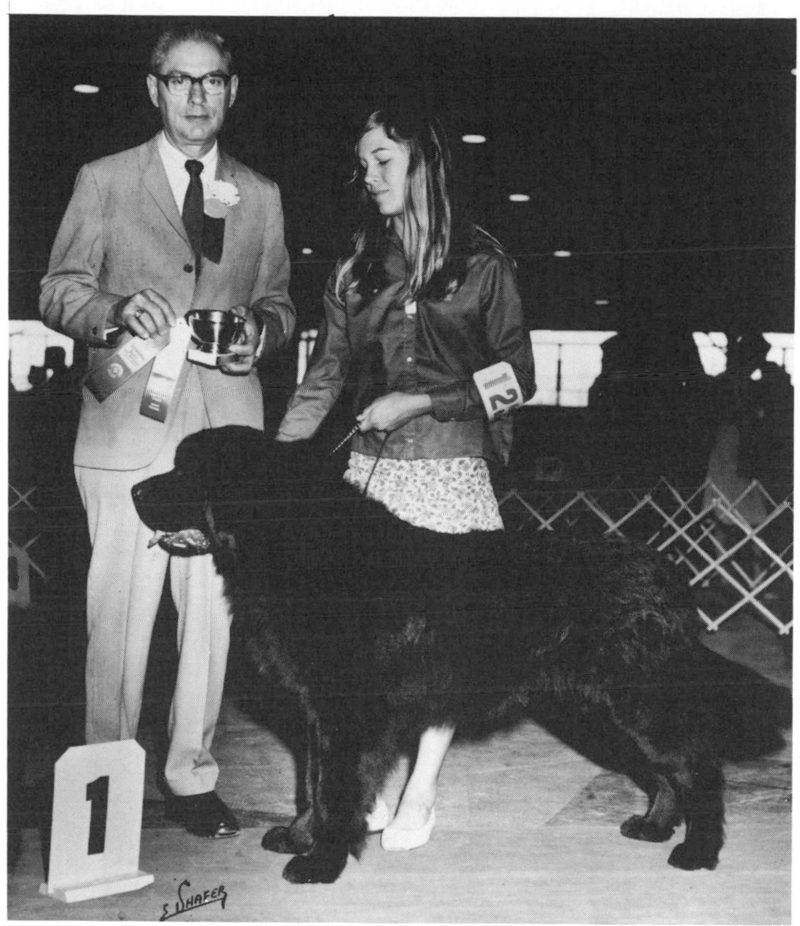

Ch. Tranquil Taylor, owned by Captain James Bellows, shown by Janice Bellows. Judge is Maxwell Riddle.

Your dog must also learn to walk and to trot (never canter) on a loose leash at your left side without dragging back or pulling forward. He must learn to turn left when you do, without getting in your way so that you do not fall all over him. If you set up a dummy ring about 25 feet by 20 fcct and practice walking and trotting around it in a counter-clockwise direction you will find that you and your dog get used to the maneuver quickly. The first few times around will be rather hectic, but you and your dog will soon get the idea and a few trial runs each day for a week should have your dog ready and mannerly for any show. A choke collar and an eight-foot lead are usually the most convenient and easiest combination to use.

Seaward's Black Bittern, C.D., C.D.X., owned by Lawrence E. Specht, taking a "high jump."

The kennel dog does not need very much training. If he is properly leash-broken when he is about five months old, knows his name so that he comes when he is called, and does not jump on people, he will have received all the training necessary and probably all that you have time to give him anyway.

Most training rules apply to all breeds, but certain characteristics of the Newfoundland must be remembered and heeded in his education, be it formal or otherwise. Of paramount importance is to know when to *stop* training. Newfoundlands are intelligent enough to become tired and disgusted with seemingly unworthy exercise. You must learn to sense when your dog becomes bored and complete the training period in a playful mood. Perhaps equally important is the necessity for keeping your temper and never becoming angry with your dog. Newfoundlands do not understand anger and as a result they become confused and bewildered. *Never* use loud verbal commands. Your dog will respond best to gentleness and firmness and will understand praise far better than punishment.

Many years ago the British Kennel Association organized a series of water trials for Newfoundlands and drafted rules for their conduct in 1876 as follows:

1. Courage to be displayed in jumping into the water from a height to recover an object. The effigy of a man is the most suitable thing.
2. Quickness to be displayed in bringing the object ashore.
3. Intelligence and speed in bringing a boat to shore. The boat must, of course, be adrift and the painter have a piece of white wood attached to keep it afloat, mark its position, and facilitate the dog's work.

4. To carry a rope from ashore to a boat with a stranger, not the master, in it.
5. Swimming races to show speed and power against stream or tide.
6. Diving. A common flag basket, with a stone in the bottom of it to sink it, answers well, as it is white enough to be seen and soft enough to the dog's mouth.

Of these trials Mr. Hugh Dalziel, their chief organizer, says: "Although they could not be pronounced a brilliant success, they were in many respects interesting and proved that, with more experience, and if well carried out, such competitive trials might become more than interesting—highly useful."

The first American Water Trials on record occurred in 1929 and Mr. Edwin H. Morris wrote of them:

The North American Newfoundland Club of which Mr. Zabriskie is one of the executives and I, myself, secretary, with the cooperation of Walter Orr, met for a water trial on Mr. Orr's lake. For this event a silver cup was donated and any dog owned by a member of the Newfoundland Club could compete whether entered for the show or not.

Mr. Orr's spacious grounds were crowded with cars and the spectators lined the banks of the lake. There were five nominees, but as one brought from Newfoundland and said to do anything but whistle did not arrive because of his owner's illness, and as another wonder did not appear, the competition was between Mr. Orr's Casey, Mr. Zabriskie's Black Knight II and Mrs. Vivian B. Moulton's dog from Maine. Mr. Moulton, on getting a letter from the secretary at night, jumped in his car the next morning at West Woolwich in Maine and reached Cornwall just in time for the trials though too late for the show. The judging started with a test of speed and endurance and Mr. Orr's dog by following the boat was fairly good in both respects. Mr. Zabriskie's dog, being naturally shy, was more so with the crowd around, so he preferred dry land. Mrs. Moulton's dog was obedient, followed the boat over the lake at considerable speed, and to show he was not exhausted Mr. Moulton gave him a rope with which the dog brought the boat to the starting place speedily and without showing effects of his exertion. A boy then dived into the lake for rescue work. The Maine dog alone jumped in and brought the boy ashore, holding to both sides of the dog's coat. At this the spectators enthusiastically announced the victory for Maine.

The judge then called for tests of obedience, retrieving, and diving, for although Mrs. Moulton's dog had scored for speed, endurance, and rescuing, there was a possibility of his losing the lead. The dogs were given a fair chance here but without change in score, and as a thunder shower was just breaking the cup was awarded to the dog from Maine and Mr. Moulton was congratulated by both clubs for his sporting and hasty trip from New England.

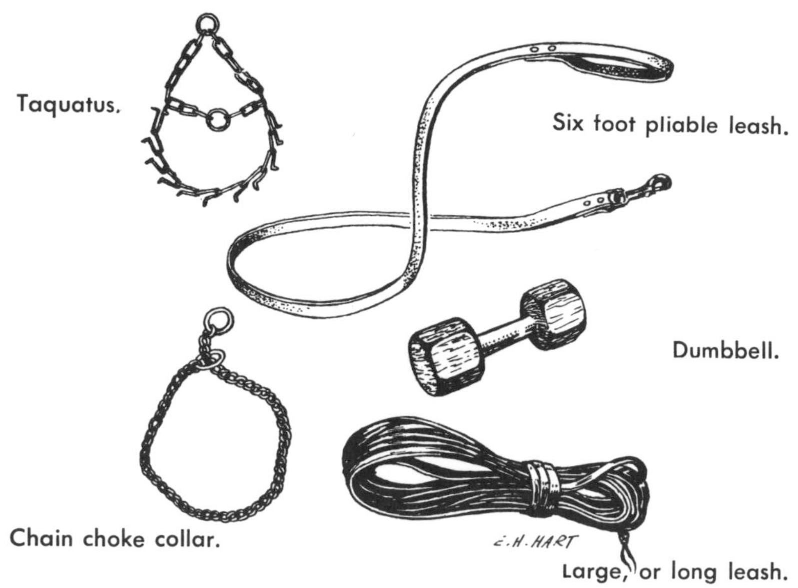

TRAINING EQUIPMENT

With the increase of the breed in this country today many owners are hopeful that similar trials may be organized in the near future. It would be highly satisfying to prove that the Newfoundland dog is all that he is claimed to be.

HINTS ON TRAINING FOR WATER TRIALS

To prepare a dog for water entry from a height, the dog must first enjoy entry from a beach and then be encouraged to enter from water-level docks and gradually higher docks until a three- or four-foot entry becomes commonplace. This type of training, just as distance swimming, takes practice and patient repetition.

Most Newfoundlands are natural retrievers. They love to carry objects and to return thrown objects. When working with floating objects, substitute a boat bumper or like object similar to what the dog has been retrieving that just barely will not float. A light color is preferable. Throw it into water a few inches deep. Gradually increase the depth as long as the dog enjoys fetching it. Alternate with a floating bumper occasionally to break the monotony and keep the activity within the realm of fun. Only experience and the individual ability of the dog as he becomes adept at it will determine the depth limit at which he can work. In order that a dog swim away or retrieve an object which he does not see at a distance and did not see fall, he must be taught hand signals. As in retriever training, the logical command is "get back" or "go back", and the logical signal is an overhand-pointing with the arm extended upward. Likewise a left-arm sweep to the left or right-arm sweep to the right should direct the dog to the left or right respectively.

To teach a dog to "get back," a bumper with which he has been working should be "planted" before he comes on the scene. From the starting position give the "get back" command and signal and walk a few steps toward the bumper. Repeat the command and walk a few more steps. Do this until the bumper is reached and the dog finds it. Praise him heartily and trot back to the starting point to receive the retrieve. With patient repetition the dog will soon learn that your signal is the beginning of "going in that direction" which he will gladly do without you as soon as he is convinced that the retrieve will be out there for him to find and bring back to you. Left or right signals can be taught similarly. Always make your signals slow and clear. Never send a dog when there is nothing for him to locate and bring back to you.

Practice having the dog retrieve a piece of line. Send him occasionally to retrieve a piece of "planted" line. The ultimate in this respcct is to send him to retrieve a painter to which a boat is attached. Make the boat a light one at first. Eventually he will probably be willing to tackle anything on the end of a rope that floats.

When your dog is willing to carry a piece of hemp line, give him the "get back" signal towards another member of the family. The other member encourages him, should he be hesitant, and praises him liberally upon his delivery of the line to them. This can be done over land or water. It will be the same to a Newfoundland.

Your dog will probably retrieve a human "instinctively," but if you wish to have an effigy rescued, fasten his bumper to it and after a couple of successful "rescues," send him for the effigy without the bumper.

A word should be said here that the Newfoundland should be trained for swimming with people, otherwise he can be a nuisance. He may try to rescue you when you just want to swim. Many owners have found that the best thing to do is to teach their dog to swim near but not at them. This is done by pushing his head away when he gets too near. Then grasp his collar or neck or tail and let him pull you into shore. He will soon learn that he is there to help you when you want help but he not to pull you in by force. It has been found that when a Newfoundland is trained as above he will swim around you in circles and be ready to pull you ashore when you want him to.

Captain Ebon, an accomplished retriever of wild game, owned by Mr. Anderson.

TRAINING FOR SHOW

OBEDIENCE ACCOMPLISHMENTS

During the past few years increased numbers of Newfoundland owners have been entering their dogs in Obedience classes. Following are dogs that have won their titles:

C.D. Titles

Captain Bob II
Carbonear Newf
Cleopatra of Waseeka
Coastwise Coal Black Rose
Lady Guenivere of Irwin-dyl
Lady Jetina of Oakwood
Little Bear Isolt of Irwin-dyl
Lord Roberts
Mark Anthony of Waseeka
Midway New
Nubia of Terra Nova
Rovalus Black Swan
Seawards Black Bittern
Shadowlawn's Black Victory
Skipper's Star
Tony's Teddy
Vivian's Boy Butch
Waseeka's Bon Voyage
Bittern Duke of Panda
Dagmar of Wakefield
Victoria Annabelle
Ch Little Bear's Seldom Come By
Latimer's Misti Lake
Latimer's Black Buttons
Happy Lad
Seaward's Sapphire Sea
Black Kelly Knight Errant
Seaward's Frosty Spray
Irwin-dyl's Cheetah May Queen
Ch Little Bear s Thunder
Ch Little Bear's Zulu Queen
Ahtuckta
Little Caesar
Irwin-dyl's Viv's Honey Babe
Irwin-dyl's Smokey Lady
Ch Caldwell's Yulie Queen Lora
Caldwell's Yulie Princess
Irwin-dyl's Cherna Momiche
Irwin-dyl's Schwarz Ritter
Irwin-dyl's Flying Dutchman
Sam's Golliwog of Windy Hill
Little Bear's Black Cinderella
Seaward's King Merasuk
Little Bear's Bmews
Irwin-dyl's Black Dinah
Bayshore's Black Storm
Black Mischief's Solo Flight
Caldwell's Duchess Ed's Brandy
Edenglen's Pilot
Heidi of Del Ray
Noah of Newfield's
Dryad's Helen of Troy
Newfield's Lively Lady
Ch Dryad's Yogi Bear
Mon Seiche Tide
Little Bear's Cabot
Irwin-dyl's Black Orpheus
Ch Dryad's Lord Nelson
Lord Jim
Irwin-dyl's Brunhilda
Ch Edenglen's Joy
Patti's Black Baby Sambo
Shipway's Avalon Holly
Princess Ebony of St John
Irwin-dyl's Poseidon
Irwin-dyl's Miss Prim
Good Time Charlie
Duke Ramaire of Lang's Acre
Don-Ru's Lady of Lourdes
Barbara Allen's Poseidon
Newfield's Nelson
Tahoe's Silver Kazan
Ebony's Samantha of Windy Hill
Little Bear's Sea Gipsey
Edenglen's Leyte Godiva
Ch Barbara Allen's Newfie Nana
Ry-Ann's Viking Rollo
Shipshape's Sea Baron
Little Bear's Bismark
Barbara Allen's Tekawitha
Henne V Schartenberg
Viv's Honey Anna John John Andy

C.D.X. Titles

Ch Carbonear Newf
Mark Anthony of Waseeka
Seaward's Black Bittern
Tony's Teddy

Rovalus Black Swan, the first Newfoundland to have earned the U.D. title in America, owned and trained by Mrs. Frances McJunkin of Vallejo, California.

Shipway's Avalon Holly, CD, CDX, UDT. Owned by Mr. and Mrs. John Carr. The first Newfoundland to garner all obedience degrees.

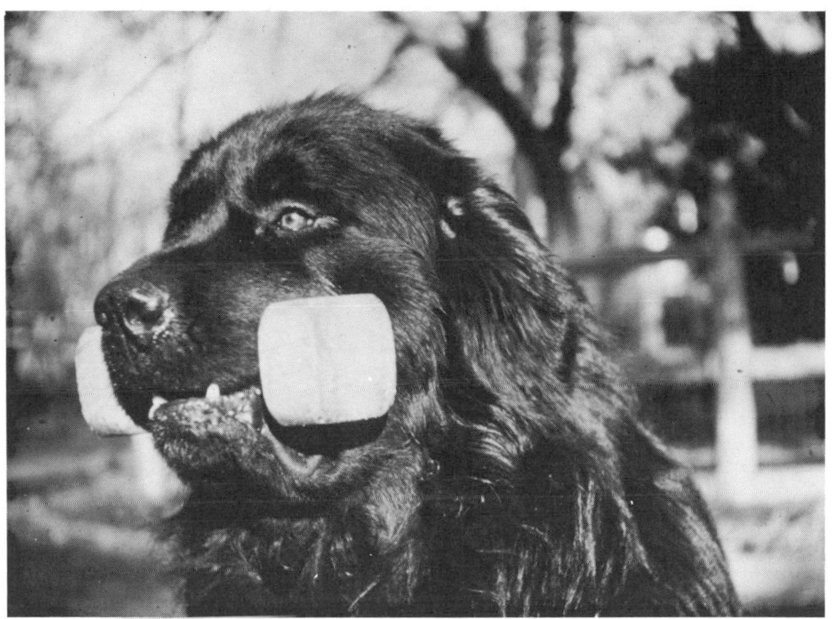

Ch. Dryad's Lord Nelson, CD, CDX, UD, T, shown, trained, and owned by Mrs. George McDonnell.

Dagmar of Wakefield
Ch Little Bear's Thunder
Ahtuckta
Irwin-dyl's Flying Dutchman
Shipway's Avalon Holly
Ch Dryad's Lord Nelson
Rovalus Black Swan

U.D. Titles

Rovalus Black Swan
Dagmar of Wakefield
Ch Little Bear's Thunder
Shipway's Avalon Holly
Ch Dryad's Lord Nelson

Tracking Degrees

Ahtuckta
Barbara Allen's Poseidon
Shipway's Avalon Holly
Ch Newfield's Nelson
Ch Dryad's Lord Nelson

Of special interest are Shipway's Avalon Holly, a dog owned, trained, and shown by Mrs. John Carr, and the first Newfoundland to earn all Obedience degrees (C.D., C.D.X., U.D.) and Tracking; and Ch Dryad's Lord Nelson, owned, trained, and shown by Mrs. George McDonnell as the first dog to have his Bench Championship and to have earned all of the Obedience degrees.

Chapter X

The Standard of Perfection

Newfoundlands are good to look at and delightful to own. Essential facts concerning the origin and improvement of a breed are useful guideposts by which breeders can survey the progress that has been made and better chart the course of their future operations. A study of past errors helps prevent the repetition of these mistakes. A study of past accomplishments makes it easier to duplicate those results. Conscientious breeders have striven throughout the years to maintain those characteristics for which their breeds have been superior and have attempted to correct their inherent weaknesses.

The principal objective of a good breeder should be uniformity and consistency. In other words, he should establish a line that will produce the correct type of dog consistently. In this connection it is well to remember that the pattern for type is set by inheritance, but its fulfillment depends on health, nutrition, and environment.

There are many terms used by people in the field of purebred dogs. Consequently, it is necessary to have a general understanding of some of the ones that are used most commonly. It is for the purpose of clarification for the layman that explanations (see Glossary) are made concerning the terms used in discussing the breed. This is not a complete glossary of terms, but is meant only to be helpful in understanding the Newfoundland Standard.

For the layman or novice the specifications of the Standard have been taken apart, analyzed, and interpreted, so that they can be applied to an individual dog or bitch. A clearly defined ideal of a Newfoundland is important to breeders and judges. Attempting to evaluate a dog without first formulating a fixed image of an ideal in your mind is synonymous to driving a car without a steering wheel. It soon ends in tragedy.

Nothing said here is intended to supersede or distort the specifications set forth in our Standard. That Standard, interpreted as best we can interpret it, must govern our breed.

THE NEWFOUNDLAND STANDARD
as approved by the American Kennel Club—November 11, 1969

The Board of Directors of The American Kennel Club has approved the following revised Standard for Newfoundlands, submitted by the Newfoundland Club of America:

General Appearance: The Newfoundland is large, strong, and active, at home in water and on land, and has natural life-saving instincts. He is a multipurpose dog capable of heavy work as well as of being a devoted companion for child and man. To fulfill its purposes the Newfoundland is deep bodied, well muscled, and well coordinated. A good specimen of the breed has dignity and proud head carriage. The length of the dog's body, from withers to base of tail, is approximately equal to the height of the dog at the withers. However, a bitch is not to be faulted if the length of her body is slightly greater than her height. The dog's appearance is more massive throughout than the bitch's, with larger frame and heavier bone. The Newfoundland is free moving with a loosely slung body. When he moves, a slight roll is perceptible. Complete webbing between the toes is always present. Large size is desirable but never at the expense of gait, symmetry, balance, or conformation to the Standard herein described.

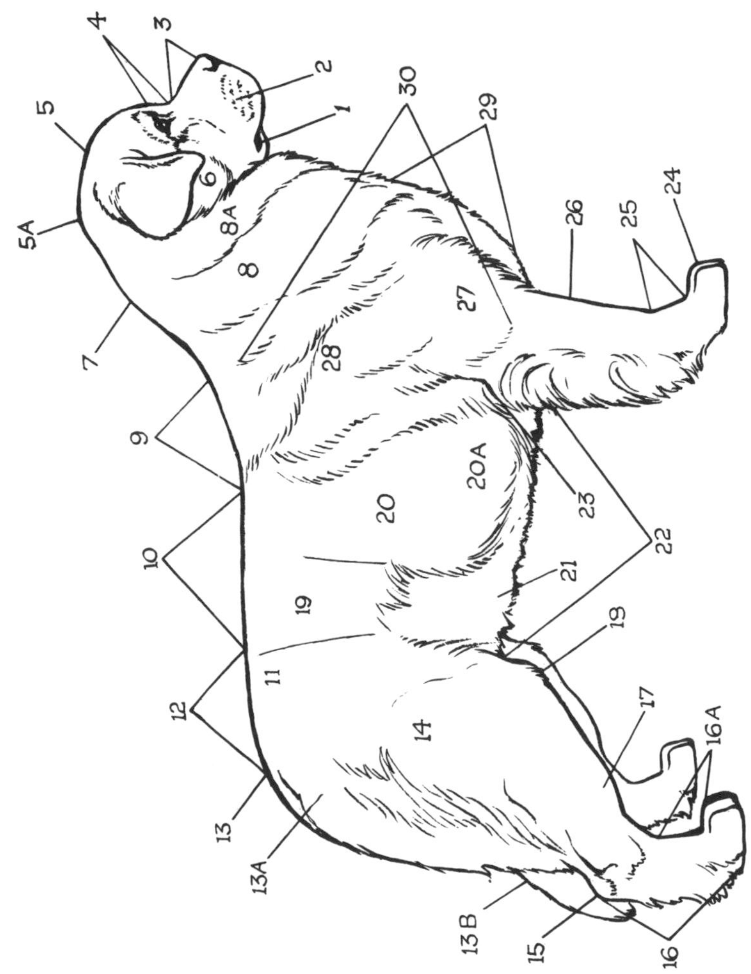

PARTS OF THE NEWFOUNDLAND

1. Lip corner (flew). 2. Muzzle. 3. Foreface, 4. Stop. 5. Skull. 5a. Occiput. 6. Cheek. 7. Crest (of neck). 8. Neck. 8a. Neck Ruff. 9. Withers. 10. Back. 11. Hip. 12. Croup. 13. Tail Set. 13a. Point of Haunch or Buttocks. 13b. Tail or Stern. 14. Thigh (quarter, haunch). 15. Point of Hock. 16. Hock. 16a. Metatarsus. 17. Lower thigh. 18. Point of Stifle (knee). 19. Loin. 20. Ribs. 20a. Chest. 21. Abdomen. 22. Bottom line. 23. Elbow. 24. Feet (paws). 25. Pastern. 26. Forearm. 27. Upper arm. 28. Shoulder blade. 29. Fore-chest. 30. Shoulder.

Head: The head is massive with a broad skull, slightly arched crown, and strongly developed occipital bone. The slope from the top of the skull to the tip of the muzzle has a definite but not steep stop. The forehead and face is smooth and free of wrinkles; the muzzle is clean cut and covered with short, fine hair. The muzzle is square, deep, and fairly short; its length from stop to tip of nose is less than from stop to occiput. The nostrils are well developed. The bitch's head follows the same general conformation as the dog's but is feminine and less massive. A narrow head and a snipey or long muzzle are to be faulted.

The *eyes* are dark brown, relatively small, and deep-set; they are spaced wide apart and have no haw showing. Round, protruding, or yellow eyes are objectionable.

The *ears* are relatively small and triangular with rounded tips. They are set well back on the skull and lie close to the head. When the ear is brought forward it reaches to the inner corner of the eye on the same side.

The *teeth* meet in a scissors or level bite.

The Newfoundland's expression is soft and reflects the character of the breed; benevolent, intelligent, dignified, and of sweet disposition. The dog never looks or acts either dull or ill-tempered.

Neck: The neck is strong and well set on the shoulders. It is long enough for proud head carriage.

Body: The Newfoundland's chest is full and deep with the brisket reaching at least down to the elbows. The back is broad, and the topline is level from the withers to the croup, never roached, slack, or swayed. He is broad at the croup, is well muscled, and has very strong loins. The croup slopes at an angle of about 30 degrees. Bone structure is massive throughout but does not give a heavy, sluggish appearance.

Forequarters: When the dog is not in motion, the forelegs are perfectly straight and parallel with the elbows close to the chest. The layback of the shoulders is about 45 degrees, and the upper arm meets the shoulder blade at an angle of about 90 degrees. The shoulders are well muscled. The pasterns are slightly sloping.

Hindquarters: Because driving power for swimming, pulling loads, or covering ground efficiently is dependent on the hindquarters, the rear assembly of the Newfoundland is of prime importance. It is well muscled, the thighs are fairly long, the stifles well bent, and the hocks wide and straight. Cowhocks, barrel legs, or pigeon toes are to be seriously faulted.

Feet: The feet are proportionate to the body in size, cat-foot in type, well rounded and tight with firm, arched toes, and with webbing present. Dewclaws on the rear legs are to be removed.

Tail: The tail of the Newfoundland acts as a rudder when he is swimming. Therefore, it is broad and strong at the base. The tail reaches down a little below the hocks. When the dog is standing the tail hangs straight down, possibly a little bent at the tip; when the dog is in motion or excited, the tail is carried straight out or slightly curved, but it never curls over the back. A tail with a kink is a serious fault.

Gait: The Newfoundland in motion gives the impression of effortless power, has good reach, and strong drive. A dog may appear symmetrical and well balanced when standing, but, if he is not structurally sound, he will lose that symmetry and balance when he moves. In motion, the legs move straight forward; they do not swing in an arc nor do the hocks move in or out in relation to the line of travel. A slight roll is present. As the dog's speed increases from a walk to a trot, the feet move in under

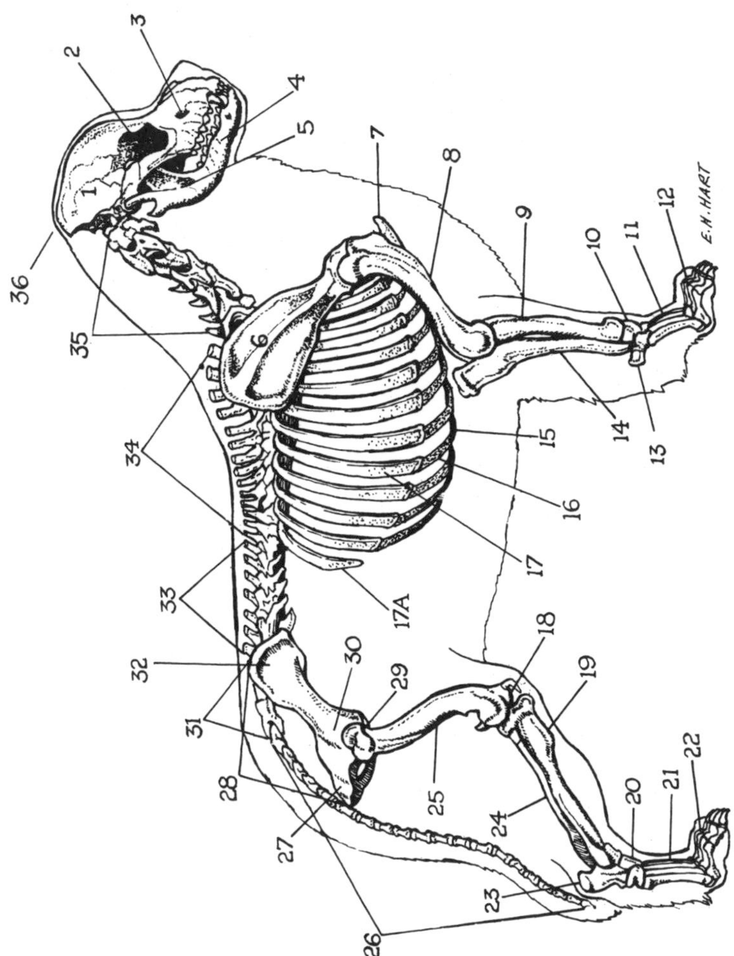

SKELETAL STRUCTURE OF A NEWFOUNDLAND

1. Cranium (skull). 2. Orbital cavity. 3. Nasal bone. 4. Mandible (jaw bone). 5. Condyle. 6. Scapula (shoulder blade, including spine and acromion process of scapula). 7. Posternum. 8. Humerus (upper arm). 9. Radius (front forearm bone—see Ulna). 10. Carpus (pastern joint. Comprising seven bones). 11. Metacarpus (pastern. Comprising five bones). 12. Phalanges (digits or toes). 13. Pisiform (accessory carpal bone). 14. Ulna. 15. Sternum. 16. Costal cartilage (lower, cartilaginous section of ribs). 17. Rib bones. 17a. Floating rib (not connected by costal cartilage to sternum). 18. Patella (knee joint). 19. Tibia (with fibula comprises shank bone). 20. Tarsus (comprising seven bones). 21. Metatarsus (comprising five bones). 22. Phalanges (toe or digits of hind foot). 23. Oscalcis (point of hock). 24. Fibula. 25. Femur (thigh bone). 26. Coccygeal vertebra (bones of tail. Number varies—18 to 23 normal). 27. Pubis. 28. Pelvic bone entire (pubis, ilium, ischium). 29. Head of femur. 30. Ischium. 31. Sacral vertebra (comprising five fused vertebra). 32. Ilium. 33 Lumbar vertebra. 34. Thoracic vertebra (dorsal, with spinal process or withers). 25. Cervical vertebra (bones of the neck). 36. Occipit.

the center line of the body to maintain balance. Mincing, shuffling, crabbing, too close moving, weaving, hackney action, and pacing are all faults.
Size: The average height for dogs is 28 inches, for bitches 26 inches. The average weight for dogs is 150 pounds, for bitches, 120 pounds. Large size is desirable but is not to be favored over correct gait, symmetry, and structure.
Coat: The Newfoundland has a water-resistant double coat. The outer coat is moderately long and full but not shaggy. It is straight and flat with no curl, although it may have a slight wave. The coat, when rubbed the wrong way, tends to fall back into place. The undercoat, which is soft and dense, is often less dense during summer months or in tropical climates but is always found to some extent on the rump and chest. An open coat is to be seriously faulted. The hair on the head, muzzle, and ears is short and fine, and the legs are feathered all the way down. The tail is covered with long dense hair, but it does not form a flag.
Color: Black. A slight tinge of bronze or a splash of white on chest and toes is not objectionable. Black dogs that have only white toes and white chest and white tip to tail should be exhibited in the classes provided for "black."
Other than black: Should in all respects follow the black except in color, which may be almost any, so long as it disqualifies for the black class, but the colors most to be encouraged are bronze or white and black (Landseer) with black head marked with narrow blaze, even marked saddle and black rump extending on to tail. Beauty in markings to be taken greatly into consideration.
Disqualifications: Markings other than white on a solid-colored dog.

SYMMETRY AND GENERAL APPEARANCE

The Newfoundland is a large, good-natured dog with an intelligent, dignified expression, very deliberate in his actions. The Standard was written for a working dog, that could double as a giant retriever, as much at home in the water as on dry land. A superior water dog, the Newfoundland has been used and is still used in Newfoundland and Labrador as a true working dog. He pulls carts and sleds and carries packs.

The Newfoundland must have symmetry and balance so that no part appears out of proportion with the other parts. A dog well balanced in all parts is preferred to one with outstanding good qualities and defects. Size and weight are important, but symmetry and balance must be maintained.

He should impress the eye with substance, strength, and agility and not appear clumsy, cloddy, or lethargic. On the other hand, a grown dog should never appear leggy, weedy, or shelly in body. He gets his height by depth of chest, not length of leg. A Newfoundland is an animal of strength rather than speed, a swimmer before he is a trotter.

His gait should be free and easy, a slight bearlike roll at a slow trot is typical of the breed. He should have a thick double coat, capable of resisting water. Above all he must have the intelligence and sweetness of disposition that are his best known traits.

EXPRESSION

The characteristics that distinguish one breed from another are usually most marked in the head, eyes, ears, expression, and temperament of the dog. A Newfoundland's expression should be intelligent, never sour; full of serene dignity, seldom sad. A Newfoundland is full of fun. He should have a face that is extremely expressive and eyes that beam with intelligence. Any appearance of sourness or ill temper is to be especially guarded against. He has a dignity of demeanor, a nobel bearing, and a sense of strength and power which, however, is softened by the serenity of his countenance and deeply sagacious look.

Sex character is the peculiarity that distinguishes one sex from another, other than the presence of sex organs. Actually it is evidenced by secondary sexual characteristics.

Masculine character is evidenced in grown males by a bolder, stronger head, greater size (the standard allows 20 to 40 pounds more weight), and generally by a more massive and rugged appearance throughout.

Feminine sex character is evidenced in grown bitches by a certain refinement in head and neck. A good female, while not lacking in substance, has a definite feminine quality about her.

Bitchy dogs and doggy bitches are to be guarded against, especially for breeding purposes.

HEAD: Skull, Muzzle, Stop, Underjaw, Teeth

The head should be broad and massive, free from wrinkles as in the Mastiff. The occipital bone is well developed. The skull should have a rounded rather than a square of flat appearance, with only enough development of the brow, or superciliary arches, to protect the eyes.

The stop should be a slope rather than a step down, and in no way accentuated as in the St. Bernard. The bridge of the nose straight, never dish-faced. The slightly rounded appearance of the broad skull as it meets the top of the ears serves to frame the face.

The muzzle should be strong, deep, clean cut, and square in shape. The depth should extend to the end of the muzzle. It should be in balance with the size of the head of the individual animal, never excessively long, pointed, snipey, or weak. The underjaw should be strong. Pronounced lower flews are not desirable. The neater the flews, the less the dog will drool. It is not depth of muzzle that makes for wet mouths but these little pockets, or flews, in the lower jaw from which the dog slobbers when hot or excited. The teeth should meet in a level or scissors bite and the jaw should be neither overshot nor undershot.

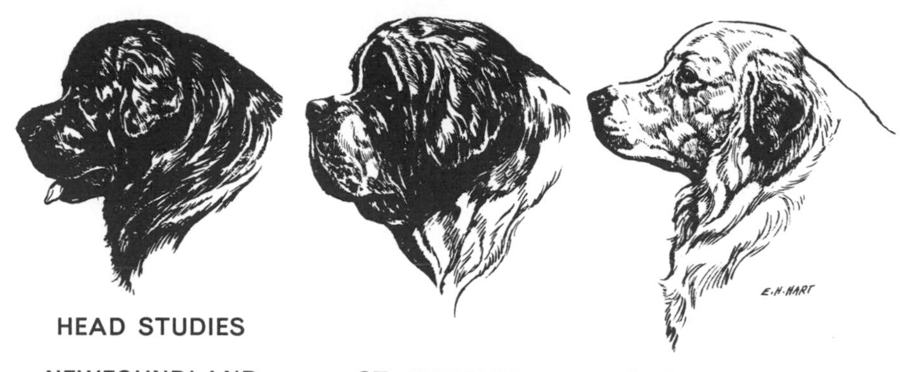

HEAD STUDIES

NEWFOUNDLAND ST. BERNARD GREAT PYRENEES

EARS

When seen from the front or back the ears of a Newfoundland should blend completely with the head. High-set ears, ears that stand away from the head, or long Spaniel-like ears are decided faults and give the dog a foreign expression. The ears should be small, neat, set well back on the skull, and lie close to the cheeks. This tends to keep water from entering when swimming. The ears are covered with short, fine hair.

Many otherwise good-headed dogs have their expression spoiled by poorly set or too large ears.

Wads of hair growing behind the ears may make an otherwise good ear stand away for the head. Fringes are objectionable and both wads of hair and fringes should be removed.

EYES

The eyes should be small, preferably of a dark brown color, deeply set, expressing great intelligence and good temper. A light eye sometimes give a startled look. A black eye can give a

CORRECT SCISSORS BITE

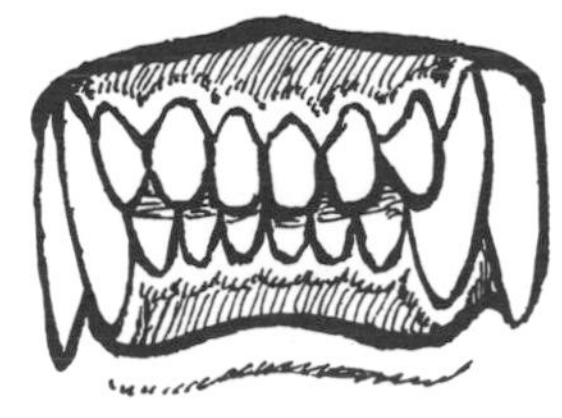

TEETH

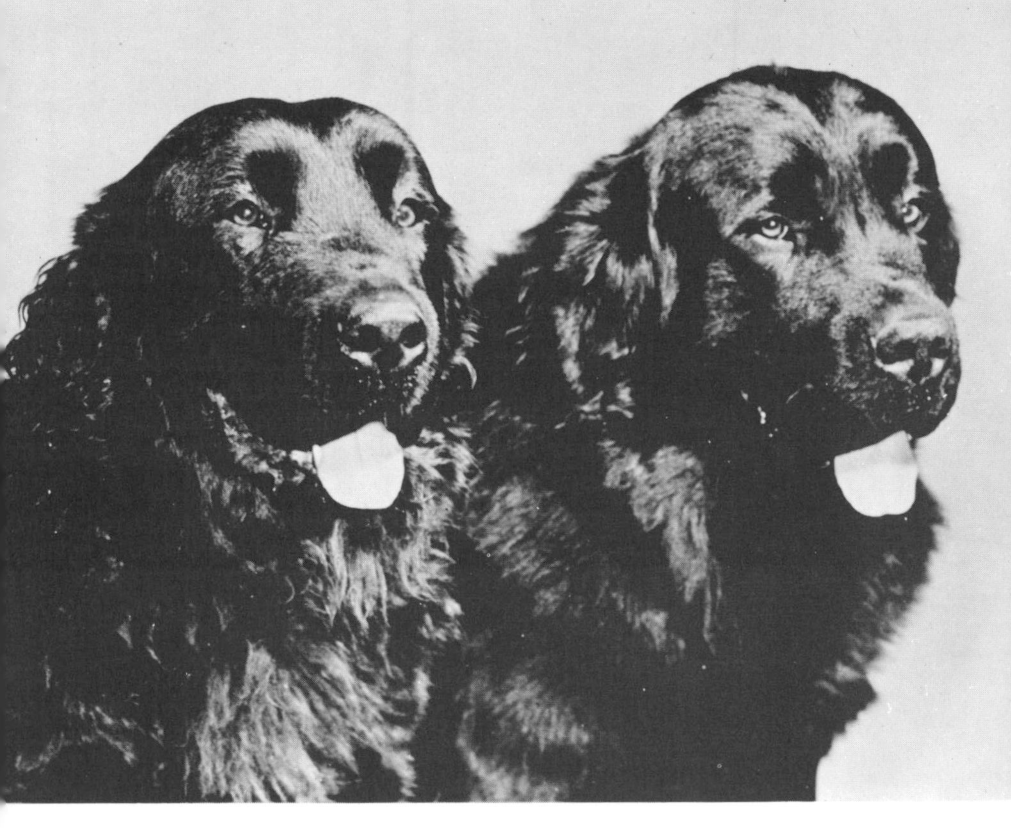

Head studies: Spinnaker's Black Magic and Spinnaker's Sinbad, owned by Mr. and Mrs. Glen Butler, Jr.

sinister look, or lack expression. Eyes should be well set apart. Prominent, bulgy eyes or eyes that are set too close together spoil the soft, sweet Newfoundland expression. No haw or inner eyelid should be visible. The eye rims must fit closely to give good protection to the eyes from water and brush.

NECK

The neck should be of moderate length, broadening toward the body. It is stout, muscular, and well set on. The set on of neck is interdependent on the placement of shoulders. It should not show surplus skin or dewlap. It should be powerful enough to carry the head without tiring and to enable the dog to perform his duties of retrieving heavy objects on land and in the water. It should be remembered that an object is grasped in the mouth but the weight is borne by the muscles of the neck.

SHOULDERS AND UPPER ARM

The structural and physical requirements needed for the Newfoundland in his general utilitarian work, both on land and in the water, are of utmost importance. Therefore, in discussing the shoulder and upper arm one must be very careful in painting an accurate picture.

Without correct structure at this point, perfection in all other body structure will suffer in proportion to the failure existing in the front end. Moreover, without the proper placement and proportion of the shoulder and upper arm it is impossible to have the required, as well as necessary, forefront or keel, which is needed in the Newfoundland's work.

The shoulder blade should be broad, have hard sinewy muscle, and be firmly placed. The upper arm should be of the same length as the shoulder blade and placed at about 90° to the latter. It should be strong of bone and hard of muscle, lying close to the ribs but capable of free movement. Such angulation permits the maximum extension of the forelegs without binding or effort.

The space between the top of the shoulder blades should not be too wide.

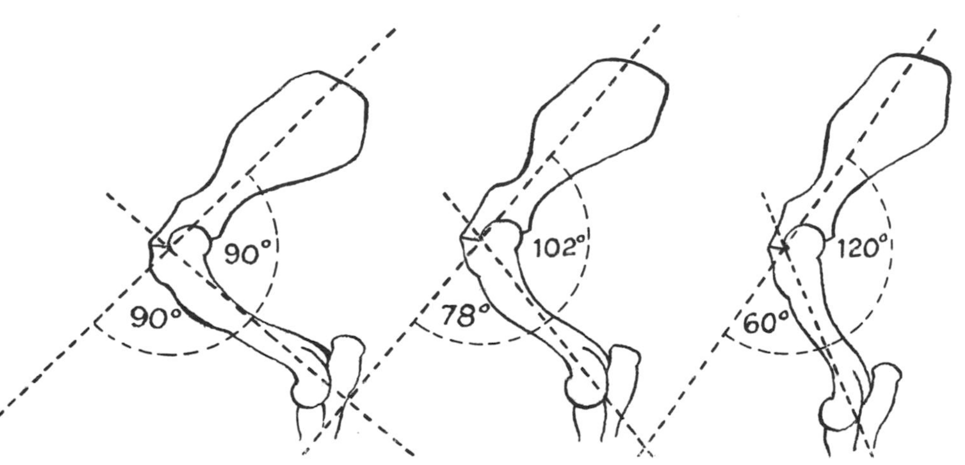

SHOULDER ASSEMBLY ANGULATION

EXTREME CORRECT STRAIGHT (POOR)

GOOD
FRONT

EAST AND WEST
PINCHED ELBOWS
TOO NARROW

BARREL LEGGED
OUT AT ELBOW
TOEING IN

CHEST AND RIBS

From the front the chest appears deep in brisket and fairly broad and well covered with hair, but not to such an extent as to form a frill. From the side the chest should extend to the elbow. If the anatomy of the shoulder and upper arm is in correct proportion, the front legs, when viewed from the side, should cover the lowest point of the breast line. Remember the Newfoundland gets his height from the depth of chest, not length of leg.

The rib cage should appear full and oval when viewed from above and by its ample capacity allow plenty of room for the development of heart and lungs. Barrel-shaped ribs would interfere with the free play of the elbows and the proper movement of the shoulders. He should never be flat-ribbed or slab-sided. In short, a Newfoundland should be well ribbed up and well ribbed back.

FORELEGS, PASTERNS, AND FEET

The forelegs should be straight, well boned, and muscular. Elbows in but well let down and legs feathered all down. Pasterns should have a slight bend or springiness as befits a working dog. This, however, does not mean a Newfoundland should be "down in pastern" or "broken down in the pasterns."

The feet should be large, strong, and somewhat round in shape. Splayed or turned-out feet are objectionable. The toes

EXCELLENT
FOOT AND PASTERN

HARE FOOT
WEAK PASTERN

should be firm and compact with webbing in between. This latter aids in swimming. Toes should be well arched, pads thick, and nails kept short.

BODY: Back, Loin, Croup

A Newfoundland stands over a lot of ground. The desirable proportions of the Newfoundland are not derived from a long back or loin but from an over-all length that is achieved by breadth of forequarters and hindquarters when viewed from the side. The distance from top of withers to bottom of chest approximately equals the distance from bottom of chest to ground.

Back. The back should be broad and lie in the straightest possible line between the withers and the slightly arched loin. A Newfoundland should not be sway-backed or hollow-backed, with an abnormal downward curve of the spine, nor should he be roached or camel-backed, with a convex curve of the spine. He should also be deep in the flank and not tucked up in the belly.

Loin. The loin should be broad and strong, well muscled up, and blending smoothly into the back without undue length. The loin must be just long enough to permit suppleness. A dog with too short a loin cannot turn easily without breaking his stride. A dog with too long a loin usually has too much play in the back, thereby losing the transmission of power from the hindquarters.

If a dog is muscular and full through the loin this compromise between litheness and power is easy without the failing of either factor. Slackness of loins is a great defect in a Newfoundland.

Croup. The croup should be wide, moderately sloping toward the root of the tail. It extends from the top of the pelvic or hip bones to the set on of tail. A flat or too sloping a croup tends to spoil the general outline of the dog. The former affects the gait and makes for high-set tails, and the latter throws the hindquarters under the dog and tends to destroy the power that should be developed there.

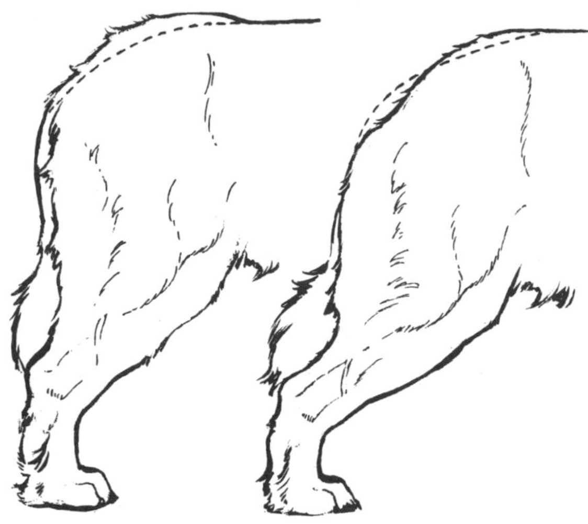

SIDE VIEW OF REAR ASSEMBLY OVERBUILT HIGH HOCK

STEEP, SHORT CROUP

HINDQUARTERS: Hips, Thighs, Stifles, Hocks, Tail, Dewclaws

Hindquarters are probably the most important part as far as gait is concerned. In evaluating a dog always remember that its power is developed in the hindquarters and transmitted through the spine to the forequarters which serve only as a point of suspension. The whole hindquarters should be powerful, the hips and thighs broad, muscular, and well developed, and the bones strong. Lack of correct angulation in the hindquarters causes a loss of power. Stifles should be well bent. Hocks should be clean and well let down.

Newfoundlands should not be cow-hocked, sickle-hocked, barrel-legged, or pigeon-toed in the hind feet.

It should be remembered that the strength in the hindquarters is made to generate power, not to carry weight. Dewclaws on the rear legs are objectionable and should be removed.

Tail. The tail should be moderate in length and broad at the base, the end of the tail bone preferably reaching as far as the hock joint. Tails with kinked vertebrae are very objectionable. When the dog is standing still, the tail hangs down. In motion it should be carried a trifle up; when he is excited it can be held straight out or slightly curved at the end. A gay tail, set on too high, or tails curled over the back, like a sled dog's, are undesirable. Tails such as this spoil the smooth general outline of the Newfoundland.

GOOD REAR

COWHOCKED, DEWCLAWS

BARREL LEGGED

COAT

The Newfoundland is a double-coated dog. The outer coat should be straight, flat, and of a coarse but not harsh or wiry texture. The outer coat is oily and capable of shedding water. The soft undercoat, which should be very dense and furlike, unless removed by season or grooming, is what protects the dog from the cold. It is this undercoat that Newfoundlands shed in hot weather; and to keep the dog comfortable, it should be thoroughly combed out when shedding. Some dogs never grow an undercoat. This is a fault and not typical of the breed. It is the combination of the two coats that makes a dense weather-

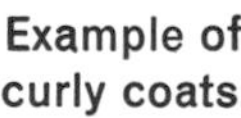
Example of curly coats.

Ch. Little Bear's. John Paul Jones, owned by Little Bear Kennels.

proof and waterproof jacket. When the undercoat is present it makes the outer coat, or guard hairs, stand slightly away from the body, making the true size of the dog deceptive to the untrained eye. The coat is heaviest over the neck, shoulders, and forechest. If brushed the wrong way, the outer coat should tend to fall back into place.

Kinky, curly, silky, or woolly coats are an abomination in a Newfoundland and not to be tolerated. Many coats have a slightly wavy appearance, especially over the hindquarters. Although this is not a disqualifying fault, this is not desirable but preferable to real curls. The length of coat is not the important factor. It is the correct texture and density that are most desirable.

An old dog saying is: "A good coat is bred in him and afterwards it is fed in him." In other words, the correct texture is an inherited factor. However, climatic conditions, feeding, and grooming determine condition.

The double coat mentioned above refers to the body coat. The hair on the muzzle, face, and ears should be short and fine. Many Newfoundlands grow an excessive amount of hair, resembling a fur hat, on top of their heads. It is wise to smooth this down to check actual skull formation.

The front legs are feathered in the back, from the elbows down. The hind legs should have longer hair on the back of the thighs and short, thick hair from the hocks down. Unsightly wads of hair between the toes can be trimmed and the hair around the feet can be shaped up. The chest is well protected with hair but not to such an extent as to form a frill. The hair on the tail should be thick, bushy, and long, but never parted in the center or forming a flag like a Setter's. The whole coat of the dog should adhere to its original purpose of protecting the dog from the long, cold winters and the icy waters surrounding his native island.

COLOR AND MARKINGS

The dominant color in Newfoundlands is black. Other whole colors are permissible. They should follow the Standard for blacks in all except color.

In the progenitors of the breed the following solid colors were found: Black, bronze, brown, blue, silver, gray, and lemon.

Black dogs having white chests, toes, and tip to tail should be exhibited in classes for blacks. If white appears elsewhere on the body it is classified as a Landseer and should be exhibited in in the classes provided for "other than black." It is very difficult to breed a well-marked Landseer and many of these black-and-white dogs are mismarked. It is interesting to note that where the hair is white on a Landseer the skin will be pink, and where

English Champion Prince of Norfolk showing good Landseer markings.

the hair is black the skin will be the usual blue-white found in black dogs. Ticking is not desirable on Landseers.

In the ancestors of the breed the following particolor, or multicolors have been found: Black and white, brown and white, gray and white, black and tan, brindle, and wolf colors.

Any particolored Newfoundland dog that resembles any other breed in coloring is considered undesirable.

Black and tan as in Gordon Setters.

Various shades of red and white, or brindle and white as in St. Bernards.

All-white, or white with gray, tan or badger-colored head markings as in Great Pyrenees.

In order to preserve the correct color in a Newfoundland our Standard calls for a disqualification for any dog of a solid color that has other than white markings.

STANCE AND GAIT

Stance. Newfoundlands should stand squarely, with the weight evenly distributed on all four legs. The hocks should not be tucked under the body and the feet should turn neither in nor out.

Gait. Movement is the crucial test of conformation. There is probably no other point at which so many dogs fail. When a Newfoundland trots he should give the impression of effortless power. He should have good reach in front and plenty of drive behind. The gait should be free and easy. The slight roll, which is typical of the breed, is shown at a slow trot and must never be confused with a pacing gait, which is undesirable.

The legs should be carried straight forward while traveling, the forelegs swinging parallel to the sides.

Perfection in action is more easily attainable if the dog possesses long thighs and muscular second thighs, well bent at the stifles.

The movement of the hind legs should be similarly true and free. This can only be accomplished if the angulation of the hindquarter is in balance with the angulation of the forequarter. This balance makes for freedom of action so necessary for easy travel. If rear angulation is correct, the dog will be able to get his hind legs well under him, enabling him to get a powerful drive or push from the muscular second thighs.

In any discussion on gait the back must not be forgotten. It is through the spine that the power created by the hindquarters travels to the forequarters. A weak back dissipates the power produced by proper hindquarters and hinders a well-made forequarter from receiving or taking advantage of this power.

At a walk or slow trot a Newfoundland tracks fairly wide apart. As he increases his speed he brings the feet inward toward the middle line of the body in order to maintain balance. This

FAULTY NEWFOUNDLANDS

Head too St. Bernardlike
Too much stop
Haw
Wrinkles over eyes
Ears too big
Down in pasterns
Sway back
Straight in stifle
Curly tail

Withers too far back
Head
  Snipey
  Long nose
  Badly placed ears
Leggy
Roached back
Too angulated stifle
Short tail
Too tucked up

E.H. HART

is not a fault as long as there is no interference.

If a dog is out at the elbows, the forefeet have a tendency to cross or weave.

The hocks should move parallel to each other. When hocks turn in (cow hocks), the stifles and feet turn outward, resulting in a serious loss of power. When the hocks turn out (barrel-legged) the hind feet may cross. This also results in loss of power and makes for an ungainly waddle instead of a free-swinging gait.

TEMPERAMENT

The Newfoundland disposition is traditionally kind and gentle, with an inherited guarding instinct, especially with children. His magnanimity is well known, his courage proverbial.

He usually investigates before he sounds an alarm and, though of mild disposition and extremely sensitive to praise or censure, he is not cowardly.

A quarrelsome or vicious Newfoundland is seldom met with, untypical of the breed, and should not be used for breeding.

He is able and willing to learn and has the intelligence to act on his own responsibility when the situation demands it.

A Newfoundland is never so well satisfied as when employed either for the pleasure or advantage of his master, and his strong propensity to fetch and carry develops naturally at an early age.

Newfoundlands are definitely not sluggish and can use plenty of exercise and are particularly fond of swimming.

The joy of living is not lost in maturity. They do not get cross with old age and most Newfoundlands remain young at heart until the day they die.

THINGS TO AVOID WHEN CHOOSING A NEWFOUNDLAND

Lack of balance
Shyness
Viciousness

Cow hocks
Slack loins
Slab sides
Splay feet
Deformed tail
Weak back
Dewclaws

Curly coat
Kinky coat
Silky coat

Light eyes
Snipey muzzle
Too much stop
Eyes too close together
Poorly set or long ears
Sloppy flews
Undershot jaw
Overshot jaw

Undesirable color
Bitchy dogs
Doggy bitches

Ch. Little Bear's Sailing Free, a specialty and group show winner owned by Mrs. William Kurth.

CONCLUSION

Remember that type, balance, and general appearance are of the utmost importance. As a breeder, shun those faults that are hard to breed out. As a judge, remember that any dog can gait soundly, but no matter how well he moves, unless he *looks* like a Newfoundland, he is not typical of the breed. Type is the embodiment of a Standard's essentials.

It does not matter whether you are an official in the ring, an interested spectator, or just appraising dogs in your own kennel, judging dogs is an art based on observation. One can read a Standard and quote it verbatim, but that does not enable one to have the proper mental picture of an ideal Newfoundland.

To appraise dogs correctly, one must possess the basic principles that underlie all good judging:

1. A clearly defined ideal in mind.
2. Power of accurate observation.
3. Sound judgement, which includes the ability to make a logical analysis and to evaluate the good and poor qualities in terms of a sound breeding program.

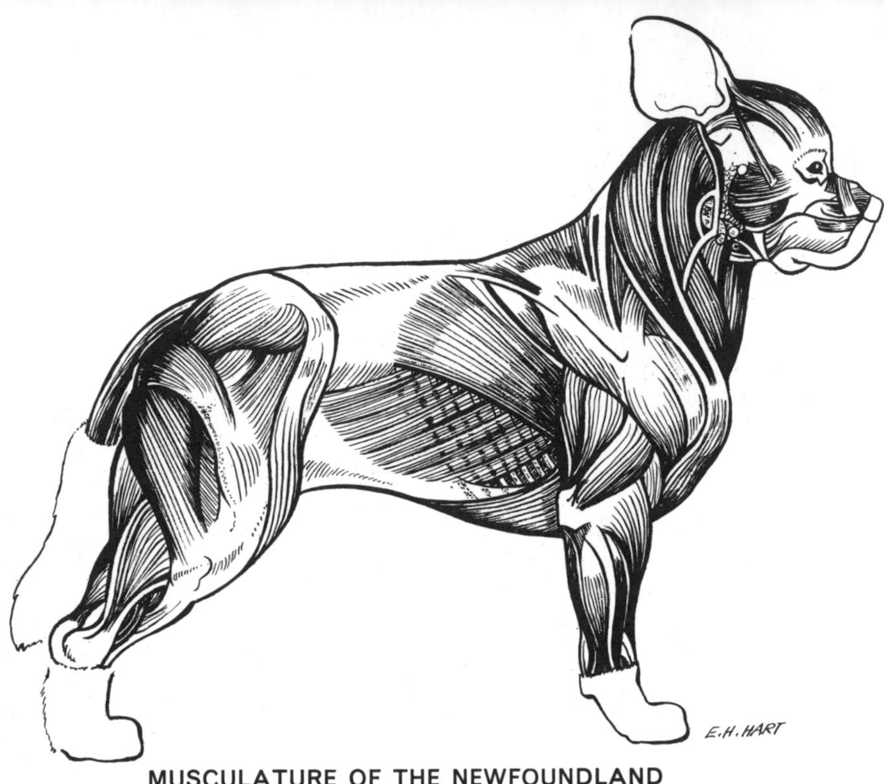

MUSCULATURE OF THE NEWFOUNDLAND

4. Courage and honesty, which includes independence of thought and decision.

5. Ability to give reasons for these decisions.

Remember, no dog is perfect. He can score well on individual points and still not be balanced. It is good for a novice to learn the parts of the Newfoundland and the relative values attached to each part. However, the animal must be considered as a whole and not as a large number of separate parts in the final analysis.

We put much emphasis on condition and handling in the show ring in America today. To be sure, fine condition and good handling of dogs are things we all like to see at shows. Judging at each show, in this country, is by comparison only with the other dogs entered and present at that particular show. When it comes to judging an individual dog, only the degree in which he measures up to his breed Standard counts. In other words, all the grooming and skilful handling cannot change a mediocre dog into a top one, nor are beauty treatments transmitted.

Finally, remember you are dealing with living things whose fate is in your keeping. Some responsibility for the welfare of Newfoundlands as well as the future of the breed is yours.

Chapter XI

Significance of the Pedigree

The most common question the layman asks about a dog is, "Has he a pedigree?" or "Is he a pedigreed dog?" Of course every living creature has a pedigree of some sort, either known or unknown, but what our novice means by his question is, "Do we know that he is a purebred dog?" This means that we must know all of the dog's ancestors for many generations and that we are sure that they are all of the same breed. It says nothing whatever about the quality of these ancestors. So simplified, the question is easy to answer as registration in the stud book of any recognized kennel club (in this country the American Kennel Club at 51 Madison Ave., New York, N.Y. 10010) is usually considered evidence that a dog is purebred. Except in extraordinary circumstances, a dog cannot be registered unless both of his parents are registered and are of the same breed. A pedigree, as a concrete article, is a written, recognized form on which is written the dog's immediate ancestors both maternal and paternal in such a way that the ancestors may be traced by name for several generations—thus we speak of a three-generation pedigree as one where all of the direct ancestors for three generations appear in order so that each generation is easily separated from the one before and the one after. When a breeder, on the other hand, starts to talk about a dog's pedigree, the subject becomes much more complex, as the serious breeder wants to know about the quality of the pedigree in order that he may be able to evaluate the dog more accurately for the good or bad qualities that he may pass on to his offspring. At first thought the novice breeder might believe that a sure way to produce champions is to procure a champion bitch and breed her to a champion dog and then sit back complacently until the puppies, all in due course, become champions. That would certainly be an easy method and, in very rare and fortunate cases, it may work, but our study of pedigrees

Ch. Amber Acres Sinbad the Sailor winning the Specialty in Canada in 1968. Judge is Robert Waters; shown is Mrs. Fred Kearsey, President of the Newfoundland Club of Canada.

must show us why such breeding cannot be a mathematical certainty and, in fact, why the results are seldom just what we may expect. In a very simple way, avoiding scientific terms as much as possible, the following description tells something about how your dog's physical characteristics are inherited and shows how these rules apply specifically to the Newfoundland.

In every dog, every characteristic such as size, color, eye color, coat, shape of skull is controlled by a pair of determiners which we call genes. At conception, when a new individual is formed, one gene is inherited from each parent so that the new individual has two genes to control each physical trait. A great many characteristics are what is known as "simple dominant" or "simple recessive" traits. This means that if a gene for a dominant trait is present the dog will show that trait even if he also carries the gene for the recessive trait from his other parent. On the contrary, if the trait is recessive it will be hidden in any case where the dominant gene is present.

This is illustrated by the inheritance of the Landseer color (white with black markings) in the Newfoundland. The color black is dominant over the black and white, so let us name the inheritance of the dominant black with a large B and the Landseer recessive with a small l. If we have a black dog that carries only the dominant black genes, we will say that his color inheritance is BB. Mated to a bitch of the same color-inheritance, the puppies produced will be as follows:

BB mated to BB

BB BB BB BB BB BB BB BB

All of the puppies will be black and will be purebred for black which means that there are no black-and-white genes present in the inheritance.

Ch. Dryad's Sea Rover, owned by Dryad Kennels, shown by Mrs. Maynard K. Drury. Judge is Mrs. Alva McColl.

Now suppose that one of these black dogs which is purebred for black is mated to a black-and-white bitch. The resulting litter will inherit their color like this:

BB mated to ll

Bl Bl Bl Bl Bl Bl Bl Bl

All of the puppies will be black, because the black color is dominant, but each one will carry the hidden factor for the black-and-white trait which is recessive. Now if two of these puppies are mated we will get the following results. (In every case a litter of eight has been used, as that is large enough for color variations to be averaged. The exact percentages, of course, will vary in individual litters.)

Bl mated to Bl

BB BB Bl Bl Bl Bl ll ll

So we can see that two puppies will be black carrying no black-and-white factor; four will be black carrying the recessive black-and-white factor; and two will be black and white carrying no genes for the solid black color. Studying these diagrams, it is easy to see that two black and whites can produce nothing but Landseers, since there is no all-black gene present to dominate over the recessive.

ll mated to ll

ll ll ll ll ll ll ll ll

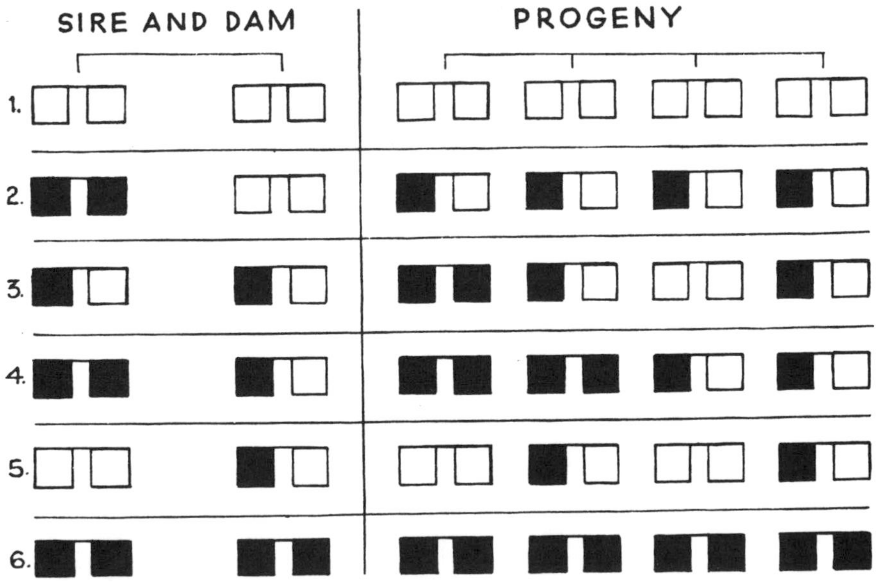

SIRE AND DAM | PROGENY

1.

2.

3.

4.

5.

6.

MENDELIAN EXPECTATION CHART

The six possible ways in which a pair of determiners can unite. Ratios apply to expectancy over large numbers, except in lines No. 1, 2 and 6 where exact expectancy is realized in every litter.

Ch. Dryad's Sea Rose, owned by Mr. and Mrs. Charles O. Webster, shown by Betty Cummings. Judge is Major Godsol.

A frequently asked question is whether you can tell whether a black Newfoundland carries the black-and-white factor. You cannot tell by looking at the dog although sometimes white paws, white on chest or possible tip to the tail indicate that the Landseer factor may be present. Mate the black dog to a Landseer bitch and if all of the puppies are black it is almost sure that no Landseer factor is present in the black.

Not enough is known about the inheritance of bronze, blue, or particolor in Newfoundlands for a definite knowledge of how these colors are inherited, but it is believed that bronze is probably a simple recessive. To our knowledge no one in recent years has had a large enough number of blues or particolors with which to do any experimental breeding.

By studying these charts you will see that when a dominant characteristic is not visible, it is not present at all, but a recessive may be carried for generations masked visibly by the dominant only to reappear after many generations when the right combination of factors occurs. Years ago, when the Waseeka Kennel was just starting, they bought a Landseer bitch, Seagrave Belle, from England bred to Ch. Siki who was a black. She had seven black puppies. At the same time Waseeka owned a black daughter of the English Landseer Ch. Black and White. The years went by and nothing but black puppies appeared. As Mrs. Homer Loring was very fond of Landseers, Waseeka eventually decided to buy a Landseer stud in England. He had not had time to cross the ocean when two well-marked Landseers were born to a black dog and a black bitch whose black ancestors had been in the kennel for generations. Their ancestry traced back to the original Seagrave Belle Landseer stock which the kennel had when it began to operate and the black-and-white trait had been carried invisibly for many generations.

From the foregoing we should now see (to revert to our novice breeder whose two champions did not produce a litter of champion puppies) that it is quite possible that traits which are inferior but recessive were inherited from grandparents and great-grandparents, to appear in the litter to spoil the chances of a super litter. This is one of the things that may spoil our best-planned efforts in dog breeding, but, after all, think how monotonous it would be if all of our paper pedigrees turned out to be flesh-and-blood champions when the puppies arrived.

There are other traits that are not simply dominant or recessive. In these the two opposing characteristics may be influenced by some other characteristic or may blend in the individual puppy. A number of breeders believe that eye color in Newfoundlands is an example of this blending. In other words, if we mate a light-eyed dog to a dark-eyed bitch we do not necessarily get some light eyes and some dark eyes but may also get all the varying shades between the light and the dark in one litter. There are other traits which are controlled by several sets of genes where the inheritance is much more complex and unpredictable. For instance, in coat we have factors which control color, texture (whether soft or harsh), amount of curl or wave, amount of undercoat, length of coat, etc. You can see that we may get several types of coat in one litter, depending upon how these factors are combined.

So now we come to realize that the quality of a dog's pedigree depends on many factors, some of which are visible in his physical make-up and others which may not be visible in either the dog or his immediate ancestors but which may be there in a

Can. and Am. Ch. Dryad's Conversation Piece, specialty show and group winner, owned by Mrs. Jean F. Hand.

recessive trait gene inherited from a remote ancestor. Since a dog passes on to his offspring only half of the genes which he carries we are certainly wise to breed from a good dog who comes from good parents and grandparents rather than to an equally good dog from indifferent parents. If this is not possible, follow the traditional advice to breed to a poor specimen from a good family rather than a good specimen from a poor family.

People are sometimes misled by the fact that a famous champion may appear as a grandsire on the paternal side and perhaps another great dog as a great-grandsire on the maternal side. This may make an impressive-looking pedigree but we must not forget that the genes from the famous ancestors may have disappeared in other generations to be replaced by those from less desirable specimens.

It should be kept in mind that after the third generation very little inheritance is contributed to an animal by a particular ancestor unless it appears repeatedly in a pedigree. The following tabulations give the percentage of inheritance that is contributed by one ancestor in each generation, and it is apparent that beyond the grandparent the contribution becomes quite insignificant; that is to say, in evaluating the pedigree of respective breeding animals considerably more attention should be paid to ancestors close up to the individual than to more distant relatives. Likewise, it should be kept in mind that both good and bad ancestry contributed the same average percentage of inheritance to the individual and consequently a pedigree in which all animals are of equally high merit is to be preferred to one in which some of the individuals are exceptionally good and some are decidedly lacking in merit. The percentage of inheritance contributed on the average by each ancestor in each generation is:

Parents (first)	50%
Grandparents (2nd)	25%
Great-grandparents (3rd)	12½%
Great-great-grandparents (4th)	6¼%
Great-great-great-grandparents (5th)	3⅛%

The pedigree of an animal is worth as much as the accuracy of the person keeping the breeding record.

This brings us to a phenomenon which every breeder knows exists but for which biology finds no complete explanation. There are individuals, both male and female, that consistently pass on their own appearance, either good or bad. These are called dominant sires and dams. The explanation that this is because they are purebred for many excellent dominant traits is certainly a partial cause for their excellency as parents, but it may be that for some unknown reason their genes tend to dominate while those from the other parent are dropped back and disappear so that no matter what sort of individuals they are bred to, the offspring closely resemble the dominant parent. Occasionally this dominance is passed on from one generation to another, but many times a dominant sire will never have a dominant son. This dominance may work to the great advantage of the breed if the dominant sire is an exceptionally good one or may be disastrous to any line of breeding if there are many faults in the opposite parent which can be carried on recessively without the breeders' knowledge, or, again, if dominant qualities are accompanied by a dominant fault, as described by Mr. Rathman later. This dominant factor in breeding is one of the reasons why line-breeding can be in some cases so spectacularly successful. Line-breeding is the repetition of one dog in several generations of a pedigree brought about by mating of closely related animals. It is done to intensify the qualities of some outstanding dog or bitch. This is an example of a line-bred pedigree:

Jo	Ch. Tom	Jack	Harry
			Nan
		Rose	Jim
			Polly
	Jane	Ch. Tom	Jack
			Rose
		Sally	Ch. Tom
			Jennie

This dog, Jo, would be said to be line-bred to Ch. Tom. If Tom was a dominant sire, it would be natural that so much repetition of the same genes could produce a dog in Jo that resembled Ch. Tom strikingly in many respects although he would carry

English Landseer Ch. Black and White.

genes for the opposite characteristics recessively in many cases. Of course the danger lies in the fact that Ch. Tom may have inherited his good points from his sire Jack who was dominant for some important points, which masked the recessive poor qualities of Rose. In the end we may have doubled up Rose's poor qualities as well as Tom's desirable ones. Anyone experimenting with line-breeding should be fully familiar with both good and bad points in the pedigree so that he can avoid breeding from the offspring that show signs of carrying the known faults of their ancestry.

Using as a model the pedigree chart accompanying this chapter, let us now turn specifically to the history of the English and

Ch. Waseeka's Ghost Ship, twice Best of Breed at the annual Newfoundland Club of America specialty shows (1953 and 1955), at eighteen months. Handled by Mrs. E. K. Annis and judged by Mr. Alva Rosenburg. Mr. L. R. Lewis, steward, at trophy table.

American Newfoundland as a show dog in modern times and see how the pedigrees of these dogs have affected both the outstanding individuals and the whole history of the breed.

Since over two thousand dogs could be listed in an eleven generation pedigree, every effort has been made not to repeat the background of any animal. For example; Eng. Ch. Siki appears in several places, but his background is traced but once.

The large numerals at the top indicate the generations.

When a pedigree is stopped to prevent duplication, a generation number frequently appears to refer you to a prior generation from which the dog's pedigree can be traced. For instance in the column under generation 8, Eng. Ch. Siki appears about one quarter of the way down with the numeral 7. You will find Siki's pedigree traced back beginning at the top of generation 7.

English Ch. Siki, owned and bred by Mr. George Bland.

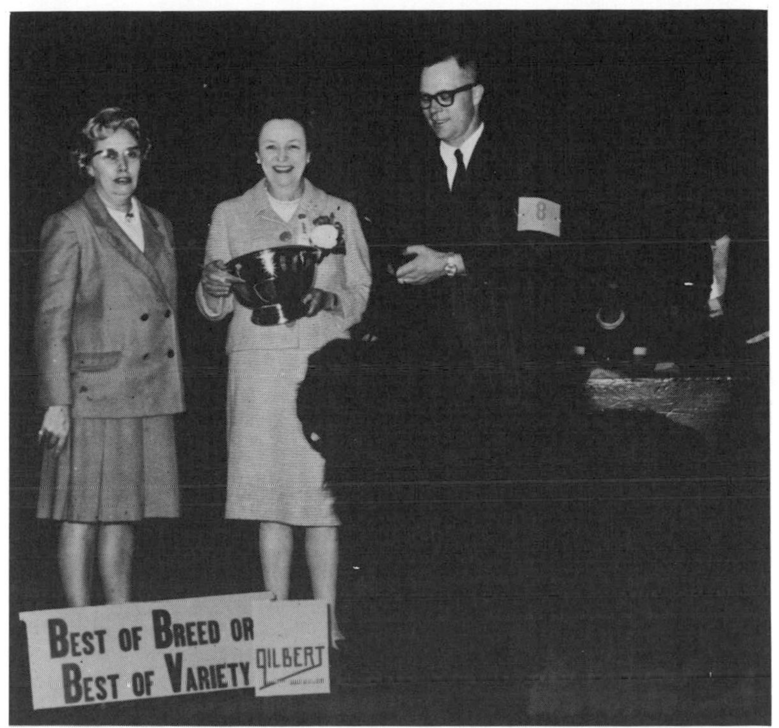

Can. and Am. Ch. Edenglen's Banner, owned by Mrs. E. W. Freeland, Lenox Newfoundland Specialty Best of Breed, shown here winning Best of Breed at the Westminster Kennel Club, 1968; judge is Mrs. Nicholas Demidoff.

When the pedigree stops and there is no number behind it, look for the same animal in that same generation for the continuation of its pedigree.

The capital letters B and L indicate whether the Newfoundland was a Black or a Landseer.

Occasionally a date numeral will appear to indicate approximately when the generation lived. For instance in generation 11 The Black Prince at the bottom of the column was whelped October 3, 1906.

A continuation of the entire pedigree to the 20th generation would of course be impossible because no reasonable way has yet been devised to accommodate the more than half million names. Two dogs have been selected from the eleventh generation and traced out to the limits of the records. These two are marked with an asterisk to aid you in finding them. Their pedigrees appear in the appendix.

Ch. Waseeka's Ghost Ship

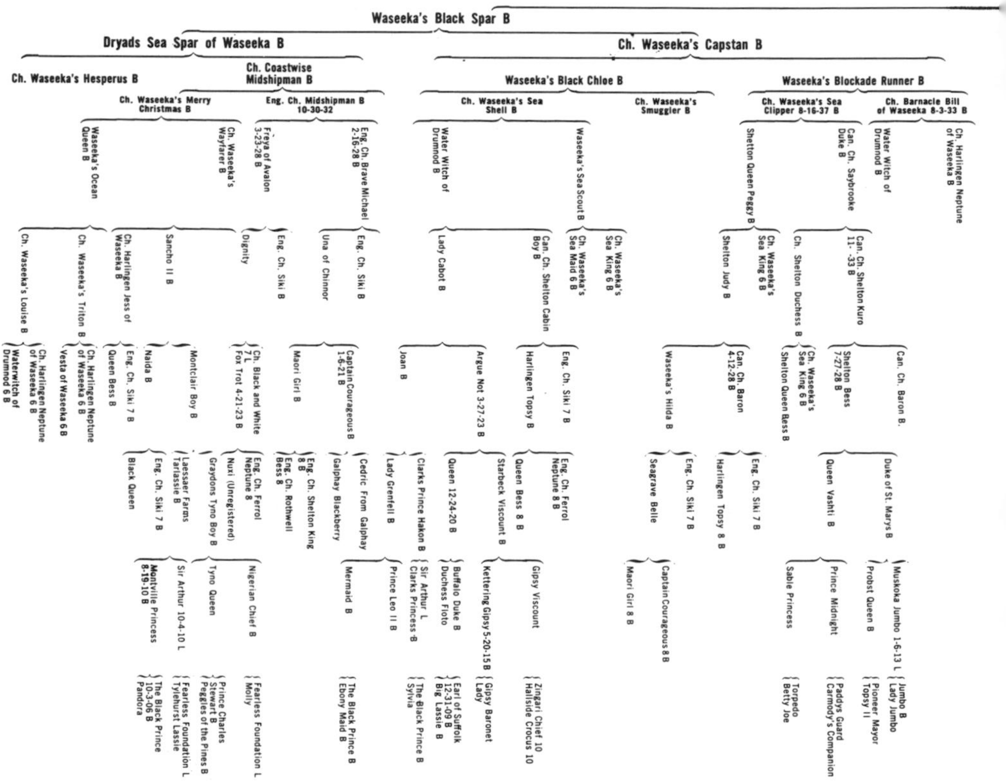

Waseeka's Black Spar B

Dryads Sea Spar of Waseeka B | Ch. Waseeka's Capstan B

Ch. Waseeka's Hesperus B | Ch. Coastwise Midshipman B | Waseeka's Black Chloe B | Waseeka's Blockade Runner B

Ch. Waseeka's Merry Christmas B | Eng. Ch. Midshipman B 10-30-32 | Ch. Waseeka's Sea Shell B | Ch. Waseeka's Smuggler B | Ch. Waseeka's Sea Clipper 8-16-37 B | Ch. Barnacle Bill of Waseeka 8-3-33 B

Waseeka's Ocean Queen B | Ch. Waseeka's Wayfarer B | Freya of Avalon 3-23-28 B | Eng. Ch. Brave Michael 2-16-28 B | Water Witch of Drummod B | Waseeka's Sea Scout B | Shelton Queen Peggy B | Can. Ch. Saybrooke Duke B | Water Witch of Drummod B | Ch. Harlingen Neptune of Waseeka B

Ch. Waseeka's Louise B | Ch. Waseeka's Triton B | Ch. Harlingen Jess of Waseeka B | Sancho II B | Dignity | Eng. Ch. Siki B | Una of Chinnor | Eng. Ch. Siki B | Lady Cabot B | Can. Ch. Shelton Cabin Boy B | Ch. Waseeka's Sea Maid 6 B | Ch. Waseeka's Sea King 6 B | Shelton Judy B | Ch. Waseeka's Sea King 6 B | Ch. Shelton Duchess B | Can. Ch. Shelton Kuro 11- -33 B

Waterwitch of Drummod 6 B | Ch. Harlingen Neptune of Waseeka 6 B | Vesta of Waseeka 6 B | Ch. Harlingen Neptune of Waseeka 6 B | Queen Bess B | Eng. Ch. Siki 7 B | Naida B | Montclair Boy B | Fox Trot 4-21-23 B | Ch. Black and White 7 L | Maori Girl B | Captain Courageous B 1-6-21 B | Joan B | Argue Not 3-27-23 B | Harlingen Topsy B | Eng. Ch. Siki 7 B | Waseeka's Hilda B | Can. Ch. Baron 4-12-28 B | Shelton Queen Bess B | Ch. Waseeka's Sea King 6 B | Shelton Bess 7-27-28 B | Can. Ch. Baron B.

Black Queen | Eng. Ch. Siki 7 B | Laessaer Farms Tarlassie B | Graydons Tyno Boy B | Nuxi (Unregistered) | Eng. Ch. Ferrol Neptune 8 | Bess 8 | Eng. Ch. Rothwell | Eng. Ch. Shelton King 8 B | Galphay Blackberry | Cedric From Galphay | Lady Grenfell B | Clarks Prince Hakon B | Queen 12-24-20 B | Starbeck Viscount B | Queen Bess 8 B | Eng. Ch. Ferrol Neptune 8 B | Seagrave Belle | Eng. Ch. Siki 7 B | Harlingen Topsy 8 B | Eng. Ch. Siki 7 B | Queen Vashti B | Duke of St. Marys B

Montville Princess 8-19-10 B | Sir Arthur 10-4-10 L | Tyno Queen | Nigerian Chief B | Mermaid B | Prince Leo II B | Sir Arthur L | Clarks Princess B | Buffalo Duke B | Duchess Floto | Kettering Gipsy 5-20-15 B | Gipsy Viscount | Maori Girl 8 B | Captain Courageous 8 B | Sable Princess | Prince Midnight | Probst Queen B | Muskoka Jumbo 1-6-13 L

The Black Prince 10-3-06 B / Pandora | Fearless Foundation L / Tylehurst Lassie | Prince Charles Stewart B / Peggles of the Pines B | Fearless Foundation L / Molly | The Black Prince B / Ebony Maid B | The Black Prince B / Sylvia | Earl of Suffolk 12-31-09 B / Big Lassie B | Gipsy Baronet / Lady | Zingari Chief 10 / Hallside Crocus 10 | Torpedo / Betty Joe | Paddys Guard / Carmody's Companion | Pioneer Mayor / Topsy II | Jumbo B / Lady Jumbo

Whelped 10-26-1951 Grey

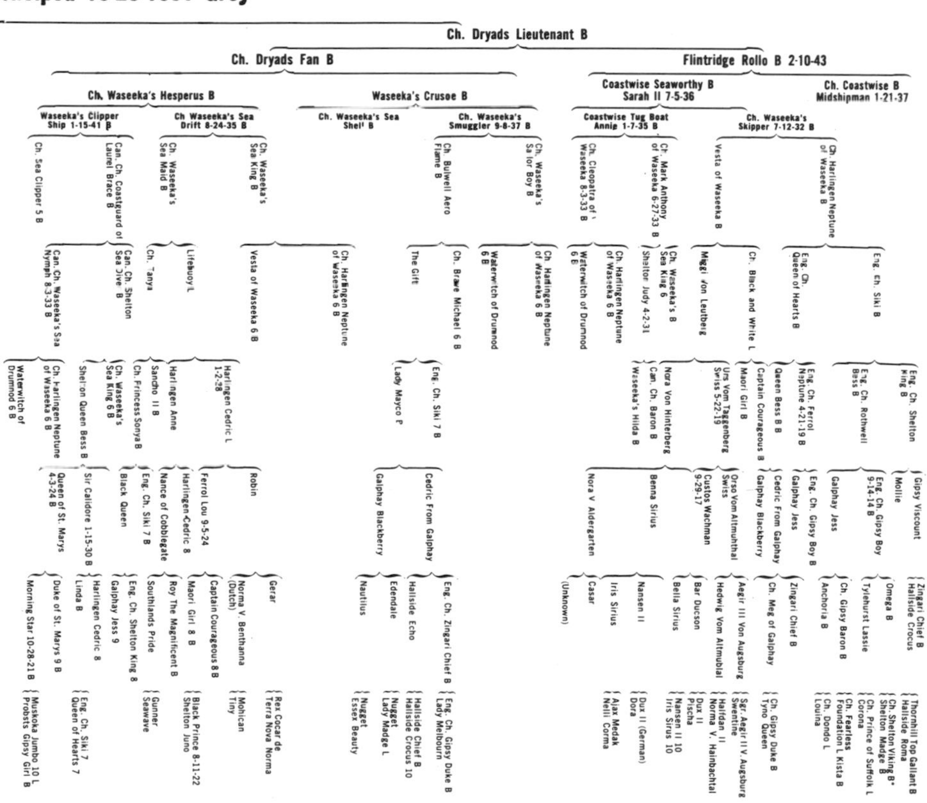

1 Ch. Dryads Lieutenant B

2 Ch. Dryads Fan B — Flintridge Rollo B 2-10-43

3 Ch. Waseeka's Hesperus B — Waseeka's Crusoe B — Coastwise Seaworthy B Sarah II 7-5-36 — Ch. Coastwise B Midshipman 1-21-37

4 Waseeka's Clipper Ship 1-15-41 B — Ch Waseeka's Sea Drift 8-24-35 B — Ch. Waseeka's Sea Shell B — Ch. Waseeka's Smuggler 9-8-37 B — Coastwise Tug Boat Annie 1-7-35 B — Ch. Waseeka's Skipper 7-12-32 B

5 Ch. Sea Clipper 5 B — Can. Ch. Coastguard of Laurel Brace B — Ch. Waseeka's Sea Maid B — Ch. Waseeka's Sea King B — Ch. Bulwell Aero Flame B — Ch. Waseeka's Sailor Boy B — Ch. Cleopatra of Waseeka 8-3-33 B — Ch. Mark Anthony of Waseeka 6-27-33 B — Vesta of Waseeka B — Ch. Harlingen Neptune of Waseeka B

6 Can. Ch. Waseeka's Sea Nymph 8-3-33 B — Can. Ch. Shelton Sea Dive B — Ch. Tanya — Lifebuoy L — Vesta of Waseeka 6 B — Ch. Harlingen Neptune of Waseeka 6 B — The Gift — Ch. Brave Michael 6 B — Waterwitch of Drummod 6 B — Ch. Harlingen Neptune of Waseeka 6 B — Waterwitch of Drummod 6 B — Ch. Harlingen Neptune of Waseeka 6 B — Shaltor Judy 4-2-31 — Ch. Waseeka's Sea King 6 B — Miggi Von Leutberg — Ch. Black and White L — Eng. Ch. Queen of Hearts B — Eng. Ch. Siki B

7 Waterwitch of Drummod 6 B — Ch. Harlingen Neptune of Waseeka 6 B — Shelton Queen Bess B — Ch. Waseeka's Sea King 6 B — Ch. Princess Sonya B — Sancho II B — Harlingen Anne — Harlingen Cedric L 1-2-28 — Lady Mayco P — Eng. Ch. Siki 7 B — Waseeka's Hilda B — Can. Ch. Baron B — Nora Von Hinterberg — Urs Vom Taggenberg Swiss 5-22-19 — Maori Girl B — Captain Courageous B — Queen Bess B B — Eng. Ch. Ferrol Neptune 4-21-19 B — Eng. Ch. Rothwell Bess B — Eng. Ch. Shelton King B

8 Queen of St. Marys 4-3-24 B — Sir Calidore 1-15-30 B — Black Queen — Eng. Ch. Siki 7 B — Nance of Cobblegate — Harlingen Cedric 8 — Ferrol Lou 9-5-24 — Robin — Galphay Blackberry — Cedric From Galphay — Nora V Aldergarten — Benna Sirius — Custos Wachman 9-29-17 — Orso Vom Altmuhlthal Swiss — Galphay Blackberry — Cedric From Galphay — Galphay Jess — Eng. Ch. Gipsy Boy B — Galphay Jess — Eng. Ch. Gipsy Boy 9-14-14 B — Mollie — Gipsy Viscount

9 Morning Star 10-28-21 B — Duke of St. Marys 9 B — Linda B — Harlingen Cedric 8 — Galphay Jess 9 — Eng. Ch. Shelton King 8 — Southlands Pride — Roy The Magnificent B — Maori Girl 8 B — Captain Courageous 8 B — Norma V. Benthanna (Dutch) — Gerar — Nautilus — Edendale — Hallside Echo — Eng. Ch. Zingari Chief B — (Unknown) — Casar — Iris Sirius — Nansen II — Bella Sirius — Bar Ducson — Hedwig Vom Altmuhlal — Aegir III Von Augsburg — Ch. Meg of Galphay — Zingari Chief B — Anchoria B — Ch. Gipsy Baron B — Tylehurst Lassie — Omega B — Zingari Chief B / Hallside Crocus

10 Muskoka Jumbo 10 L / Probsts Gipsy Girl B — Eng. Ch. Siki 7 / Queen of Hearts 7 — Gunner / Seawave — Black Prince 8-11-22 / Shelton Juno — Mohican / Tiny — Rex Cocar de / Terra Nova Norma — Nugget / Essex Beauty — Nugget / Lady Madge L — Hallside Chief B / Hallside Crocus 10 — Eng. Ch. Gipsy Duke B / Lady Melbourn — Ajax Medak / Nelli Corma — Dux II (German) / Dora — Nansen II 10 / Iris Sirus 10 — Dux II / Pischa — Haldan II / Norma V. Hainbachtal — Sgr. Aegir II V. Augsburg / Swentine — Ch. Gipsy Duke B / Tyno Queen — Ch. Dondo L / Louina — Ch. Fearless / Foundation L Kista B — Ch. Prince of Suffolk L / Corona — Ch. Shelton Viking B / Shelton Madge B — Thornhill Top Gallant B / Hallside Roma

11

Canadian Ch. Baron, imported by Mr. D. R. Oliver.

Canadian Ch. Shelton Cabin Boy, imported by Montague Wallace.

Ch. Harlingen Neptune of Waseeka, imported by Waseeka Kennels.

The modern history of the American Newfoundland as a show dog could be said to start in 1922, when George Bland's Ch. Rothwell Bess was sent to be bred to Colonel and Mrs. Wetwan's Ch. Shelton King. (See generation column marked 8.) We have pictures of both of these dogs and descriptions written by well-known judges of their day. Mr. T. Hooten, for example, describes Shelton King as follows: "He is thoroughly sound. His head is magnificent, he has great bone, great depth of brisket and good quarters, and well-let-down in hocks. He carries a sea-resisting coat and is a lover of a daily swim and perfectly docile." Rothwell Bess looks in her pictures like a good-sized but not overlarge bitch of excellent type. From this mating came a great winner and even greater sire, Ch. Siki. His owner, Mr. George Bland, showed the young Siki most successfully, and it was not long before his reputation as a sire far outshadowed his show record. Siki proved to be that much-sought-after animal—a superlative show dog who was also a dominant sire. Bitches from all over England were mated to him and from almost every litter came one or more champions.

In the meantime the Newfoundland in America had almost disappeared as a show dog. There were a few outstanding specimens to be had and a few breeders who showed valiantly (without the spur of much competition) at the shows, both in this country and in Canada, but many of the dogs in the ring at that time would hardly be recognized as Newfoundlands today and bad faults such as light eyes, very curly coats, unsoundness, and lack of bone were very common. However, there was a small group of people who had clung to the true type of Newfoundland and who had a few dogs of high quality. These people heard of the magnificent specimens which were being produced by Ch. Siki and his near relatives and, in the late 1920's, three stud dogs were imported to the United States and Canada and it can be safely said that these dogs have influenced every show Newfoundland on this continent today. The dogs were Canadian Ch. Shelton Cabin Boy, a son of Ch. Siki out of Harlingen Topsy, who was purchased by Mr. Montagu Wallace of Saskatchewan; Canadian Ch. Baron, also a son of Ch. Siki out of Harlingen Topsy, who was imported by Mr. D. R. Oliver of St. Mary's, Ontario; and American Ch. Harlingen Neptune of Waseeka, a son of Ch. Siki from Queen of Hearts who was imported by Mrs. Elizabeth (Loring) Power. (As Queen of Hearts was a daughter of Ch. Ferrol Neptune and Queen Bess, she was a full sister to Harlingen Topsy.) Therefore, these three dogs were of almost identical breeding. They all proved to be outstanding show dogs, but what is more important to the history of the breed, they were all good sires and were dominant for their better characteristics.

At the same time quite a few good females of similar bloodlines came from England to join the best of what remained of the good stock on this continent. These bitches were bred to the three sons of Ch. Siki and we soon found that they were producing winning stock from practically any bitch which was bred to them. Victories in the working group became common, and even the great award of Best in Show was being won many times by dogs of these bloodlines. On the island of Newfoundland the Honorable Harold Macpherson was following the same lines of breeding by crossing the best stock which he had in his kennels with the best bitches which he could buy in England or with the daughters of the three famous sons of Ch. Siki which were available in Canada and America.

For the next ten or twelve years the Newfoundland flourished in North America and we continued to breed consistently to the Siki stock, producing dogs which not only approached the ideal of Standard but which were very uniform within a specific litter.

So strong is the influence of these three dogs that there were thirty-seven Newfoundland dogs and bitches whose completed championships were announced in the *American Kennel Gazette* during the five-year period from January, 1950, through December, 1954, and every one of these dogs and bitches traces back to one of the three imported sons of Ch. Siki.

List of Newfoundland A.K.C. Champions of Record
1950 through 1954

1950
- Midway Black Ledge Sea Raider
- Midway O'Lady Sea Romain
- Midway Black Ledge Lelonga
- Swivy of Camayer
- Seaburn Sea Change
- Dryads Fan
- Dryads Lieutenant

1951
- Midway a Sea King
- Bonnavista
- Topsails Captain Cook

1952
- Waseeka's Zunzibar
- Dryads Admiral
- Birchmount Sea Nymph
- Perivale Sea Ranger
- Dryads Decorative Accessory

1953
- Midway a Sea Queen
- Skippers Star
- Coastwise Nan Tucket
- Waseeka's King Toxzon
- Claverie Barnacle
- Midway Sea Raider
- Waseeka's Ghostship
- Little Bear Isolt of Irwin-dyl
- Little Bear's Merasheen

1954
- Carbonear Newf
- Perivale Rocky Shore
- Little Bear's Big Chance
- Little Bear's Seldom Come By
- Dryad's Cherie of Spinnaker
- Irwin-dyl's Sir Aliking
- Little Bear's James Thurber
- Midway Black Ace
- Spinnaker's Sinbad
- Irwin-dyl's Lady Beale Isoud
- Little Bear's Gander
- Midway Lady Baldor
- Dryad's Pilot

Am. and Can. Ch. Dryad's Trademark O'Golly, owned by Roger Richards, shown by E. J. Carver. Judge is Willis Linn.

Not listed are the champions of record from 1955 through 1969 in the United States and Canada because there are over 200 of them. However, they are all on record with the American Kennel Club in the United States and with the Canadian Kennel Club in Canada for those interested in research.

The pedigrees of all the champions bred on this continent have been checked and we find they all trace back to Baron, Cabin Boy, or Neptune.

Many have two in their pedigrees and a few of them can claim all three as ancestors. This is certainly a clear proof of what great dominant sires can do for a breed. However, there are serious disadvantages in depending on a few dominant sires to carry the whole burden of quality in the male line of any breed. In the first place, there were, of course, dominant bitches during these years, but the influence of any bitch, no matter how great a producer, is less than a great male because the number of her progeny is so limited by comparison with a popular stud that sires may litters in one year. There is also a tendency to disregard the faults in a bitch if you intend to breed her to a sire that is sufficiently dominant to produce good or even excellent puppies from poor bitches. In this way recessive faults crept into the bloodlines and we did not always realize that they were lurking there ready to reappear in future generations.

The next problem to arise was realized in England much earlier than in this country. Suddenly breeders found that in their eagerness to produce wonder dogs they had bred all of their bitches to Siki or his close relatives and that when these puppies grew up there was no stock to breed them to except their near relatives.

The English turned to the Continent for outcross stock. There they found dogs with good bone, excellent bodies, fine coats, but with a very different-looking head—snipier in the muzzle, less depth in the lips, less development of the occipital bone, and a tendency to a larger eye. These differences gave the dogs a strange and rather foreign look in the head which many people did not like. However, if they were to get out-crosses the English had little choice, so they tried several imported dogs with more or less success: Miggi von Leutberg, Roland von Gunzthal, Judith van de Neyerhut, Harlingen Cedric (these were only partial outcrosses, as some of their ancestors were English dogs imported to the continent) and a few others were bought in Germany, Switzerland, and Holland. We were quick in this country and Canada to avail ourselves of these different bloodlines and bought their sons and daughters as an outcross for our stock.

The immediate results of these crosses seemed to be good. There is often a good reaction when a very closely bred and dominant dog is bred to a bitch which is almost a complete outcross. In many cases we get an upsurge of what is called "hybrid vigor" without losing the type of the line-bred stock. So for some years it looked as if our outcrosses were successful. We were producing very large, sound dogs of excellent type and they were winning all sorts of awards in the show ring. If anyone thought of those recessive genes of a very different type of head which must have been present in many of the dogs, we did not know enough about the science of breeding to be alarmed. However, a generation or two later we found that our type was not quite as good as it had been—heads were not as typical, dogs were leggier with less spring of rib, and eye color was inclined to be lighter, with many eyes a bit too prominent. So we had to go back again and by selective breeding (eliminating as breeding stock dogs whose faults we were trying to avoid) try to re-establish the standard type. This time we were not fortunate enough to find any strongly dominant sire that did not also prove dominant in some less desirable qualities, so there was no easy way back to "the good old type."

Taking heed of the above, and in an endeavour to produce stud dogs that would strengthen the breed, Coastwise and Dryad Kennels imported two linebred bitches from Holland: Saskia and Beatrijs v't. Zeepardje. They were fine bitches but lacked our head type. Therefore they were bred to dogs linebred for our type head and in turn their offspring were bred to dogs linebred for head type. The results of this breeding program is evident today in stud dogs such as Ch. Dryad's Sea Rover, Ch. Edenglen's Beau Geste, Ch. Edenglen's Banner, Ch. Dryad's Lord Nelson, and Ch. Shipshape's Cuttysark.

This pedigree of Ch. Edenglen's Banner (twice winner of National Specialty shows—under Mrs. Power and Mrs. Godsol) shows how such a breeding is made.

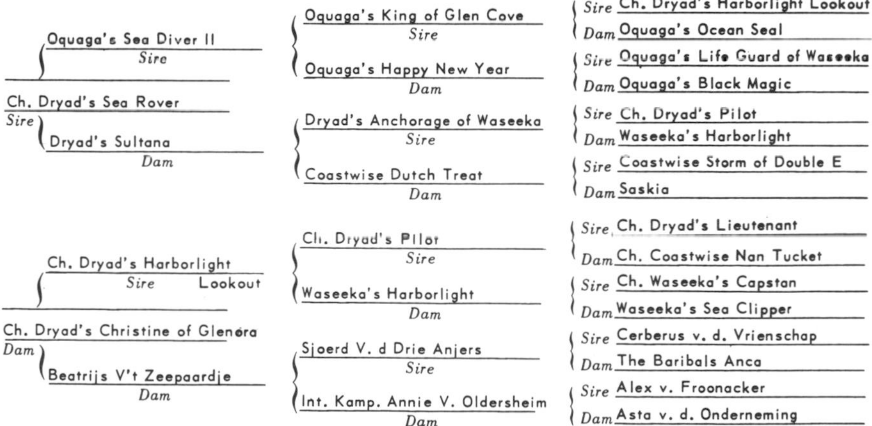

Today we believe that we are gradually getting back to the desired type. When asked how the Newfoundland of today compares with the great dogs of twenty-five years ago, Mrs. Power says that the general average of dogs seen at the shows today and also of those living with acquaintances as pets is much higher than years ago. There are practically none of the doubtful specimens that resembled other breeds as much as Newfoundlands. She believes that our general average at the shows is improving each year, and that there are some top dogs at shows in North America that compare with the best of Siki's sons and grandsons: Ch. Seafarer, Ch. Shelton Cabin Boy, Ch. Baron, Ch. Waseeka's Sea King, Ch. Coastguard of Laurel Brae, Ch. Naida III, Shelton Atlanta, and Ch. Waseeka's Skipper. Those of us who remember these dogs or can study them should make every

Ch. Shipshape's Cuttysark, owned by the Shipshape Kennels of Mr. and Mrs. Robert Lister.

effort to breed and choose our breeding stock with such care that we can someday produce dogs which could equal them.

Today we hear a great deal about hereditary or congenital defects. These terms are often confused. Briefly heredity means "deriving by inheritance." Thus a quality a dog has what was also present in the ancestor from whom he inherited it. Congenital means "born with or existing from birth." This means that a quality or condition which is hereditary is also congenital but a quality or condition which is congenital is not necessarily hereditary.

To refer to Newfoundlands. Eye color and shape, shape of head, ears, webbing in the feet, disposition, coat color, and many other characteristics are hereditary. However, defects of the heart, kidneys, hips, shoulders etc. with which some puppies are born are usually called congenital because we do not know if they are hereditary or not.

To add to the confusion there is a vague area of dog characteristics which we cannot place in either of these categories. Environmental is about as close as we can get. Injuries in delivery, or "in the nest" can cause lasting defects in the shape of the hips, back, shoulders, and even in the mouth. Distemper can cause brown teeth. Sun and salt water tend to make a brown coat.

Ch. Little Bear's James Thurber, owned by Dowling Realty Company.

Ch. Waseeka's Skipper, owned by Coastwise Kennels.

Ch. Dryad's Coastwise Showboat, bred by Dryad Kennels and owned by Coastwise Kennels.

Ch. Waseeka's Square Rigger, owned by Waseeka Kennels.

Ch. Waseeka's Sea King.

Ch. Edenglen's Beau Geste, owned and shown by Mrs. Robert Dibble. Judge is Percy Roberts.

Traumatic accidents at any age can cause lameness. And so the list can go on.

Thus good and bad points in our grown dogs are a result of any or all of these. In breeding, we must take all of them into consideration in judging parental lines and breed a balanced good dog. We must take each characteristic and consider it in proportion to others. Do not put all the emphasis on one characteristic. Remember too that it is not good breeding practice to breed to a dog with a bad hereditary or congenital defect.

The reason for the above discussion is that in recent years there have been "fads" in breeding. Some have bred for a particular, as for head or coat or hips or shoulders. In the Newfoundland, remember, we want a sweet dispositioned, big, sound moving dog that is as much like the Standard as possible. Breed for these things but don't be disappointed if every puppy in a litter does not turn out as you planned. The chances are that only one or two will come up to your expectations.

Chapter XII

The Brood Bitch and the Stud

If we want to succeed in improvement within our breed we must have an even greater trueness to breed type in our bitches than we have in their breeding partners. The productive value of the bitch is comparatively limited in scope by seasonal vagary, and this, in turn, increases the importance of every litter she produces.

In America, over a span of fruitful years, we were fortunate in possessing many bitches of true and uniform type, and through them perpetuated the breed type we desired.

To begin breeding we must, of necessity, begin with a bitch as the foundation. The foundation of all things must be strong and free from faults, or the structure we build upon it will crumble. The bitch we choose for our foundation bitch must, then, be a good bitch, as fine as we can possible acquire, not in structure alone, but in mentality and character and health as well. She is a product of her heredity, and this most important facet of her being must be closely analyzed so that we can compensate, in breeding, for her hidden faults. Structurally, the good brood bitch should be strongly made and up to standard size. She should be deep and not too long in body, for overlong bitches are generally too long in loin and weak in back, and after a litter, tend to sag in back line. She must possess good bone strength throughout, yet she should not be so coarse as to lack femininity. Weakness and delicacy are not the essence of femininity in this breed and should be avoided in the brood bitch.

A bitch will first come in season when she is between eight and twelve months of age. Though this is an indication that nature considers her old enough and developed enough to breed, it is best to allow her to pass this first heat and plan to breed her when she next comes in season. This should come within six months if her environment remains the same. Daylight, which is thought to affect certain glands, seems occasionally to

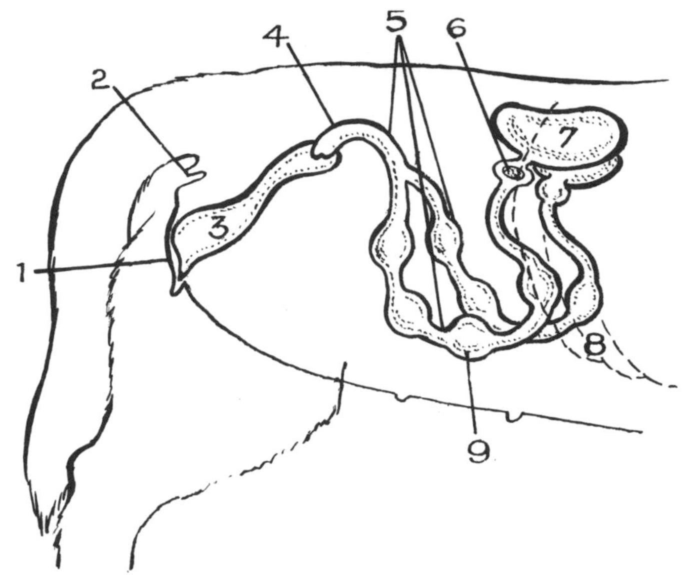

REPRODUCTION SYSTEM OF BITCH

1. Vulva. 2. Anus. 3. Vagina. 4. Cervix. 5. Uterus. 6. Ovary. 7. Kidneys. 8. Ribs. 9. Feotal Lump.

influence the ratio of time between heats, as will complete change in environment.

When your bitch is approaching her period of heat and you intend to breed her, have her stool checked for intestinal parasites, and if any are present, worm her. Feed her a well-balanced diet, such as she should have been getting all along. Her appetite will increase in the preparatory stage of the mating cycle as her vulva begins to swell. She will become restless, will urinate more frequently, and will allow dogs to approach her, but will not allow copulation. Within the bitch other changes are taking place at this stage. Congestion begins in the reproductive tract, the vagina and the horns of the uterus thicken, and the luteal bodies leave the ovaries.

The first sign of blood from the vulva ushers in the second stage of the mating cycle. In some bitches no blood appears at all, or so little that it goes unnoticed by the owner, and sometimes we find a bitch that will bleed throughout the cycle. In either circumstance we must depend upon other signs. The bitch becomes very playful with animals of her own and the opposite sex, but will still not permit copulation. This, of course, is a condition which is very trying to male dogs with which she

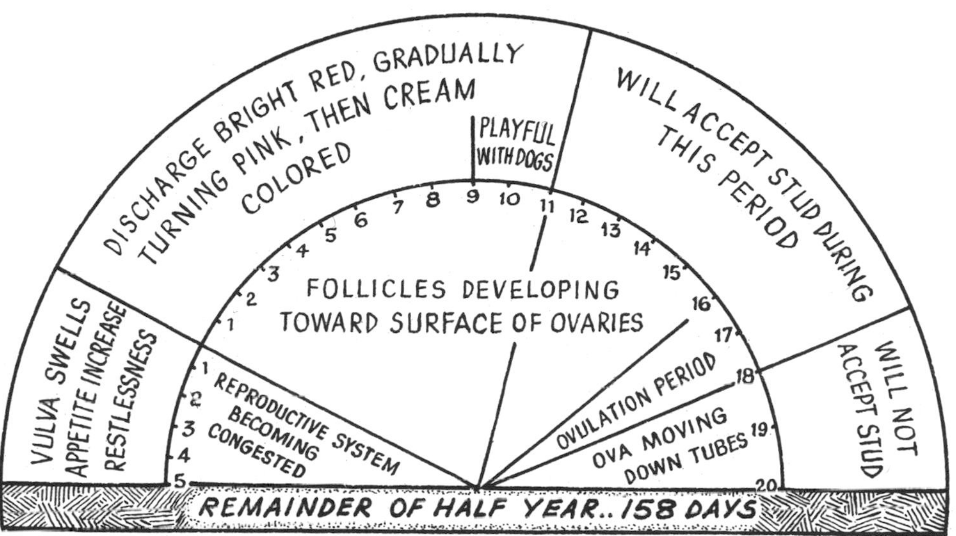

NORMAL BITCH MATING CYCLE

comes in contact. Congestion within the bitch reaches a high point during this period. Ova develop within the follicles of the ovaries, and, normally, the red discharge gradually turns to pink, becoming lighter in color, until it becomes straw color and is no longer obvious. Her vulva is more swollen, and she becomes increasingly more playful with males. This period is generally of about ten days' duration, but the time varies greatly with the individual. Rather than rely upon any set time period it is best to conclude that this period reaches its conclusion when the bitch will stand for the stud and permit copulation. This generally occurs at about the tenth day, but can take place as early as the fourth or fifth day of this period or as late as the twenty-second day.

The third period in the cycle is the acceptance period. The bitch will swing her hind end toward the dog, her tail will arch and fall to the side, and she will permit copulation. The bitch may be sensitive and yelp and pull away when the stud's penis touches the lining of the vagina. If this occurs several times, it is best to wait another day, until the sensitivity has left this region. A very definite indication that the bitch is in the acceptance period is the softness and flaccidity of the vulva, from which the firmness and congestion have gone. Within the bitch the ovarian follicles have been growing ever bigger, and approximately midway in the acceptance period some of them burst and the eggs are ready for fertilization.

If the bitch has a normal mating cycle, as shown on the diagram, the best time to breed her is about the thirteenth or fourteenth day of the mating cycle, when ovulation has occurred. This time also varies with the individual bitch, so that until you have bred your bitch once or twice and feel that you know the best time for her, it is better to breed her on the eleventh day and every other day thereafter until her period of acceptance is over. This last, of course, is generally only possible when the stud is owned by you. If copulation is forced before the bitch is ready, the result is no conception or a small litter, since the sperm must wait for ovulation and the life of the sperm is limited. The acceptance period ceases rather abruptly, and is signaled by the bitch's definite resistance to male advances.

If your bitch is maiden, it is best to breed her this first time to an older stud that knows his business.

THE MECHANICS OF BREEDING NEWFOUNDLANDS

For owners of Newfoundlands who have no professional help available and who have never bred the larger breeds, the following explanation of the mechanics of breeding from a practical standpoint will prove helpful.

Both dog and bitch should be in good health. They should be as free of worms as possible and not too heavy. An overweight stud dog may not be able to even get up on a bitch and may become exhausted from the effort involved. An overweight bitch may never conceive; and, if she should, she may have a more difficult time whelping. It is best to have them both on the lean side.

The area where they are to be bred should be enclosed so that they cannot run away. The footing should be firm and not slippery. Dogs cannot get a purchase on a slippery floor and may slip when they are tied causing injury to one or both of them. Grass is the best.

When is the correct time to breed them? An active, healthy stud dog can be bred anytime. He is ready if the bitch is ready. A young inexperienced dog may be overanxious and try to breed a bitch before she is at the correct time. An experienced stud on the other hand is often the best judge of the correct day. Although it is possible for a veterinarian to tell by smears when the bitch is ovulating, the average and easiest way is to check her. She should switch her tail to one side when touched in the rear, she should have passed from a bright red discharge to a straw colored one and when you insert two fingers into her vagina and turn them around she should not object and it should not be tight. A novice bitch may be very tight and you will have

Bulwell Aero Flame.

WELL KNOWN BROOD BITCHES

Ch. Coastwise Shore Leave.

Canadian Ch. Daventry Grace Darling.

to stretch the opening. All this is usually possible from about the 10th day onwards to about the 18th day. However there is no true rule and bitches have been bred on the first day they start to bleed and have been known to breed on the 22nd day. This is why a bitch should be confined the entire time she is in season.

Both dogs should be thoroughly aired and empty. Both dogs should have choke chain collars and a lead should be on hand for the bitch. Put them in the area together and let them play for a few minutes. There is usually some love play of licking each other's ears and genitals. The bitch may even ride the dog. If she growls and snaps, separate them at once. This will frighten a novice stud and may prove dangerous if she actually bites him. However, if they both seem desirous and he starts to mount her, proceed as follows.

Do not just leave them together and hope they breed. They may, but most likely they will not. They may work for hours and both get exhausted. This is not good for any stud dog. If you help them, you are sure they are bred and will be able to more accurately foretell the whelping day.

Always, for a novice dog and bitch, and for ease at any breeding, it is a good idea to have three persons available. One holds the bitch at her head so she can't go forward or turn or snap. It is very rarely that she would have to be muzzled. One person holds the stud dog while the bitch is being set up. The third person is the most important. This one holds the bitch and directs the one who is holding the stud. This person kneels on his left knee with his right under the bitch's belly on the right hand side of the bitch. The right hand is then placed between the bitch's rear legs and holds the lips of the vagina apart. He is now in a position to guide the opening over the dog's penis and can tell if the dog is too high or too low and guide it accordingly. The left hand holds the bitch's tail out of the way.

Once the bitch is set up as described let the dog loose and he will most likely mount her right away. If he goes to the side or to the front, pull him off or shove him around to the back. If he is too high or too low on the bitch, pull him off and have him try again. As soon as the penis enters the vagina, the dog pulls up and starts a quick agitation, and will tie almost immediately (10–30 seconds). If he penetrates, but not far enough to cause a tie, the person holding the bitch should place his left arm under the rear of the stud dog and pull him in with an upward motion. In some cases it is a good idea to have the third person put his hands on the buttocks of the dog and shove him in.

When you are sure they are tied let go. When the dog has finished, he will move his front legs to one side of the bitch. You

Ch. Dryad's Compass Rose, owned and shown by Christine Lister. Judge is Mrs. Nicholas Demidoff.

should then lift the rear leg of the dog over so that both dogs are back to back. It is wise to hold the bitch for a few minutes as she may become excited and jump around. Do not worry if they pull against each other and wander around a bit. However, any effort to really separate them will cause damage to both. You will notice that the bitch will contract every once in a while. This is normal. The tie will last from 30 seconds to over an hour. The average tie is about 15 minutes. If the male starts dragging the bitch around it is wise to hold him too.

Once they have separated let the dog take care of himself. He will usually lick himself and the penis will go back into its sheath without help. The bitch should be held up for a few minutes to keep the semen in and then should be given a quick run and put in a place where she cannot urinate for at least half an hour.

Frequently in the process of breeding, the penis and knobs will come out of the dog's sheath. If this happens let the bitch and dog both go. He will ride her for a minute or so and they will go right back in. Then try again. Occasionally the stud will ejaculate. Then you may have to wait a couple of hours to try again. You can tell this because the penis will swell up and semen will drip out. He may be in a hunched stand.

Do not touch the male's genitals during breeding as this may cause him to ejaculate prematurely.

Length of tie is no indication as to how many puppies will be in a litter. Some dogs never tie but may penetrate and ejaculate semen. A minute tie can result in as many puppies as a 30 minute one.

It is not necessary to trim off the hair around the vagina if you are holding the bitch and guiding the dog.

A bitch will usually accept a dog many times during her breeding period. She is completely indiscriminate regarding the breed of the dog. For this reason be sure she is confined the entire season.

Small dogs can breed big bitches and *vice versa*. Bitches have been known to lie down for a small dog. Don't think your Terrier can't breed your Newfoundland.

If your Newfoundland bitch gets tied to another breed, do not forcibly separate them. This will injure both dogs. Either let her have the pups or take her (right after they have become untied) to your veterinarian for shots that may keep her from having them. If she should have a litter, dispose of all but one of the pups. Having one to nurse will keep her from going into an emotional spin.

It is an old wive's tale that a bitch is ruined once she is bred to other than her breed. Just be sure she is bred correctly the next time.

Stud dogs will sometimes vomit; it indicates nothing.

Have water available at all times. Both dogs may want it.

Dogs should be started at stud at about a year of age. For the first year, use him about once a month. It will not harm him to be used several times a month on different bitches. One bitch might be bred three times in one week to the stud.

If you can't get two dogs bred after a couple of days trying, take them to a professional.

Occasionally the dog or bitch may bleed a little after a tie. Unless it is profuse, don't worry about it.

Don't force breeding. It will usually result in two dogs that have a bad experience breeding and you may have trouble with them another time.

It is advisable to breed a bitch twice, skipping a day between breedings. This will cover a greater number of days when the bitch is fertile.

Be particularly careful in breeding a novice stud. Be gentle and encouraging. Praise him when he mounts correctly. If handled with care you will have a valuable animal that is easy to handle.

If you are breeding the dogs with no help, or only have one to help you, remember that the key position is for holding the bitch from underneath and guiding.

If a male seems to lose interest (as in an older dog), rest him and take him out to air.

Opinion varies as to whether a bitch should be bred on her first or second season. It depends on how mature she is. Ask advice.

Should you skip a season after a litter to breed your bitch again? This depends on the condition of the bitch and the number of pups she had. Again ask advice from an expert.

A bitch may be bred for many years. They have been known to produce fine puppies at nine or ten.

Occasionally fertile bitches, whether bred or not, will have phantom pregnancies and show every physical manifestation of true gestation up to the last moment. In some cases a bitch may be truly bred and then, after a month, resorb her fetuses. The only way of differentiating between pseudo-pregnancy and fetal resorbtion is by palpation, or feeling with the hands, to locate the fetal lump in the uterus. This is a difficult task for one who has not had vast experience.

Let us assume that your bitch is in good health and you have had a good breeding to the stud of your choice at the proper time in the bitch's mating cycle to insure pregnancy. The male sperm fertilizes the eggs and life begins. From this moment you will begin to feed the puppies which will be born in about sixty to sixty-three days from ovulation. Every bit of food you give the bitch is nutritionally aiding in the fetal development within her. Be sure that she is being provided with enough milk to supply calcium, meat for phosphorus and iron, and all the other essential vitamins and minerals. A vitamin and mineral supplement may be incorporated into the food if used moderately. She must be fed well for her own maintenance and for the development of the young *in utero*, particularly during the last thirty days of the gestation period. She should not, however, be given food to such excess that she becomes fat.

Your bitch, her run, and house or bed should be free of worm and flea eggs. She should be allowed a moderate amount of free exercise in the prenatal period to keep her from becoming fat and soft and from losing muscular tone and elasticity. If your bitch has not had and enough exercise prior to breeding and you wish to harden and reduce her, accustom her to the exercise gradually and it will do her a great deal of good. But do not allow her to indulge in unaccustomed, abrupt, or violent exercise, or she might abort.

The puppies develop in the horns of the uterus, not in the "tubes" (fallopian tubes), as is commonly thought. As the puppies develop, the horns of the uterus lengthen and the walls expand until the uterus may become as long as three and a half feet in a Newfoundland bitch carrying a large litter. A month before the bitch is due to whelp, some breeders incorporate fresh liver in her diet two or three times a week. This helps to keep her free from constipation and aid in the coming necessary production of milk for the litter. If the litter is going to be small, she will not show much sign until late in the gestation period. But if the litter is going to be a normal or large one, she will begin to show distention of the abdomen at about thirty-five days after the breeding. Her appetite will have been increasing during this time, and gradually the fact of her pregnancy will become more and more evident.

Some advance preparations should be made several days before she is due to whelp. The whelping box should be prepared. It should be located in a dimly lit area removed from disturbance by other dogs or humans. The drawing shows a suitable whelping box. The purpose of the step on the inside is to keep the bitch from accidentally smothering a puppy that gets behind her.

If she has a superfluous amount of hair around the vaginal opening it is a good idea to trim some of it off. This will keep it from getting matted. Also trim some from around the nipples if there is so much there that a puppy can't find them. Be sure she is clean and that her nipples are clean.

If the puppies are born at a time of year when it is cold, the problem of heat comes into consideration. There are several methods of heating a whelping box. 1. The whole room can be kept warm. When the bitch has a place to go out and cool off this is a good method. 2. Chicken-brooder heaters can be attached to the bottom of the box in various places. This has the advantage of keeping the pups in one place, as they will all congregate near the heat. Also, the bitch can get away from the heat. 3. Heat lamps can be placed above the box directed to any spot. This method is the easiest and very effective. By lowering or raising the bulbs, a warmer or cooler temperature can be obtained. It also keeps the puppies in one place, and if they are too hot they can move away. The bitch, too, can move away from the heat. The temperature in the area for newborn pups should be in the 80's for the first few days. This can gradually

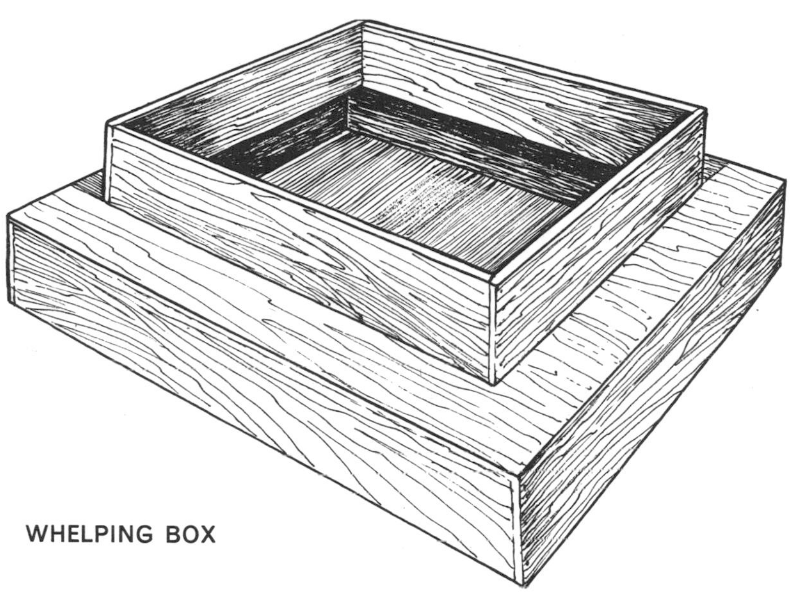

WHELPING BOX

be lowered until it is the same as outdoors. At this point it is good to get Newfoundland puppies out. Their coats will grow thicker than those kept indoors and there is less chance of their catching cold if they get used to the colder temperatures.

As the time approaches for the whelping, the bitch will become restless; she may refuse food and begin to make her nest. The normal temperature for a Newfoundland is 101.5. If you check her temperature every day for four or five days before she is due to whelp, you will notice that it drops usually a few tenths of a degree each day. The day that it drops to 99 degrees you can expect her to whelp. She will also show a definite dropping down through the abdomen. Labor begins with pressure from within that forces the puppies toward the pelvis. The bitch generally twists around as the puppy is being expelled to lick the fluid which accompanies the birth. Sometimes the sac surrounding the puppy will burst from pressure. If it doesn't, the puppy will be born in the sac, a thin, membranous material called the fetal envelope. The navel cord runs from the puppy's navel to the afterbirth, or placenta. If the bitch is left alone at whelping time, she will rip the fetal caul, bite off the navel cord, and eat the sac, cord, and placenta. Should the cord be broken off in birth so that the placenta remains in the bitch, it will generally be expelled with the birth of the next whelp.

After disposing of these items, the bitch will lick and clean the new puppy until the next one is about to be born, and the process will then repeat itself. Under completely normal circumstances your Newfoundland bitch is quite able to whelp her litter and look after them without any help from you, but since the whelping might not be normal, it is best for the breeder to be present, particularly so in the case of bitches that are having a first litter.

If present, the breeder may choose to remove the sac, cut the umbilical cord, and gently pull on the rest of the cord until the placenta (assuming that it has not yet been ejected) is detached and drawn out. Some breeders keep a small box handy in which they place each placenta so that, when the whelping is completed, they can check them against the number of puppies to make sure that no placenta has been retained. The navel cord should be cut about three inches from the pup's belly with a dull instrument to close off the blood vessels. The surplus will dry up and drop off in a few days. There is no need to tie it after cutting. You need not attempt to sterilize your hands or the implements you might use in helping the bitch to whelp, since the pups will be practically surrounded with bacteria of all kinds, some benign and others which they are born equipped to combat.

If a bitch seems to be having difficulty in expelling a particularly large puppy, you can help by wrapping a towel around your hands to give you purchase, grasping the partly expelled whelp, and gently pulling. Do not pull too hard, or you might injure the pup. The puppies can be born either head first or tail first. Either way is normal. As the pups are born, the sac broken, and the cord snipped, dry them gently but vigorously with a towel and put them at the mother's breast, first squeezing some milk to the surface and then opening their mouths for the entrance of the teat. You may have to hold them there by the head until they begin sucking.

The following advice is very important but should not be used by the novice. It should be done only under the supervision of a veterinarian.

Often several puppies are born in rapid succession, then an interval of time may elapse before another one is born. If the bitch is a slow whelper and seems to be laboring hard after one or more pups have been born, regular injections of Pitocin, at three-hour intervals, using a little less than one half c.c., can help her in delivery. Pituitrin, one half to one c.c., is a similar drug and the one most often used, though Pitocin brings less nausea and directly affects the uterus. Both of these drugs should be administered hypodermically into the hind leg of the bitch at the rear of the thigh. After the bitch has seemingly completed her whelping, it is good practise to administer another shot of the drug to make sure no last pup, alive or dead,

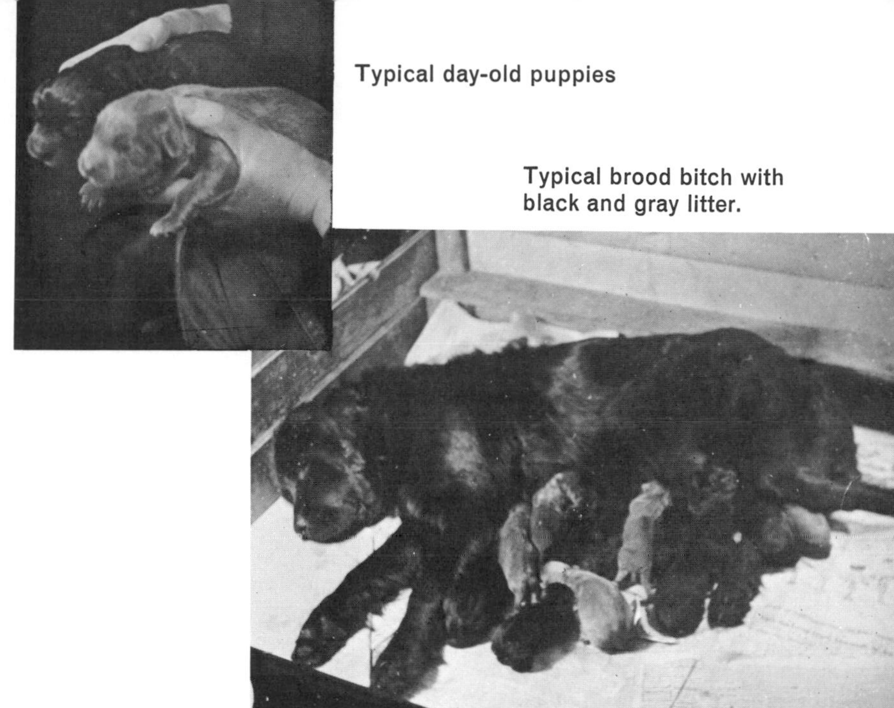

Typical day-old puppies

Typical brood bitch with black and gray litter.

is still unborn and to cause her to clean out any residue left from the whelping. Never use either of these drugs until she has whelped at least one pup.

Allow her to rest quietly and enjoy the new sensation of motherhood for several hours, then insist that she leave her litter, though she won't want to, and take her out to relieve herself. Offer her some warm milk. From then on feed her as recommended during the gestation period, with the addition of three milk feedings per day. Sometimes milk appears in the udders before birth, but generally it comes in when the pups begin to nurse, since it is manufactured by glands, from blood, while the pups are at the breast.

Now is the time to cull the litter. Of course all young which are not normal should be culled immediately at birth. If the bitch whelps six or fewer pups and all seem strong and healthy, no culling is required. Quiet puppies are healthy ones. Constant crying and squirming of the pups are danger signals, and a check should be made to see what ails them. It may be that the bitch is not providing enough milk and they are hungry, or perhaps they are cold. Sometimes the trouble is parasitic infection, or possibly coccidiosis, or navel infection.

Except for the removal of dewclaws on the hind legs, the pups, if healthy, need not be bothered until it is time to begin their supplementary feeding at about three weeks. Dewclaws should be removed on about the second day after birth.

There are several ills that might befall the bitch during gestation and whelping which must be considered. Eclampsia, sometimes called milk fever, is perhaps most common, This is a metabolic disturbance brought on by a deficiency of calcium and phosphorus in the diet. If your bitch gets plenty of milk and a good diet such as is recommended, she should not be troubled with this condition. Should your bitch develop eclampsia—evidenced by troubled shaking, wild expression, muscular rigidity, and a high temperature—it can be quickly relieved by an injection of calcium gluconate in the vein.

Should your bitch be bred by accident to an undesirable animal, your veterinarian can cause her to abort by the use of any one of several efficient canine abortifacients. With the aid of stilbestrol, he can also aid old bitches that have been resorbing their fetuses to enable them to carry full term and whelp.

Mastitis, an udder infection, is a chief cause of puppy deaths. It is generally mistaken by the uninformed for "acid milk," a condition which does not exist in dogs because the bitch's milk is naturally acid. Mastitis is an udder infection which cuts off part of the milk supply and the whelps either die of infection, contracted from the infected milk, or from starvation, due to the lack of sufficient milk. It is not necessary to massage the dam's breasts at weaning time with camphorated oil. They will cake naturally and quickly quit secreting milk if left completely alone.

Growths, infections, injuries, cysts, and other and various ailments can affect the female reproductive system and must be taken care of by your veterinarian. The great majority of bitches that have been well cared for and well fed are strong and healthy, and the bearing of litters is a natural procedure—the normal function of the female of the species to bear and rear the next generation, and in so doing fulfil her destiny.

THE STUD DOG

Rittmeister von Stephanitz in 1930 wrote: "Modern breeding research has taught us that it is not so much the appearance of an animal that indicates its breeding values, but rather its hereditary picture, which means the sum total of the qualities and characteristics which it has inherited from its ancestors." This is particularly applicable to the stud dog.

If what we have said about the unrivaled importance of the brood bitch is true, it may be difficult to understand why we pay so much attention to the male lines of descent. The reason is that stud dogs tend to mold the aspects of the breed on the

Brood Bitch Class Specialty Show, 1949; left to right, Ch. Waseeka's Hesperus, Ch. Dryad's Coastwise Showboat, Ch. Dryad's Coastwise Gale.

Stud Dog Class Specialty Show, 1952; Judge Mrs. Francis V. Crane awarding trophy to Ch. Dryad's Lieutenant, handled by Mr. M. K. Drury. Four of Lieutenant's sons out of three bitches. Left to right: Ch. Waseeka's Ghost Ship handled by Jack Cypress, Waseeka's White Sails handled by Mrs. E. K. Annis, Ch. Dryad's Decorative Accessory handled by Mrs. Robert Schirmer, and Harforidge Beachcomber handled by Mr. Alfred Forest.

whole and in any given country, or locality, to a much greater extent than do brood bitches. While the brood bitch may influence type in a kennel, the stud dog can influence type over a much larger area. The truth of this can be ascertained by the application of simple mathematics.

Let us assume that the average litter is comprised of five puppies. The brood bitch will then produce a maximum of ten puppies a year. In that same year a popular, good producing, well-publicized stud dog may be used on the average of three times weekly (many name studs, in various breeds, have been used even more frequently over a period of several years). This popular stud can sire fifteen puppies a week, employing the figures mentioned above, or 780 puppies a year. Compare this total to the bitch's yearly total of ten puppies, and you can readily see why any one stud dog wields a much greater influence over the breed in general than does a specific brood bitch.

The care of the stud dog follows the same procedure as outlined in the chapter on general care. He needs a balanced diet, clean quarters, and plenty of exercise, but not the special care required by the brood bitch. There is no reason why a healthy young dog cannot be used at stud for the first time when he is twelve months old. He is as capable of siring a litter of fine and healthy pups at this age as he ever will be. He should be bred to a steady, knowing bitch that has been bred before, and when she is entirely ready to accept him. Aid him if necessary this first time. See that nothing disturbs him during copulation. In fact, the object of this initial breeding is to see that all goes smoothly and easily. If you succeed in this aim, the young dog will be a willing and eager stud for the rest of his life, the kind of stud that it is a pleasure to own and use.

After this first breeding, use him sparingly until he has reached sixteen or seventeen months of age. After that, if he is in good health, there is no reason why he cannot be used once a week or oftener during his best and most fertile years.

The male organs vital for reproduction consist of testicles, where the sperm is produced; epididymis, in which the sperm are stored; and vas deferens, through which the sperm are transported. The dog possesses no seminal vesicle as does man. But, like man, the male dog is always in an active stage of reproduction and can be used at any time.

When the stud has played with the bitch for a short period and the bitch is ready, he will cover her. There is a bone in his penis, and behind this bone is a group of very sensitive nerves which cause a violent thrust reflex when pressure is applied. His penis, unlike that of most other animals, has a bulbous enlargement at its base. When the penis is thrust into the bitch's

Seward Kennel's team at Lenox. Champion Seaward's Frosty Morn, Ch. Seaward's Maharanaee, Ch. Seaward's White Ranee, Ch. Seaward's Ermine, handled by Betty Cummings.

vagina, it goes through a muscular ring at the opening of the vagina. As it passes into the vagina, pressure on the reflex nerves causes a violent thrust forward, and the penis, and particularly the bulb, swells enormously, preventing withdrawal through the constriction band of the vulva. The stud ejaculates semen swarming with sperm, which is forced through the cervix, uterus, fallopian tubes, and into the capsule which surrounds the ovaries, and the breeding is consummated.

Ch. Dryad's Bambi and Ch. Sunny Lane's Black Bucko with owner Harry Lehr.

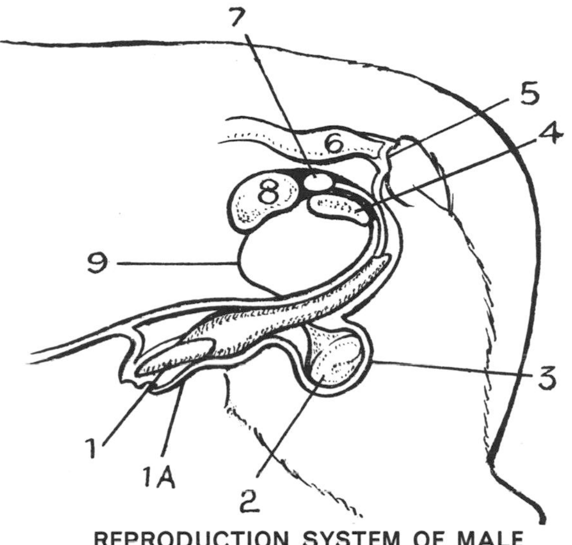

REPRODUCTION SYSTEM OF MALE

1a. Sheath. 1. Penis. 2. Testicle. 3. Scrotum. 4. Pelvic Bone. 5. Anus. 6. Rectum. 7. Prostate. 8. Bladder. 9. Vas deferens.

The dog and bitch are tied, or "hung," and the active part of breeding is completed.

There is not much more that can be written about the stud, except to caution the stud owner to be careful of using drugs or injections to make his dog more eager to mate or more fertile. The number of puppies born in any litter is not dependent upon the healthy and fertile male's sperm, but upon the number of eggs the bitch gives off. Should your dog prove sterile, look for basic causes first. If there seems to be no physical reason for his sterility, then a series of injections by your veterinarian might prove efficacious.

It is often a good idea to feed the dog a light meal before he is used, particularly if he is a reluctant stud. Young or virgin studs often regurgitate due to excitement, but it does them no harm. After the tie has broken, allow both dog and bitch to drink moderately.

Chapter XIII

The Newfoundland in Europe

Although the Newfoundland has been in Europe for several centuries originally taken there by sailors, he entered on a larger scale by way of England in the later 1800's. He spread little by little over Germany, Switzerland, the Netherlands, Scandinavia, Finland, Austria, Italy, France, Ireland, Belgium and, central and Eastern Europe.

He conquered the hearts of many by his impressive, massive body and by his fine character. However, and fortunately so, he has never become a "fashionable" dog. But on the street and at the shows, everybody admires this majestic animal.

Although the Newfoundland originated on the west side of the Atlantic, he is thought of in Europe as an English breed, and the English Standard is binding for all the countries affiliated with the Federation Cynologique Internationale (International Kennel Federation).

There is a close relationship between several of the European countries: England and Ireland; Switzerland and Germany (Mr. Emil Burkhard, president of honor of the Swiss Club, was breeding counsellor of the German Club for years); Netherlands and Finland, as the Finnish breeding is mostly based on imports from the Netherlands, under the guidance of Mr. Johan Pieterse; and more and more they are working together for mutual advantage in their breeding programs.

In America, England, Western Europe, Scandinavia, and Finland, the Landseer is considered a white and black Newfoundland and is judged in classes with the blacks and "other colors." In Central Europe (Germany, Switzerland, and Austria) the Landseer is considered a separate breed. There has been a difference of opinion for years; in 1961, the Federation Cynologique Internationale especially pressed by Germany and Switzerland, acknowledged the "Landseer-European-Continental-Type" as a separate breed with its own Standard. All the European countries affiliated with the F.C.I. (England is not included) have to accept this. However, it is still very confusing; in talking about Landseers on the continent, misunderstandings are avoided only by being specific. For example, Hollanders are giving up the name of Landseer and speaking of white and black Newfoundlands or spotted ones.

The difference between the black and the brown Newfoundlands is very evident. The brown ones have a more angular head with a decided stop, ears high set up on the head, bigger eyes, shorter and softer coat, less undercoat, are higher on legs with shorter back, are missing feathers on fore legs, and roll in gait is not wanted, bigger than a black and of a different character. In short, everything that would bc a fault in a black is considered desirable in a brown.

It is well known that the Newfoundland has long been used for hauling fishnets, drawing sledges and carts, as a watch dog, and in other work. Less known is the fact that he is an excellent guide dog for the blind. The Newfoundland Liane has escorted her master, Xavier Fleck, for years. They live in Storkensohn, a little village in the Vosges (France). They walk together every day over highways and small mountain paths. Liane warns immediately of every object in the way. Mr. Fleck trained the dog with the help of his children. They used to lay objects in her way and she soon caught on to her job. She is the light in the life of Mr. Fleck.

Judging on the European continent differs from that in England or the United States and Canada. Dogs are rated from first through fourth in order of excellence in England and North America; on the Continent, each dog receives a card marked with a "Qualification." Qualifications are "Excellent" for beautiful dogs with very few faults; "Very good" for beautiful dogs with somewhat graver, but acceptable faults; "Good" for dogs with objectionable qualities, and "Poor" if judged fully unacceptable. In some countries there are intermediate qualifications.

To become a Champion of a show, a dog must first win the qualification "Excellent." To earn the definitive Champion title, the dog must win four championships under two different judges. For the International Champion title, the dog must win four certificates (C.A.C.I.B. international certificate of beauty) in three different countries under three different judges, of which one must be in the homeland.

The result of judging with qualifications is that an owner knows the qualities of his dog and won't bother to show him again if he is rated "poor" at his first show. Therefore, the quality of most of the dogs shown is high.

The classes in shows on the Continent are: Youth class (9–18 months), Open class (9 months and older), Breeders class (at least 9 months and the owner must be the breeder). Classes are separated for dogs and bitches. Brace classes are also included.

Professional handlers are unknown and owners show their own dogs.

Names of dogs always include the breeder's name and not that of a future owner.

We are very much indebted to Mr. W. Mohr (Austria), Miss Birgitte Gothen and Mr. Flemming Uziel (Denmark), Miss Jeanne Davies (England), Mrs. Beatrice Ahonius (Finland), Mrs. Lampert (France), Mr. Peter Gale (Ireland), Mrs. Ulla Andersson (Sweden), and Mr. E. Burkhard (Switzerland) whose contributions, information, and pictures made this European chapter possible.

ITALY

Although the climate of Italy is less than perfect for raising Newfoundlands, Mr. Silvio Cipolla of Dell'Agagna Kennels has been breeding them there since 1928, starting with an Austrian bitch and an English dog. It has been necessary, however, to continually import dogs from Holland, Switzerland, England, and German in order to maintain coat quality.

AUSTRIA

Austria Newfoundland lovers, thus far, are breeding very few dogs. No Newfoundland Club exists, although some twenty-five fanciers, members of the "Verein Für Grosse Hunde" Association (Association of big dog breeds) expect to create one shortly. Familiar breeding kennels are Haus am Echofels, v.d. Schneebergeiche, and Schwanenhaus am Attersee.

Prominent among the total of fifty Newfoundlands in the country are:—

Delf von Schwanenhaus am Attersee
Anuk v.d. Schneebergeiche
Konga v.d. Juliana
Anna vom Haus Bussard
Bella v. Windbichl
Bessy v.d. Schneebergeiche.

BELGIUM AND LUXEMBURG

There is no breeding of Newfoundlands in Belgium and Luxemburg at the present time, although there are several dogs which have been imported from Germany, Holland, and France. Dog shows in Brussels and the township of Luxemburg, probably because of the convenience of their locations, attract many

Katja v. Haus Bussard, owned by W. Mohr.

Kennel deel 'Agogna, owned by Silvio Cipolla of Italy

Delf v. Schwanenhaus a. Attersee, owned by W. Mohr.

Newfoundland entries and bring together exhibitors from Germany, Holland, and France who are seeking the C.A.C.I.B. (International Certificate of Beauty).

NORWAY

Norway provides an ideal climate for the Newfoundland dog. Moreover, with such easy access to Denmark, Finland, and Sweden, where excellent breeding programs are underway, the establishment of the breed in that country could easily be developed. At the present time, however, no Newfoundland activity is reported in Norway.

DENMARK

There have been Newfoundlands in Denmark for many years and there is record of three having been entered in 1898 for a show at Copenhagen. Not until approximately ten years ago, however, were there many dogs or active breeders.

Pedigrees show that most of Denmark's stock are descendents of dogs imported from the Helluland Kennel of the late Miss Betty Berg of Sweden, who bred successfully for many years. Eventually, however, the stock suffered because of intensive interbreeding. In recent years, the situation has vastly improved as the Danes imported breeding dogs from Sweden, Finland, Switzerland, Newfoundland, Germany, England, and Holland.

Until 1964, a Landseer was seldom seen in Denmark but several have lately appeared in different litters. Shows are well supported with an entry of fifteen to twenty dogs; not many have as yet earned their championships, but it is indeed reasonable to expect improvement in the breed in Denmark.

Miss Birgitte Gothen, an enthusiastic lover of the breed, assisted by Mrs. E. Straarup, has worked diligently for the cause of the Danish Newfoundland. As a result of their combined efforts, the Newfoundlandklubben was formed on September 10, 1967, with a membership of 60 and Mr. Fleming Uziel as President.

All champions: Black Cesar (Swedish); Alderbay-Bamse (Finnish); Bjornegaards Tom (Danish); Finnbear Ikaros (Finnish); Klams Black Bluff (Swedish); Chicka (Swedish).

Black Ido v. Helluland, owned by Birgitte Gothen.

Swedish and Danish Ch. Nero, owned by Fleming Uziel.

Kolkjears White Label, owned by B. Gothen.

Ch. Rys Ambrosijus, owned by H. Heggelund.

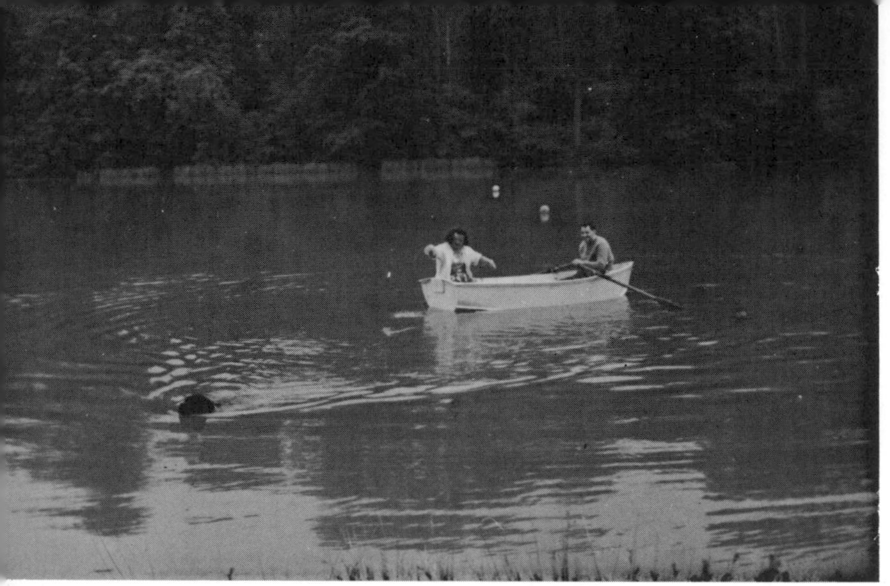

The Water Trials Match Meeting at Alcester in 1967.

ENGLAND

The first Newfoundland club in England was founded in 1886. Known simply as The Newfoundland Club, its purpose was to establish the standard and type for the breed now acknowledged by Newfoundland Clubs through the world. Among the founders of this organization were Mr. Bailey, Mr. Gillingham, Mr. van Weede, and Mr. van Oppen, Mrs. Charles Roberts, daughter of founder van Oppen, served for thirty years as secretary of the club.

After World War II, the club membership was reduced to ten, but has increased steadily until now there are one hundred members, led by Mrs. K. Rowsell as President, Mr. Charles Roberts as Vice-President, Mrs. C. Handley as Treasurer, and Miss J. M. Davies as Secretary.

Miss Davies writes of the activities of The Newfoundland Club as follows:

"With the British Newfoundland population now numbering approximately 150, the last decade has shown a distinct rise in the popularity of the breed. Whilst the blacks still outnumber the Landseers, the latter are on the increase and are regularly seen on the show benches today.

"The British bred Newfoundlands retain their benevolent temperament, typical head and expression, plus sound conformation and are in demand as breeding stock in many countries, including Australia, Denmark, and the United States.

Sparry's Sea Rover of Perryhow, C.C. and Best of Breed, Crufts 1955, owned by Sparry Kennels, England.

Ch. Harlingen Sand Piper, owned by Mrs. Hamilton Gould.

"Recently British breeders have imported from America, Canada, Holland, and Finland, so as to obtain outcrosses which, together with the well-established bloodlines are providing a sound breeding foundation, auguring well for the future of the British Newfoundland.

"Simultaneously, the Club's activities are expanding with the re-introduction of the water trials in 1965, which are proving very successful and the publication of a bi-annual Newsletter which is sent to all known Newfy owners as well as to Club members.

"In 1966, the Club celebrated its 80th birthday with a dinner party, at which the late Mr. Leo Wilson was the guest of honor. On this occasion some of the Club's many trophies were on display, including the pre-World War I Challenge Cups which are awarded annually one to each sex in both black and Landseer. The Club is particularly lucky to be the recipient in recent years of additional trophies and can, as a result, offer perpetual awards at most shows.

"With the membership of the Club having risen to nearly 100, thus showing a significant reflection of the overall trend of the

Black Jet of Little Grange, owned by Fran Warren.

Faithfull of Little Grange, owned by Miss J. Davies.

Ch. Sea Irchin, Best of Breed at Crufts in 1959, 1960, and 1962, owned by F. Cassidy.

breed in the British Isles, it is confidently expected that the high standard of the British Newfoundland will be maintained and even enhanced by the enthusiasm and interest shown by all lovers of the breed."

There are several magnificent Landseers in England, among them Ch. Harlingen Sandpiper, owned by Mrs. Hamilton Gould. Other Champions are Little Creeks Son of Rex, Drift of Little Creek, Mossie of Little Creek, Bonnybay Jasmine, Storytime Whaler, Bonnybay Mr. Barrel, Bonnybay Mona of Sparry, and Bonnybay Musette of Sparry.

The import of dogs into England is made difficult by strict quarantine regulations, and it is much to the credit of the British breeders that they have spared neither labor nor expense in order to obtain Newfoundlands from other countries.

FINLAND

Although it is a comparatively young club, founded in 1952, the Suomen Newfoundlandinkoirayhdistys, led by its original president, Mr. Gerold Blomberg, has achieved for Finnish dogs a reputation of quality that is well known among Newfoundland fanciers throughout the world. Exports to Holland, England, Germany, Sweden, Norway, and the United States have won fame and award in their new lands both in the ring and in breeding kennels.

Club membership now numbers some three hundred, and it is estimated that there are approximately 350 Newfoundland

Finland—Finnish Sieger Gerogeest Attan—Finland's present most outstanding Newfoundland.

The 1967 Jubilee Edition of the Finnish Newfoundland Club magazine featured these fine specimens of the breed: Muotovalio Punnilan Morri Ski, Harmongttan O'Key, Gerogeest Burre.

DEUTSCHER NEUFUNDLÄNDER-KLUB E.V.
(ehem. Neufundländer-Klub für den Kontinent · Gegr. 1893) · Sitz München
Vom Verband f. d. Deutsche Hundewesen e.V. allein anerkannter zuchtbuchführender Neufundländer-Klub

Suomen Newfoundlandinkoirayhdistys
Finska Newfoundlandshundföreningen
(THE FINNISH NEWFOUNDLAND ASSOCIATION)

AFFILIÉ A LA S. C. C.
(reconnue d'utilite publique)

Letterheads of some of the European Newfoundland clubs.

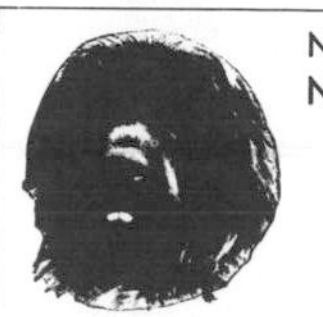

NEDERLANDSE
NEWFOUNDLANDER CLUB

OPGERICHT 16 FEBRUARI 1917
KONINKLIJK GOEDGEKEURD
ERKEND DOOR DE RAAD VAN BEHEER
GIRO : 287128

dogs in the country. A news bulletin is published on a regular basis and the club provides for every member a booklet defining rules of the Association, standard of the breed, breeding instructions, and an extract of the international rules.

A breeding program, under the direction of Mr. Blomberg, controls what dogs and bitches may be bred, and *a litter may consist of only six pups*, all of which are sold by an intermediary of the club.

Once a year, in conjunction with the International Show of the Kennel Club, the Suomen Newfoundlandinkoirayhdistys conducts its own Specialty Show which is judged by an expert selected by the association. It is an impressive parade of from thirty-five to forty Newfoundlands competing for highly treasured awards, many of which are donated by Newfoundland Clubs of other lands.

It is indeed a fine commentary on the success of the program of the Finnish Club when an impartial reporter says, "It is very difficult at the present time to select an outstanding dog in Finland as there are many excellent ones, all of whom are highly awarded."

French Champion Jaloute du Dakala.

A scene from the French Newfoundland Club's show at Paris in 1965.

FRANCE

Until 1963, there was no Newfoundland Club in France, and breeders were forced to carry on their programs without support or direction. However, with the formation of the Club Francais du Chien Terre Neuve, and under the leadership of President, Mr R. Montenot, much is being accomplished for the improvement of the breed in matters of showing, breeding, and importing new breeding stock.

The Club membership is four hundred, and it is estimated that there are approximately 450 dogs (perhaps six of them Landseers) in France.

The emblem of the Club Francais du Chien Terre Neuve which shows the head of a Newfoundland dog encircled by a lifebuoy is very attractive. Believing he is primarily a rescue dog, the French Club has organized and carried on an extensive water trials program. So successful was the endeavor that M. Montenot plans to seek approval from the Societe Centrale Canine for a rescue program which will earn for a dog a "brevet of rescue" and which may, in time, be required for his championship.

Of the several Champions listed in France, the most outstanding is considered to be Buck v.d. Niederburg. Dogs well known for their rescue ability are Orphee de Men ar Groas, Marquise de Men ar Groas, and Max v. Schwabenland.

GERMANY

The Newfoundland Club of the Continent, the second oldest of Newfoundland clubs, was established in Germany in 1893. This club is known to have worked closely with those persons interested in the breed, even when outside of their normal sphere of influence. For instance, we find much cooperative effort with those in Switzerland. One of these close associations is described by Mr. Burkhard as follows:

"Most of the competent Swiss breeders and a number of Newfoundland devotees had been members of the Newfoundland Club of the Continent (N.K.) prior to 1925 and were represented on its board of directors. In 1926 an agreement was reached between the N.K. and the S.N.K. whereby the S.N.K. was recognized as a specialty club for a single breed. The purposes

Ikarus v. Giskadi.

Eileen v. Giskadi.

International Champion Cito v. Zschimmeroth, owned by Gisela Hoffman.

Germany, 1954 winner. Sieger Janko von den Peck-Bergen.

and aims of both clubs remained the same. The only difference was that the S.N.K., as the special breed club of the all-breed Swiss Kennel Club (S.K.G.), was limited to operating in Switzerland. The N.K. agreed to set aside for the Annual Specialty Show in Switzerland the same cash prizes and club awards, cup awards, and ribbons as at the Annual Specialty Show in Germany. The N.K. also made available its periodicals to the Swiss club not only for informing the members about the breed but also providing space for club notices, announcements, etc."

Unfortunately such wonderful working arrangements had to be terminated in 1933 when a change in the German government forced a reorganization of all canine associations in Germany.

Under this organization there are six Landesgruppe or geographical divisions of the country. Each landesgruppe is autonomous. We are indebted to letters from Herr Fritz Rathmann, president of the Berlin Landesgruppe and to Professor Dr. Otto Fehringer of the Landesgruppe Bavaria and his book *Der Neufundlander* for much of the data contained here.

Herr Rathmann tells us:

"We keep to our standard and recognize three types. They are the heavy Newfoundland of middle size, the somewhat higher-legged dog, and the typey small dog handing down the best characteristics of the breed.

"We pay particular attention to the coat, which must show thick undercoat, to the dark eye, to the strong, well-boned build, to the well-placed tail, and to the broad chest.

"We place particular weight on teeth, preferring those that close like scissors. Unfortunately two of the lower cutting teeth protrude all too often. Years ago this was introduced by an imported male dog, the well-known Satan. Being otherwise a wonderful dog, a sound mover, perfect as to coat, dark eyes, tail carriage, his two protruding teeth were not considered too serious a fault. Now we are having considerable trouble eliminating the fault."

The breed, like the people of Germany, has suffered considerably from the effects of the war. Berlin in particular is having a hard time re-establishing the Newfoundland to his rightful place because of the restrictions on travel to and from the city.

However, the shows are still well supported and there is much hope for the future.

HOLLAND

Traditionally the Netherlanders have been good breeders (of cattle, horses, and poultry) and thus their success in breeding Newfoundland dogs might well have been expected.

Mrs. S. Roorda began breeding Newfoundlands sometime in 1913 or 1914, using imported stock from Germany. The most

Joschi v. Giskadi.

Jabal v.h. Zuiderzeeland, owned by W. Hanegraaf.

outstanding animal imported was Norma, the daughter of Halfdan III; of the inbred line from the brilliant Halfdan I, a relative of Thirzen imported from Newfoundland. Also imported was Moro the son of Winner Hannibal von Hardtwald, an offspring of the outstanding Buchner.

Mr. Johan Pieterse, whose name was to become very familiar in the Newfoundland world, describes his entry among the Newfoundland lovers as follows:

"It was a cold November evening (1916) that my eldest son and I were standing on the platform of the Heerenveen Station, waiting for our first Newfoundland.

Ch. and Int. Ch. Duke v.h. Zeepardje, owned by E. Leeftink.

Ch. Tom, ancestor of the Dutch Newfoundland stock.

Adrian van Sijl-Ralli and Hestia.

Johan Pieterse and Puck v. Nordwige, 1950.

Holland: Mrs. Johan Pieterse with Pere Noble van Nordwige and Theresin von Die Angers, winners in 1952.

"Louwerse, the unforgettable (Dutch) writer of our youth, had given so complete a picture of the dog that we were prepared to receive him.

"And so Tom arrived, our own honest, good-natured Tom, a bit tired after the long trip, being only a pup, but trying to take in the strange new faces and surroundings. Tom was the star, and he is still the ultimate criterion for all breeders. The credit for this goes to the breeder, Mrs. S. Roorda." (To this day, Newfoundland lovers in the Netherlands claim "that Tom has not yet been equalled in his beauty).

The following February, in the Cafe Restaurant Central in Haarlem the Nederlandse Newfoundlander Club was founded. Mr. E. L. Duicker was elected president and Mr. Pieterse, secretary-treasurer, by the Club's eleven members. Although Mr. Duicker retired as president and passed the office along to Mr. van Gelderen, Mr. Pieterse continued as secretary until 1932, when he became president. Miss Jetske Kalkman succeeded Mr. Pieterse as secretary of the N.N.C. and became his wife in 1952. Mr. Pieterse died in 1958 having served the Club as secretary for 15 years and as president for 26 years; Mrs. Pieterse retired

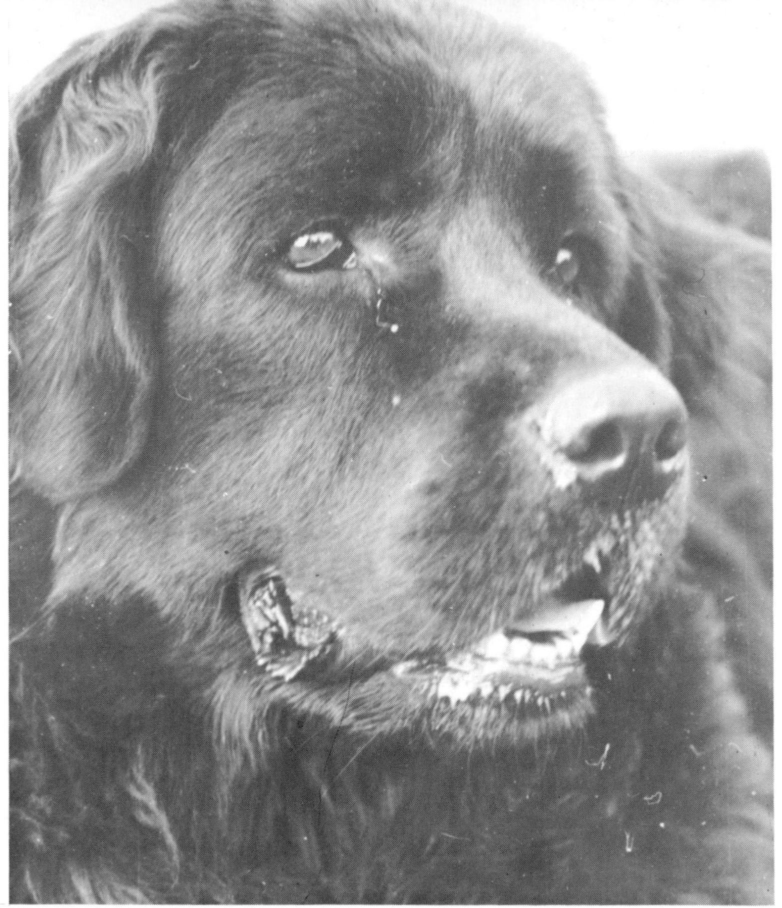

Avalon's Hestia, owned by G. te Dorsthorst.

in 1964, having been secretary for 32 years. It is an extraordinary record from the point of view of both time and valuable service.

In 1961, in Mr. Pieterse's memory, the Johan Pieterse Trophy was established and is awarded annually to the dog or bitch that has accumulated the greatest number of points during the year. The dog or bitch finishing in second place (but not of the same sex) is awarded the Nederlandse Newfoundlander Club Cup. Both cups may be won only once by the same dog.

From the time the Club was founded, Johan Pieterse guided the breeding of Dutch dogs. He raised the quality of the breed to a very high standard, and it is due to his influence that nowhere else in the world does the Newfoundland dog appear in such conformity.

Eaglebay Mariner, owned by J. W. Woodman.

Ch. Avalon's Demeter, owned by M. Rackwitz.

Avalon's Heracles, owned by W. Stoks.

Since Netherlanders were never tempted to adapt their type to fashion but bred systematically to their type, there are few Landseers in Holland; brown and bronze dogs are whelped regularly and are used for breeding, crossed with blacks, for it is felt that they favourably influence the coat quality.

The first Specialty Show was held in Amsterdam on December 25, 1920 with twenty-four dogs entered; starting in 1947, the N.N.C. has celebrated its 30-, 40- and 50-year anniversaries with Speciality Shows, each one more festive and with a larger entry list than its predecessor. A record entry of sixty-three at the time of the "Golden Jubilee" in 1967 clearly revealed the conformation, similarity, and splendid character of the breed.

Some of the best known breeding and show dogs of the past ten years are:

Dorine & Duke v.h. Zeepaardje (Achilles X Brigitte v.h. Zeepaardje)

Avalon's Athena & Aphrodite & Ariadne (Achilles X Cabot Doeschka).

Pere Noble & Taru van Thamen (Taaran Trulle X Carmen v.d. Toren).

Achilles & Brigitte v.d. Papenhof (Duke v.h. Zeepaardje X Avalon's Aphrodite).

Avalon's Demeter & Dionysos (Duke v.h. Zeepaardje X Cabot Doeschka.

Avalon's Ganymedes (Nattanin Ralli X Avalon's Athena)—who won the Pierterse Trophy in 1967.

Avalon's Ganymedes, owned by F. Leeman.

Nattanin Ralli, 1964 Youthwinner, owned by A. v. Zijl.

Avalon's Ion, owned by P.v.d. Werff.

Ch. Dryad's St. Johns, owned by Mr. and Mrs. Douglas Marshall; this dog is the son of Beatrijs v't Zeepardje, "Sinjun."

Brunte (brown), owned by Mrs. Anita Ringert.

Beatrijs v't Zeepardje, an import from the Netherlands, owned by Dryad Kennels.

The past two decades have produced many dogs and bitches that are noted particularly for their fine breeding qualities, some of them are as follows: Puck van Nordwige, Cerberus v.d.Vriendschap, Goliath v. Froonacker, Sjoerd v.d. Drie Anjers, Alex v. Froonacker, Remo v.d. Oude Plantage

Carla v.h. Singelhius, Brigitte v.h. Zeepaardje, Rena & Rhoda v.d. Drie Anjers, Annie v. Oldersheim and The Barribals Anca (of Perryhow) that was exported to England in whelp in 1949, Anca's descendents have been sent from England all over the world and, presumably, no bitch in the history of the breed has had so much influence on the development of the breed.

Mr. A. van Leeuwenberg is the present president of Nederlandse Newfoundlander Club, and its secretary is Mr. K. H. Versteeg. Three hundred members were recorded at the time of the fiftieth anniversary of the Club's founding, and the Dutch Newfoundland dog population has increased to 350. Among the novelties offered by the N.N.C. are silver demi-tasse spoons bearing a Newfoundland head, and silver brooches marked by the same distinctive feature.

IRELAND

The Newfoundland breed became established in Ireland in 1958. At about that time, Mr. Peter Gale, owner of Rathpeacon Kennel, imported Sea Breeze of Sparry and Achilles of Fairwater. Soon thereafter several other dogs were brought into the country, and the Newfoundland Club of Ireland was founded with Mr. Peter Gale (still in office) as its president.

The Club members number some thirty, and the Newfoundland dog population of Ireland is approximately twenty.

In 1960, Achilles became the first breed champion, also winning the "Supreme Award" at the Limerick Show. The following year Micmac of Rathpeacon (a son of Achilles) earned his title after winning eight certificates at consecutive shows. Champion Micmac continued to dominate the scene for some time.

Mr. Gale's Rathpeacon Kennel is still the only breeding kennel in Ireland. As a result, the number of young dogs in Ireland is limited, although several have been imported from England. English influence and bloodlines will undoubtedly always be strong in Ireland because of quarantine regulations and the proximity of the islands.

SWEDEN

Although Newfoundland fanciers of Sweden organized a club some years ago, it has never actually been active because distances between members were so great. Indeed, it was frequently impossible to assemble even the Board of Directors of the Club.

In order to provide some degree of communication and companionship, several smaller organizations have been formed, with members of each being owners of Newfoundlands bred by a particular kennel. Meetings occur once a month, with a different member each time serving as host, and discussion covers matters of interest common to all Newfoundland lovers.

At the first Swedish show in 1886, four Newfoundlands (one of which was named Wotan) were shown. At the end of that century there is record of the fact that Captain Aaby Ericson bred some Newfoundlands from Danish stock. It has been learned that an English import, Champion Waterman, owned by Mr. W. Withington, and a bitch named Bella were entered in several shows in 1910.

Breeding in Sweden, however, moved ahead in 1915–16 when Mr. Eric Lundin imported Champion Harras and three bitches, Berna and Toska von Hardtwald and Champion Rolandine von Frankenthal. One of the best known and most successful breeders in Sweden until she became ill in 1959 was the late Miss Betty Berg of Helluland Kennels. Her first litter, whelped in 1929, was sired by Champion Wotan out of Champion Katja av Eskenas.

Avalon's Daphne, owned by U. Ekholm, and her litter.

Ch. Finnbear Ikaros, owned by Mrs. Ulla Andersson.

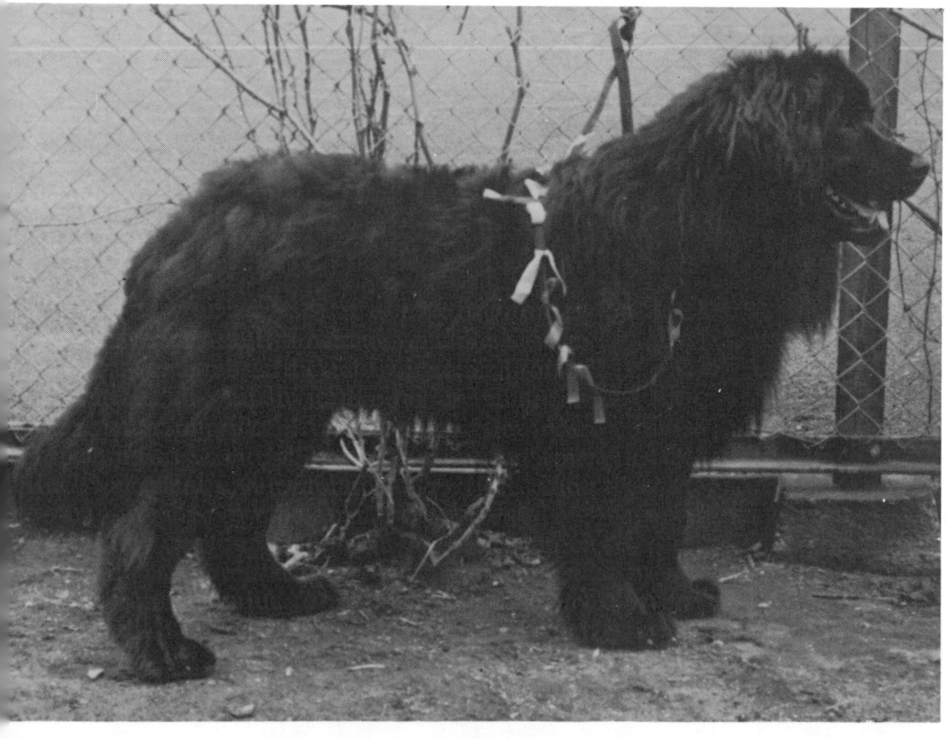

Punnilan Turja, owned by U. Ekholm.

A majority of the present Swedish dogs are descendents of Helluland stock from Kennel Auricco, owned by Mrs. Sandra Larsen. Champion Auricco Black Archibald Andersson, a son of the Finnish import, Champion Gerogeest Bero, brought great renown to his breeders in 1942. Black Archibald's most famous descendent, Champion Chika of Klams Kennel, recently won her International Certificate at the age of nine.

Since 1960 there have been many imports into Sweden from Finland, Holland, and Switzerland and many of them have become champions: among these, two of the most prominent were Champion Nattanin Rita (out of Champion Alderboy Attila and Harmonattan Nina) and Champion Finnbear Ikaors (out of Champion Punillan Turja and Avalon's Daphne).

SWITZERLAND

As far as can be ascertained from show reports and the stud books, the breeding of Newfoundlands in Switzerland first began about 1880. At the first Swiss dog show, which was held at Zurich in 1881, there were two male Newfoundlands among the 200 entries. Stud-book records show the first English import to have been made in 1886.

In 1887 Professor Albert Heim, probably the most outstanding promotor of the Newfoundland breed, obtained his first dog, Pluto, whelped in 1886 at Mr. Burger's kennels in Leoburg, Germany. A year later he added the bitch Thetis, from the kennels of Mr. Hartstein in Plauen. Mr. Hartstein was founder of Newfoundland breeding programs on the European continent. Thus began the planned breeding of Newfoundlands in Switzerland.

From 1884 until 1914, when World War I began, 197 Newfoundland dogs were registered in the Swiss Stud Book. Although there was no compulsory registration, most dogs that were successfully shown were entered.

Professor Heim devoted himself not only to popularizing the breed but also to the task of producing enough specimens to supply the growing demand. Besides simply propogating the dogs he had, he made special efforts to improve their disease

Brown Newfoundlands from Kennel "v. Gollorina" at age of nine months.

Roland von der Waldstatte, bred by R. & E. Burkhard in 1941.

Ottoline van de Oude Plantage, owned by R. & E. Burkhard—Swiss-Siegerin in 1942.

Gido v. d. Schurz, bred and owned by W. Amsler—Swiss-Sieger in 1954.

resistance and general health. Early in the Swiss breeding program there appeared symptoms of degeneration and organic debility which were believed to be the result of excessive inbreeding. Professor Heim, assisted by his friends Junzli and Dr. Rikli, therefore imported a number of dogs from their island home. These imports provided gratifying results in the improvement of the breed.

World War I almost resulted in the extinction of the breed in Switzerland. Again it was Professor Heim who came to the rescue with his friend U. Meier-Bosch who saved for the world what is now known as the Toggenburg Strain. This is a basic strain now among the Swiss dogs and appears in our American and Canadian pedigrees by way of Miggi von Leutberg, imported to England following the excessive inbreeding there in the twenties.

Following the war, many breeders were so desirous to return the breed to its former prominence that they neglected to be sufficiently selective in their imports and in their breeding programs. This was the situation that spurred Emil Burkhard,

Hexe v.d. Schürz.

Int. Ch. Ares v. Landseehof, owned by E. Amstad.

Pit v. Margarethe.

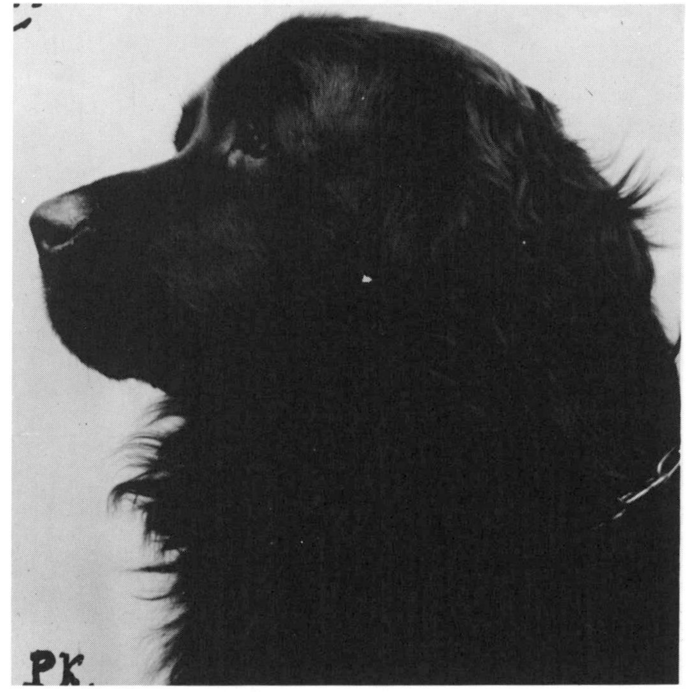

Pan v.d. Schürz, owned by Franz Willi.

Professor Heim, and about twenty faithful followers, to found the Schweizerischer Neufundlander Klub on June 7, 1925. They met in the restaurant Zum Safran in Basle as a result of a small notice in the May issue of *Schwizer Hunde-Sport.* About forty persons consider themselves to be founding members and Mr. Emil Burkhard was elected first president of the organization.

Mr. Burkhard tells of his club's activities as follows: "Because a number of breeders and fanciers in Switzerland had belonged to the Neufundlander Club fur den Kontinent (now the German Club), a mutual interest relationship continued between the two clubs. Likewise good relationships were maintained with the Dutch Club. This friendship makes possible an exchange in bloodlines which is very important in offsetting excessive inbreeding in a country as small as Switzerland. This is true despite the fact that the uniformity of our Blacks is not so strongly pronounced as in some countries. Although uniformity can be achieved only by inbreeding, we have always considered it our first duty to uphold the health of our dogs and are satisfied that by our practice we are getting the best results."

Arbo v. Chiemsee.

Int. Ch. Bob v.d. Warte, owned by Rosy Burkhard.

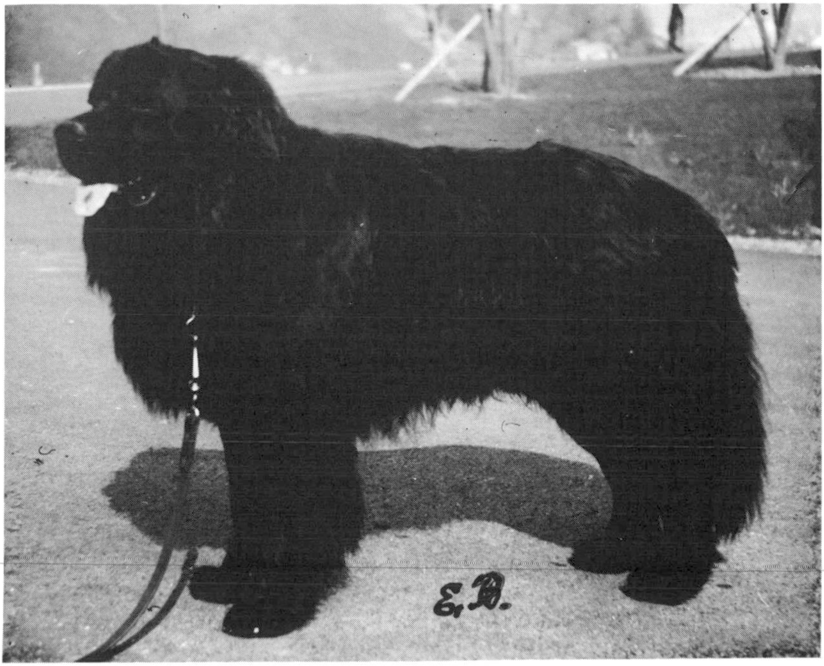

There are approximately 450 Newfoundlands and Landseers in Switzerland and, since 1950, the Swiss Newfoundland Club has grown from a membership of 220 to 280. From the beginning of the Swiss Stud Book, there have been entered 2,990 Newfoundlands and 126 Landseers. (From 1955 through 1966, 194 litters were whelped with a total of 884 pups, an average of 4–5 per litter, and entries numbered 23 imports from Germany, Holland, Austria, and Sweden.

For some years, the Swiss Club has operated under its own breeding regulations. These rules control the use of dogs for stud purposes and bitches for breeding. In Switzerland, as in Germany and Austria, the breeding programs of black Newfoundlands and black and white Landseers are absolutely separated. They are considered to be two different breeds, each coming from Newfoundland, but of different origin, thus presenting distinctive anatomical and physical qualities. Each breed has its own standards; blacks and browns are judged by the English standard as interpreted by the German and Swiss Newfoundland clubs. Landseers are held to a standard defined by the F.C.I.

Each year, two or three international shows are held in Switzerland with entries of between 30 and 50 dogs. In 1965, the Jubilee Specialty boasted some 73 entries. The Swiss "Sieger" show is held annually, and the coveted title is awarded only if the quality of the dog merits it.

NEWFOUNDLAND CLUBS AROUND THE WORLD (1969)

England: THE NEWFOUNDLAND CLUB Founded 1886 Members: 100:
President of the Club:
Mrs. K. Rowsell, Brick House Farm, Mundon, Maldon, Essex.
Hon. Secretary:
Miss J. M. Davies, Old Shelve Manor, Lenham, Maidstone, Kent.

Germany: DEUTSCHER NEUFUNDLANDER KLUB e.v.
Founded 1893 Members: 500
President:
Heinz Hofman, Dyckerhofstr. 407, 8919 Utting/Ammersee
Secretary:
Wolf Diery, Wittelsbacherstr. 7, 8 – Munchen – 19

Netherlands: NEDERLANDSE NEWFOUNDLANDER CLUB
Founded 1917 Members: 300
President:
A. van Leeuwenberg, van Brakellaan 31, Hilversum
Secretary:
K. H. Versteeg, van de Sande Bakhuysenlaan 25, Leiden

Switzerland: SCHWEIZERISCHER NEUFUNDLANDER KLUB
Founded 1925 Members: 280
President of Honor:
E. Burkhard, Sternhalde 14, 6000 Luzern

President:
P. Greiner, 8967 Widen bei Bremgarten
Secretary:
Frau G. Schwab, Giacomettistrasze 8, 3000 Bern
Breeding Counsellor:
M. Jeannot, Waldhof, 5032 Rohr AG

Finland: SUOMEN NEWFOUNDLANDINKOIRAYHDISTYS
Founded 1952 Members: 300
Chairman of the Association:
Mr. Gerold Blomberg v.d. Geest, Kirkkoherrantie 2, Helsinki 65
Secretary, Treasurer and Editor of the Bulletin:
Mrs. Beatrice Ahonius, Jokiniementie 12, Helsinki 65

Ireland: NEWFOUNDLAND CLUB OF IRELAND
Founded 1958 Members: 30
Chairman of the Club:
Mr. Peter Gale, Ballyduff, Ashford, Co. Wicklow
Secretary:
Mr. Edmund Lueders, 114, Terenure Road West, Dublin, 14

Canada: CANADIAN NEWFOUNDLAND CLUB
President:
Donn Purdy
Vice-Presidents:
Thomas Harrison and Mrs. Eliz. Sellars
Secretary:
Miss Natalie Elias, 368 Ellerslie Ave., Willowdale, Ont.
Ass't Secretary:
Mrs. Bert Basterfield, 61 Brimley Road, Scarboro, Ont.

United States: THE NEWFOUNDLAND CLUB OF AMERICA, INC.
Founded 1932 Members: 500
President:
Mrs. Maynard K. Drury, R.D. #1, Phelps, N.Y.
Corresponding Secretary:
The Rev. Canon R. Curry, Shattuck School, Faribault, Minnesota
Recording Secretary:
Mrs. E. A. Gleason, Jr., 21 Kemble St., Lenox, Mass.

France: CLUB FRANCAIS DU CHIEN TERRE NEUVE
Founded 1963 Members: 400
President of the Club:
Mr. R. Montenot, 29, avenue Jean Jaurès, 93-Villetaneuse
Secretary:
Mme Lampert, "La Petitte Maison", 62-Cucq

Denmark: NEWFOUNDLAND KLUBBEN Founded 1967 Members: 60
1st President of the Club:
Leif Poulsen, Herringlöse, 2640 Hedehusene
2nd President:
Miss Birgitte Gothen, Borghaven 8, 2500 Valby
Secretary:
Bernt Creutzburg, Kamstrupvej 119A, 2610 Rodovre

Contact address for Sweden:
Mrs. Ulla Andersson, Kläms Kennel, Norra Bygget Postlada 1665, Kallinge.

Austria: VEREIN FUR GROSSE HUNDERASSEN
The founding of a special Newfoundland Club is in preparation.

Canadian Ch. Laurel Brae's Gale and Canadian Ch. Laurel Brae's Life Guard.

Chapter XIV

The Newfoundland in Canada

The history of the Newfoundland in Canada is as old as the breed itself. However, no actual records were kept until The Honorable Harold Macpherson started breeding Newfoundlands at Westerland. He bred them for over fifty years and sent dogs all over the world. Most of his breeding stock was imported from England, the United States, and the Canadian mainland. The two most famous dogs he bred were Seiger, portrayed on stamps, and Newton, the top-winning Newfoundland of all time.

During the critical years for the breed, the 1930's and 1940's, five Canadian breeders vied for the position of most significant breeder. It may be some years before their efforts are fully appreciated. Mr. Edric Emmet of Islington, Ontario, although not active for a long span of time, earned a magnificent reputation for his Laurel Brae Kennels by breeding such famous dogs as Ch. Laurel Brae's Life Guard and Ch. Laurel Brae's Gale. He worked closely with Mr. D. R. Oliver of St. Mary's, Ontario, who continued the Shelton prefix established by Colonel and Mrs. Wetwan. Mr. Oliver will long be remembered not only as the importer of the famous Siki-sired Canadian Ch. Baron, but also for having used this stud so effectively in building up the breed in Canada. Mr. Oliver added considerable glory to the Shelton Kennels name by breeding such magnificent dogs as Ch. Shelton Queen Juno and Ch. Shelton Sea Diver.

Mrs. Mercedes Gibson, using the Perivale prefix while residing in Ontario, and later when she moved to Vancouver Island, B.C., established her place in the breed history by her work with both blacks and Landseers. Her most famous dogs were Perivale Coast Guard King, Perivale Sea Urchin, Perivale Uncle Remus and Ch. Perivale Sir Timothy.

Mr. J. J. Patterson of Edmonton, Alberta, established the Millcreek Kennels, and contributed many excellent specimens to the improvement of the breed.

Mr. Montague Wallace of Saskatoon, Saskatchewan, got well

Ch. Edenglen's Black Sambo, owned by Hal Duffett and featured on Newfoundland post cards and telephone directory.

started in Newfoundlands when he bred the early group winner Ch. Knight of Drumnod. He added fame to his Drumnod Kennel name by importing another of the famous Siki sons, Can. Ch. Shetton Cabin Boy, which became a Canadian best in show. He, too, used this stud to good advantage and bred the famously productive brood bitch, Waterwitch of Drumnod.

The Topsail Kennels of Mr. and Mrs. Leroy Page produced the Canadian and American Ch. Topsail's Captain Cook, a Canadian Best in Show winner and a fine stud, and Ch. Captain Henry Morgan, grandsire of many of today's fine dogs.

The Black Ledge Kennels of Mr. and Mrs. Richard Hockridge in Nova Scotia, was founded with the purchase of Mr. Oliver's last two Shelton bitches. Black Ledge was famous as the breeder of the Canadian and American Ch. Midway Blackledge Sea Raider, that won many groups and was a Best in Show winner.

The Newfoundland dog is Canada's national dog, in fact if not yet in name. From the tangy, salt shores of the Atlantic provinces, through the rolling farm lands of Quebec and Ontario, with their islands of urbanization at Mortreal and Toronto, up past the northern shores of the Great Lakes, out onto the grain-clad plains and through the Canadian Rockies to the shores of the Pacific and the bright lights of Vancouver, the Newfoundland has had an unprecedented surge of popularity. Breeders in Canada, closely knit through the club which they formed in 1963, have long lists of puppy buyers. They are Canadians from all walks of life. The Newfoundland dog is no longer an estate dog, pet of the wealthy few. He can be found in the homes of trades people, farmers, business men, and even on a picket line in a central Ontario newspaper strike.

Mrs. S. J. (Nona) Navin sparked the formation of the Canadian club, along with other long-time Ontario breeders. Many of the early members were also members of the Newfoundland Club of America, which extended encouragement, financial support through the contributions of interested members, and advice on organizational matters.

Fourteen persons attended the September 1963 organizational meeting convened by Mrs. Navin at her Shipmate's Kennels in Gormley, Ontario. Others had answered her invitation with expressions of support. The charter members were:

Bank notes circulated in Newfoundland around 1890; each note portrays a Newfoundland in one form or another.

Topsail's Captain Bob Bartlett and Honorable Harold Macpherson.

Mrs. S. J. Navin	Mrs. E. Jameson
Mrs. Mercedes Gibson	Mr. & Mrs. D. G. Suckling
Mr. & Mrs. Daniel Hanington	Mrs. J. H. Daniell-Jenkins
Mr. J. A. Latimer	Mr. & Mrs. J. Loring Jr.
Mr. & Mrs. Donn Purdy	Mr. & Mrs. W. A. Gibson
Mr. & Mrs. R. T. Seaman	Dr. H. W. Jacobs
Mr. Wayne Wettlauffer	Mr. & Mrs. W. F. Cochrane
Mr. D. H. Irwin	Mrs. A. R. MacKenzie
Mrs. Lois Duncan	Mr. & Mrs. F. G. Kearsey
Mr. V. A. Hutt	Mr. & Mrs. J. Dawes
Rev. Gordon Smythe	Mr. J. Geerts
Mr. & Mrs. Dennis Moon	Mrs. K. Drury
Mr. & Mrs. R. Riddell	Mr. & Mrs. R. Nutbeem
Mr. Hugh Baird	Dr. & Mrs. D. Munro

The first president was Mr. Douglas Irwin, of Nobleton, Ontario, whose Swiss Landseer import, Fjord v.d. Arx, has been instrumental in a revival of Landseers in Canada. Mrs. Navin modestly assumed the position of Vice-President and shortly after moved with her physician husband to wilderness area mines in Northern Ontario and British Columbia. In grateful appreciation of her efforts, the club in 1965 made her its first life member. Mrs. Alison Seaman was the club's first secretary and made contact with breeders and fanciers throughout Canada. Membership grew rapidly from the initial fourteen to one hundred twenty-five in 1968.

The executives of the club early recognized the difficulties of maintaining contact with members strung out along the vast

Mr. J. J. Patterson, owner of the Millcreek Kennels, showing Canadian Ch. Perivale's Sea Urchin—Best in Show, Edmonton, May 7, 1953.

cross-continent distances of the country and established the newsletter *Newf News*. This bi-monthly publication keeps the membership informed of club activities and actions of the executive, reports new members, new litters, publishes historical items, feeding programs, and other items of interest. Donn Purdy, a hobby printer and club president, edits and publishes the newsletter.

Featured in the *Newf News* have been articles by Mrs. Navin and Mrs. Mercedes Gibson. Mrs. Navin's contributions covered the history of Newfoundlands as mascots attached to military units. Mrs. Gibson, who has also been honored with a life membership in the club, described her thirty-five years of owning and breeding black and Landseer Newfoundlands in an article

Windjammer Fjord v.d. Arx, owned by D. H. Irwin, imported from Switzerland in 1966.

entitled "Farewell to Newfs," which was reprinted in *Dogs in Canada*, the official magazine of the Canadian Kennel Club.

The Newfoundland Club of Canada has adopted as its official symbol the famous Ch. Westerland Sieger that appeared on 1932 and 1938 Newfoundland stamps, set against the outline of the maple leaf taken from Canada's flag.

The Newfoundland Club of Canada in 1967 turned its efforts, as a Centennial year project, toward official cognizance of the Newfoundland as Canada's national dog and has a committee working towards such designation. Newfoundland is a relatively new province of Canada, having confederated in 1949, and recognition of the origin of the breed in that province assumes a prominent place in the study. The club is also concerned about ensuring that interest in maintaining conformity of the breed will continue strong enough to withstand the demands for dogs aroused by publicity and that the Standard will be maintained through ethical breeding practices. Mr. John Waller of Ottawa is chairman of the committee, assisted by Mrs. Megan Nutbeem and Mr. Donald Mercer of Newfoundland, Mrs. Joyce Mac-

Am. and Can. Ch. Dryad's Domino, owned by Mae S. Freeland, winning the Canadian National Specialty in 1969. Judge is Mrs. Maynard K. Drury.

Can. Ch. Thelma's Boy, CD, owned and handled by Arne Berg.

Hostess for Air Canada airlines delivers codfish for annual Newfoundland Club of Canada dinner at Toronto to Mrs. Elizabeth Sellars and T. J. Harrison. Observers are Ch. Brumhill's Upper Case, Ch. Newfield's Phantom Lady, and Windjammer Samson.

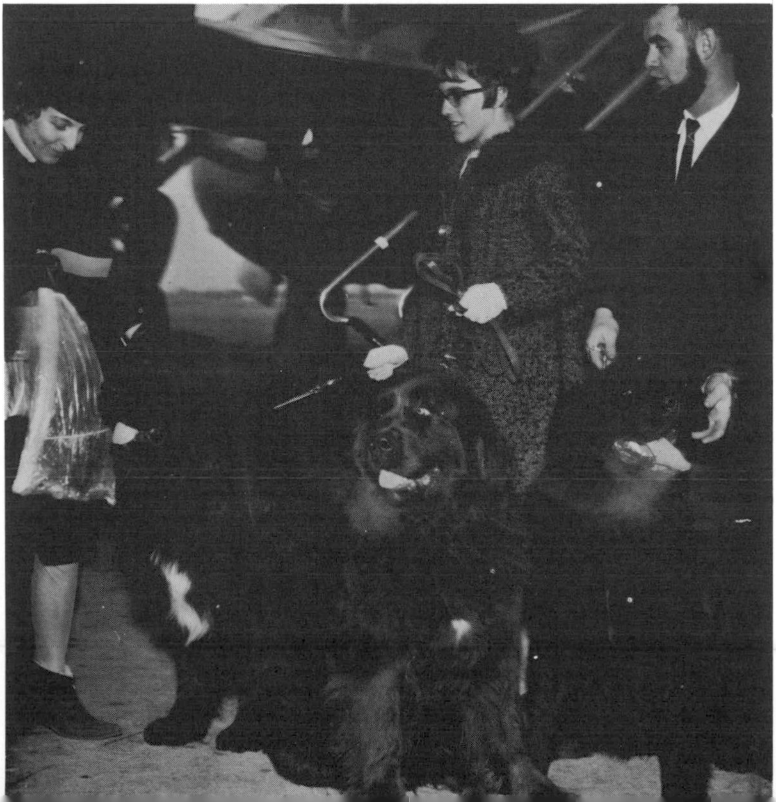

Int. Ch. Newton winning his first specialty show at Sportsman's; owned by Hugh Baird.

Kenzie and Mrs. Margaret Suckling of Ontario, and Mrs. Margaret Cochrane of British Columbia. The club's life members, Mrs. Navin and Mrs. Gibson, are advisers to this and other committees.

Under the two-term leadership of Mrs. F. (Madeline) Kearsey, the club promoted interest in the breed and cooperation between owners and breeders. Mr. Michael Davis, immediate past president, encouraged Newfoundland gatherings and matches. The annual Spring Booster Show, held at the Sportsmen's Show in Toronto each year in March, is one of the principal attractions of this largest dog show in Canada.

Mr. and Mrs. J. Loring Jr. (Joe and Polly) were active in club affairs during a three-year residence in the Toronto area. Their original breeding stock was of United States dogs but by 1967 they had introduced Canadian stock and left their Newfield Kennels' mark on Ontario breeding programs.

Specialty show winner Can. and Am. Ch. Kimtail's Schooner Bounty, owned by Mr. and Mrs. A. R. MacKenzie.

The present executive of the club is:
President: Mr. Donn Purdy
1*st Vice-President:* Mr. Thomas Harrison
2*nd Vice-President:* Mrs. Elizabeth Sellars
Secretary: Miss Natalie Elias
Assistant Secretary: Mrs. Julie Basterfield
Treasurer: Mr. J. A. (Sandy) Latimer
Public Relations Officer: Mrs. Joyce MacKenzie
Directors: Mrs. Nona Navin, Mrs. Megan Nutbeem, Mr. William Cochrane, Mrs. Mercedes Gibson, Mrs. Alison Seaman, Mrs. Margaret Suckling, Mr. Harold Multhaupt and Mrs. Polly Loring.
Past Presidents: Mr. Douglas Irwin, Mr. Daniel Hannington, Mrs. Madeline Kearsey, Mr. Michael Davis.

The future looks bright for Newfoundlands in Canada. There are dedicated breeders from coast to coast, and the first National Specialty show was held in October 1969 at Greenwood.

Can. and Am. Ch. Topsail's Captain Cook being shown by his master, Mr. Leroy Page, winning the Working Group at Guelph, Ontario.

A LITTLE PRAYER FOR LARRY

Is there a country, Lord, where Thou dost keep
A place reserved for dogs that fall asleep?
Large airy kennels, yards for hiding bones,
A little river chattering over stones,
And wide, green fields for those that never knew
A smoky town, an old, worn rug or two
Before a fire, where sparks do not fly out—
Sparks are such nasty things to have about.
I like to think there is, and so I pray
For one small Newfoundland that died today.
He was so full of fun, not very wise,
The puppy look still lingered in his eyes.
But he was very dear—he'd come to me
And rest his soft, black chin upon my knee,
Thou knowest him. One night not long ago,
He tramped with me across the frozen snow
And there, beyond the wood peaceful and still,
We met Thee walking on the moonlit hill.
Lord, keep him safe, wherever he may be,
And let him always have a thought of me;
That I may hear, when I pass through the dark,
Thy soothing voice, and then a friendly bark!

Appendix A

TERMINOLOGY

This is not meant to be a complete glossary of terms. It is intended only to be helpful in understanding the Newfoundland Standard as outlined in this book and as a source of general knowledge to give an over-all picture of the breed.

ACTION: The way in which a dog walks, trots, or gallops.

ANGULATION: The angles formed by the meeting of certain bones at their joints, such as shoulder blade (scapula) and upper arm (humerus), or the angles between the bones of the back leg assemblies.

APRON: See Frill.

BACK LINE: See top line.

BAD MOVER: A dog with a gait not typical of the breed, or with a gait that lacks freedom and soundness.

BALANCED: A consistent whole; symmetrical, typically proportioned as a whole, or as regards its separate parts; i.e., balance of head, balance of body, or balance of head and body.

BARREL LEGS: The opposite of cowhocked. The legs appear rounded from hip to foot like a barrel stave.

BITCH: An expression carried down from the old English to describe a canine female and quite proper to use in mixed company.

BITCHY DOG: Descriptive of a male dog which is overrefined, usually in head, giving an impression of feminity.

BLOOM: The sheen on a coat in prime condition.

BOSSY: Overdevelopment of the shoulder muscles.

BREED CHARACTER: Expression, individuality, and general appearance and deportment as typical of the breed.

BRISKET: The heavy cartilage and bone formation at the base of the thorax, or rib section, to which the ribs are attached; sternum, breastbone. It lies between the forelegs.

BROOD BITCH: A female used for breeding; brood matron.

CAMEL BACK: A roached back, convex curvature of the spine.

CAT-FOOT: The short, round, compact foot like that of a cat.

CHARACTER: See breed character.

CHEST: The part of the body enclosed by the ribs and breastbone.

CLOSED COAT: A coat that lies down flat and, if rubbed in the wrong direction, tends to fall back into place.

COBBY: Short-bodied, compact.

CONDITIONING: Feeding, exercising, and grooming in order to bring a dog to top physical form.

COW HOCKED: Hocks turning inward toward one another.

CONFORMATION: Formation of the dog by the symmetrical arrangements of its parts, the form or outline of the animal.

CRABBING: Front quarters and hind quarters moving out of line. Suggestive of crab movement.

CROWN: The highest part of the head: the topskull.

CROUP: That part of the top of the back from the hip bones to the tail.

CRYPTORCHID: A male dog with neither testicle descended nor visible.

DEWCLAWS: An extra claw on the inside of the hind legs. Rarely found in Newfoundlands but, if present, should be removed when the puppy is a few days old. The extra toe on the front legs is not a dewclaw and should not be removed.

DEWLAP: Superfluous loose skin under the throat.

DISH-FACED: A concave line from the eyes to the nose tip, so that the nose tip is higher than the stop, and the bridge of the nose appears to be hollowed out.

DISQUALIFICATION: A fault that makes a dog ineligible for competition at a dog show. (Usually designated in the breed Standard as disqualifying.)

DOG: A male dog.

DOGGY BITCH: Descriptive of a female dog that is coarse, usually in head, giving an impression of coarseness and masculinity.

DOUBLE COAT: A coat that has a soft furlike undercoat and a coarser outer coat consisting of guard hairs.

DOWN IN PASTERNS: Due to a weakness of the supporting tendons and muscles or to faulty pastern joints, the pasterns bend back and down at an angle rather than being perpendicular.

DRIVE: The power in the rear legs.

EAR FRINGES: Long hair on ears.

ELBOW: The joint between the upper arm and the forearm.

ELBOWS OUT: See Out at Elbows.

ELEGANCE: Symmetrical and stylish conformation.

EVEN BITE: Front teeth meeting in an even, level bite.

EXPRESSION: This is usually formed by the ears, eyes, and shape of head.

FEATHERING: Long hair on legs, tail, and hindquarters.

FEMUR: The thigh bone between the pelvis and the stifle in the upper thigh.

FIBULA: The smaller of two bones in second thigh.

FIDDLE FRONT: Or French front. Bowed front legs with pasterns turned in and feet turned out, usually out at elbows,

FLAG: A long-haired, fringed tail. Tail carried high.

FLANK: The lower side of the body between the last rib and the hip.

FLAT-SIDED: See Slab-sided.

FLEWS: Pendulous lips.

FOREARM: The part of the front legs between the elbow and the pastern joints. (Radius and ulna bones.)

FORECHEST: Front part of brisket or breastbone.
FOREFACE: The front part of the head before the eyes, the muzzle.
FRILL: Or apron, the long hair on chest and lower side of neck.
GAIT: The manner in which a dog walks, trots, or gallops.
GAY TAIL: A tail which is carried above the back line. It is usually due to a flat croup or from being set on too high.
GOOSE RUMP: A croup that falls away too sharply from the hip bones to the tail.
HACKNEY MOTION: The legs move almost straight up and down with little reach. Typical of some of the Terrier breeds.
HARE FOOT: A long, somewhat narrow foot, close toes.
HAW: A third eyelid, the red membrane inside the lower eyelid. It shows if the lower eyelid is too loose.
HEIGHT: The distance measured from the top of the withers to the ground. Shoulder height.
HIGH-STATIONED: See Leggy.
HIP DYSPLASIA: A malformation of the hip joints, which in its most serious form, causes crippling.
HIP JOINT: The ball-and-socket joint between thigh bone (femur) and pelvis.
HOCKS: The joint between the bones of the lower thigh (tibia and fibula) and the bones of the metatarsus.
HOCKS WELL LET DOWN: When the distance from the hock joint to the ground is comparatively short. Hocks close to the ground.
HOLLOW BACK: See Sway-back.
HUMERUS: Bone in upper arm.
KENNEL BLINDNESS: The inability to see faults in one's own dogs.
KINK TAIL: Twisted, bent tail.
KNEECAP: See Patella.
KNITTING AND PURLING: An expression used to indicate poor movement of the front and rear legs. The legs cross and the movement is sloppy. A serious fault in Newfoundlands.
KNUCKLING OVER: Insecure knitting of the pastern joint.
LAYBACK: The angle of the shoulder blade as compared to the vertical.
LEGGY: Where there is too much daylight under a dog. Legs out of proportion (too long) for the rest of the dog.
LEVEL BITE: See Even Bite.
LOADED SHOULDERS: Overdevelopment of the muscles in this area.
LOIN: Located between the last rib and the hindquarters.
LOWER THIGH: Or second thigh. (Tibia and fibula bones.)
MINCING: Taking short awkward steps.
MONORCHID: A male dog with only one testicle descended and visible.
MUZZLE: Foreface. See Foreface.
NEWF.: The nickname for a Newfoundland.
OCCIPUT: The bone on the top of the back part of the skull. (Prominent in Newfoundlands.)

OPEN COAT: A coat that stands up straight like that of a Chow. A serious fault in a Newfoundland.

OUT AT ELBOWS: Elbows that protrude from the body.

OVERSHOT: Upper front teeth overlap the lower teeth, leaving a space in between.

PACING: A way of movement in which the left foreleg and left hindleg advance in unison, then the right foreleg and right hindleg.

PADS: The sole of the foot.

PIGEON TOES: The feet turning in towards the center line of the body.

PADDLING: Throwing of the front feet to the side when the dog is in motion.

PASTERNS: The collection of bones forming the joint between the radius and ulna and the metacarpals, i.e., between the forearm and the top of the foot.

PATELLA: A caplike bone at the stifle joint. Functions the same as the human kneecap.

PILE: Dense furlike undercoat on double-coated breeds.

POINT OF SHOULDER: At the joint of the shoulder blade (scapula) and upper arm (humerus).

REACH: The extent the front legs go forward from the shoulders.

RADIUS: Front bone in forearm.

RIBBED UP: See Well Ribbed Up.

ROACH BACK: Excessive convex curve on the top line—camel-like.

RUFF: Thick, long hair growth around the neck.

SCAPULA: The shoulder blade.

SCISSORS BITE: When the upper front teeth slightly overlap the lower front teeth (the inner surface of the upper teeth should touch the outer surface of the lower teeth.)

SECOND THIGH: The part of the back leg between the stifle and the hock.

SHELLY: Shallow, narrow body, lacking in substance.

SHORT COUPLED: Short and compact in the loin.

SICKLE TAIL: A tail which is carried out and up in a semicircle.

SINGLE TRACK: The way the feet fall when a dog is moving fast. To maintain balance the feet move closer as the dog moves faster until the feet follow one another in a single line.

SHUFFLING: Sliding of the feet on the walking surface. The feet are not picked up properly.

SLAB-SIDED: Flat ribbed.

SLOPING SHOULDERS: See Well-laid-back Shoulder.

SNIPEY: A pointed, weak muzzle.

SPLAY-FOOTED: A flat foot with spreading toes and usually with flat thin pads.

SPRING OF RIBS: The degree of: usually refers to the degree of roundness of ribs.

STANCE: Manner of standing.

STATION: Comparative height from ground.

STIFLE: The joint of the hind leg between the upper and lower (second) thigh.

STRAIGHT HOCKED: Too little angulation at the hock joint.

SUBSTANCE: Sufficient development of bone and muscle for size of animal.

SUPERCILLARY ARCHES: Ridge, projection, or prominence of the frontal bone of the skull over the eyes.

STOP: The depression at the juncture of the nose and skull.

SWAY-BACK: See Hollow Back.

THIGH: The hindquarter from the hip joint to the hock, divided by the stifle joint into upper and lower (first and second) thighs.

THROATINESS: An excess of loose skin under the throat.

TIBIA: The larger of the two bones in the second thigh.

TOP SKULL: Top part of the skull.

ULNA: Bone in forearm behind radius bone.

UNDERSHOT: Lower front teeth project beyond the upper front teeth.

UPPER ARM: See humerus. Bone between the shoulder blade (scapula) and the forearm (radius and ulna).

UPRIGHT IN SHOULDER: Insufficient angulation at the juncture of the shoulder and upper arm. Shoulder is not well laid back.

WEAVING: The front feet cross when the dog is gaiting.

WEBBING: The skin between the toes that is found in all dogs but to a greater extent in Newfoundlands.

WEEDY: Lacking in substance and bone.

WELL LET DOWN: See Hocks Well Let Down.

WELL PUT DOWN: A dog that is well groomed.

WELL SPRUNG: Refers to ribs well sprung, or nicely rounded.

WELL RIBBED UP: Long ribs that are properly rounded.

WELL-LAID-BACK SHOULDER: A shoulder blade (scapula) that slopes sufficiently to form a proper angle with the upper arm.

WITHERS: The ridge between the shoulder blades. The peak of the highest dorsal verteabra, the top part of the body just behind the neck.

WRINKLE: Excess skin that forms folds on the head or face.

WRY MOUTH: A lower jaw that is twisted or tilted to one side.

Les Retrievers et Leur Dressage
Illustrations de O'Klein et Jean Herbert
Count J. DeBonvouloir
Libraire Des Champs Elysees, 1948
The Cabinet of Natural History and Rural Sports in America (Vol. I)
T. & H. Doughty
Philadelphia, 1830, 1834
History of Dogs for Defense
Fairfax Downey
Daniel P. McDonald (Distributor)
New York, 1955
How To Raise and Train a Newfoundland
Kitty Drury and Bill Linn
T. F. H. Publications
Jersey City, New Jersey
British Dogs
W. D. Drury
L. Upcott Gill
London, 1903
Homo et Canis (The Autobiography of Old Cato and Some Account of His Race)
John P. Dudley
Edited by T. L. Townleigh
The Republic Publishing Company
Chicago and Cincinatti, 1892
Animal Stories Old and New
Edward Evans
Illustrated by Harrison Weir
1875
Der Neufundlander
Prof. Dr. Otto Fehringer
Deutscher Neufundlander-Klub, 1952–53
Landsgruppe, Bavaria
Deutscher Neufundlander-Klub, 1952–53
Paul Revere and His Times
Esther Forbes
Boston
Memories (Reference Good Book of the Dog by Goodman)
John Galsworthy
Charles Scribner's Sons
New York, 1916
Diseases and Surgery of the Dog
Raymond J. Garbutt
Orange Judd, New York, 1948
The Gentleman Farrier
London, 1878
Neufundlander
Prof. Victor Goerttler
Koskos Verlag, Stuttgart
This Is the German Shepherd
Goldbecker and Hart
T. F. H. Publications
Jersey City, New Jersey

Illustrated natural history of the animal kingdom
Samuel Griswold Goodrich
New York, Derby and Jackson, 1861
Fifty Years of Peter Pan
Roger Lancelyn Green
Neptune or the Autobiography of a Newfoundland
Grefich, Farrar, O'Keder, and Welsh
Illustrated by A. L. Ewes, London, 1838
E. P. Dutton & Co., New York
Peter Davies, London, 1954
Animal Sagacity
Edited by Mrs. S. C. Hall
Illustrated by Harrison William Weir, J. Bateman, Piloty and a photograph by Bullock Brothers, Leamington
London, S. W. Partridge, 1867
Encyclopedia of Dog Breeds
Ernest H. Hart
Illustrated by the author
T. F. H. Publications
Jersey City, New Jersey, 1968
Der Neufundlanderhund (in German)
Dr. Albert Heim
Gustav Buchner, Mannheim-Waldhof
Switzerland, 1937
The Sorely Trying Day
Russell Hoban
Harper & Rowe
The British Museum; or Elegant Repository of Natural History
William Holloway and John Branch
Vol. I—Quadrupeds
John Babcock, London, 1803
Discovery of America by Northmen
Eben Norton Horsford
Houghton Mifflin Co.
Cambridge, 1888
The Landfall of Lief Erikson A.D. *1000*
Eben Norton Horsford
Boston, 1892
Lief's House in Vineland
Eben Norton Horsford
Boston, 1893
Our Four-Footed Friends
Mary Howitt
Illustrated by Harrison William Weir
London, S. W. Partridge & Co., 1868
Dog Breaking
General W. N. Hutchinson
John Murray
London, 1909
Hutchinson's Dog Encyclopedia (Vol. II)
Edited by Walter Hutchinson
Hutchinson and Co., Ltd.
London, 1934–35
Naturalists Library
Jardine's
Edinburgh, 1840
Picture Books for Children. Animals
Rev. C. A. Johns
London, Society for promoting Christian knowledge (1873)
(The Picture Library. Second series. No. 2)
The natural history of domestic animals
Dublin, J. Jones, 1821
Arctic Expedition (2 vols.): *The Second Grinnell Expedition in Search of Sir John Franklin 1853–1855*
Dr. Elisha Kent Kane, USN
Childs and Peterson
Philadelphia, 1856
Lion Ben of Elm Island
Elizah Kellog
Boston, 1896
Kennel Review
California
August 1969
The Labrador Retreiver 1931–1944
Labrador Retriever Club, Inc., 1945
The Red Book of Animal Stories
Selected and edited by Andrew Lang
With numerous illustrations by H. J. Ford
London, etc. Longmans Green and Co., 1899
Iron Men and Their Dogs
Ferdinand C. Lathrop
Privately printed, Baltimore 1941
The Story of the Good Dog Rover
E. L. Lecky
Modern Dog (Vol. II)
Rawdon B. Lee
Horace Cox
London, 1897
The New Book of the Dog
Robert Leighton
Cassell and Co., Ltd.
London, 1911—Special edition
Newfoundland Specialty Pictorial
Lenox
Vanderbrook Press
Newark, New Jersey, March 18, 1967
The Care and Handling of Dogs
John Lynn Leonard
Garden City Publishing Co., Inc.
New York
The English Governess at the Siamese Court
Anna Harriette Leonowens
Fields, Osgood, & Co.
Boston, 1870

Your Dog
Natalie Willits Lewis
G. P. Putnam's Sons
London, 1931
Decorative Arts of the Victorian Era
Francis Lichten
Charles Scribner's Sons
New York, 1950
Natural history of forty-eight quadrupeds
London, Darton, Harvey, & Darton and J. Harris, 1815
A miniature book. Binder's title: *Beasts*
The Dog in Action
Lyon, McDowell
Orange Judd
New York, 1950
The Newfoundland Dog
Honorable Harold Macpherson
Richard Clay and Sons, Ltd.
Bungay, Suffolk, 1937
Nos Chiens
Paul Magnin
J. B. Bailliere et Fils
Paris, 1929
Le Chien and Ses Races
Pierre Magnin
Vincennes
Paris, 1900
History of the Dog
W. L. Martin
London, 1845
The treasury of natural history
Samuel Maunder
Second edition
London, Longmans, Brown, Green and Longmans, 1849
McGuffy's First Grade Reader
"Alice and Her Dog"
Dogs of the World
Edwin Megargee, 1942
A Handbook of Old Mechanical Banks
John D. Meyer
Privately printed at Tyrone, Pa., 1948
The Labrador Dog: Its Home and History
Lieutenant-Colonel Lord George and Sir John Middleton
H. F. and G. Witherby Ltd.
London, 1937
Natural history in anecdote. Illustrating the nature, habits, manners and customs of animals, birds, fishes, reptiles
Arranged and edited by Alfred H. Miles
Hutchinson & Co.
London, 1895
Gallery of American Dogs
Miller and Mawhinney
McGraw-Hill
New York, 1950
Our Home Pets
O. T. Miller
Harper Bros.
New York, 1894
The Book of Dogs
National Geographic Society
(With plate by Louis Agassiz Fuertes)
Washington, 1927
Natural history of quadrupeds for children
By the author of *The Decoy*
Darton, Harvey, and Darton, London 1813
The Dog
Woodroffe Nile
London Swan Sommerschein and Co.
Macmillan and Co.
New York, 1900
Dogs (A selection of 100 photos)
Oxford University Press
New York (Plate LX)
Sporting Pictures of England
Guy Paget
London, 1945
Dogs and People
George and Helen Papashvily
J. B. Lippincott
Philadelphia, 1954
Dogs, Their Sagacity, Instinct and Uses
George Frederick Pardon
James Blackwood
London, 1857
Peter Parley's Animals
Darton and Co.
London, 1855, 1865, 1866, 1868
The annuals were not the works of Samuel Griswold Goodrich, 1793–1860, the genuine Peter Parley, but were probably edited by William Martin, one of the spurious English Peter Parleys.
The Shaggy Dog Story
Eric Partridge
For the Philosophical Library, Inc.
Great Britain, 1954
Currier and Ives
Printmaker to the American People
Harry T. Peters
Doubleday & Co.
New York, 1929
The Newfoundland, How He Lives and Is Bred
Johann Pieterse
J. M. Meulenhoff
Amsterdam, 1937
A Book about Animals
The Religious tract society
London, 1852
Mascot of the Melroy (novel)
Keith Robertson
Viking Press
New York, 1953
Diego Velazquez
Text by Margaretta Salinger
Department of Paintings
The Metropolitan Museum of Art
Harry N. Abrams, Publishers, N.Y.
The Complete Book of Dog Obedience
Blanche Saunders
Prentice-Hall
New York, 1954
Training You to Train Your Dog
Blanche Saunders
Doubleday and Co.
Garden City, N.Y.
Schweizer Hunde-Sport
Berne, Switzerland
Issues of February, 1935 and 1945, March, 1933
Castle Blair
Flora L. Shaw
Little, Brown & Co., 1922
The Odyssey of Homer
Translated by T. E. Shaw
Oxford University Press
New York, 1932
The Illustrated Book of the Dog
Vero Shaw
Cassell, Petter, Galpin & Co.
London, 1881
The American Book of the Dog
Edited by G. O. Shields ("Coquina")
Rand McNally and Co.
New York, 1891
The Dog and the Sportsman
J. S. Skinner
Lea and Blanchard
Philadelphia, 1845
The Book of Newfoundland (Vol. I)
Edited by J. R. Smallwood
Newfoundland Boon Publishers, Ltd., 1937
About Our Dogs
A. Croxton Smith, O.B.E.
Ward Lock and Co., Ltd.
London, 1931
British Dogs
A. Croxton Smith
Sun Engraving Co., Ltd.
London
Everyman's Book of the Dog
A. Croxton Smith
Hodder and Stoughton
London, 1909

Famous Dogs of Famous People
Mae Trevillion Smith
Dodd, Mead & Co.
New York, 1943
George Stubbs and Ben Marshall
Walter Shaw Sparrow
Cassell & Co., Ltd., London, 1929
Charles Scribner's Sons, New York
Sporting Magazine (Vol. 3)
London, 1804
The Sporting Magazine, Vol. XLIV, No. CCLX
London, May, 1814
Vol. XLIX, Plate II, December 1816
Vol. XXIII, December, 1804
Sportsman Annual
A. H. Baily and Co.
London, 1836
Ladies' Dogs as Companions
Dr. Gordon Stables
London, 1879
Our Friend the Dog
Dr. Gordon Stables
Dean and Son
London, about 1885
The Dog in Health and Disease
Stonehenge
Longmans, Green, Reader and Dyer
London, 1873
The Dogs of Great Britain, America and Other Countries
Stonehenge
Orange Judd Co.
New York, 1880
Stonehenge on the Dog
Longmans Green and Co.
London, 1857
Man's Best Friend
Captain A. B. Trapman
The Macaulay Co.
New York, 1928
Dogs of All Nations (Vol. II)
Count Henry A. Graff Van Bylandt,
K. Paul, T. Trubner, and Co., Ltd.
London, 1905
Les Races des Chiens
H. A. Graff Van Bylandt
Hendernassen-Door
Brussels, 1904
Fünf Langhaarige Groszhunde
Otto Meissners Verlag
Scholsz Bleckede a.d. Elk
The Book of the Dog
Brian Vesey-Fitzgerald
Borden Publishing Co.
Los Angeles, 1948
Instinct displayed
Priscilla Wakefield
Fourth edition
London, Harvey and Darton, 1821
First published 1811
Dogs of the British Islands
J. H. Walsh (Stonehenge)
"The Field" office
London, 1878
Dog Transportation FM 25–6
War Department Field Manual
August 19, 1944
The Dog Book
James Watson
Doubleday, Page & Co.
Garden City, N.Y., 1920
Dogs
Henry Webb
London, 1872
Animal stories old and new, told in pictures and prose
Harrison Weir
Sampson Low, Marston, Searle & Rivington
London, 1886
This Is the Beagle
Dr. George Whitney
Practical Science Publishing Co., 1955
Feeding Our Dogs
Leon F. Whitney
D. Van Nostrand Co., Inc.
New York, 1949
How to Breed Dogs
Leon Whitney
Orange Judd
New York, 1949
Illustrated Natural History for Young People
Rev. J. G. Wood, M.A., F.L.S.
DeWolfe, Fiske & Co.
Boston, 1901
The New Illustrated Natural History
Rev. J. G. Wood
London and New York, 1885
George Routledge and Sons
Working Dogs of the World
C. (A) Sedgwick & Jackson, Ltd.
London, 1942
"A Good Danish Specimen"
Yankee Magazine
Dublin, New Hampshire
February 1968
The Dog
William Youatt
N. Y. World Pub. House
New York, 1877
Lea and Blanchard
New York, 1846
De Hond Staat Model
Dr. Annie N. Zadoks
Kosmos, Amsterdam

Appendix C

ART AND LITERATURE

List of Illustrations, Paintings, or other Works of Art Relating to the Newfoundland Dog

The Basalt Dog	Louvre Museum	Roman epic
Plaster Figure of 18th Dynasty Egyptian Dog	Louvre Museum	
The Kill, a hand illumination from the Duke de Berry's "Book of Hours"		
Depart En Foret, a hand illumination from Les Chasses de Chantilly, 16th Century		
The County Fair	Rubens	1635
Phillip Sydney—Earl Romney	Sir Peter Lely	1656
The Maids of Honor (Las Meninas)	Diego Velásquez: The Prado Museum, Madrid	1656

Illustrations

Bung, a woodcut after Bewick		1778
The Newfoundland Dog	Phillip Reinagle	1803
The Newfoundland Dog	Orrin Smith	1859
Dick	Vaughan Davies	1881
Leonberg Dog	Vero Shaw	1881
Berghund	Vero Shaw	1881
Newfoundland Dog (Dandie)	Harrison Weir	1875
Newfoundland Dog (Photograph)	Henry Webb	1872
Newfoundland Dog	Thomas Doughty	1830
Newfoundland Dogs	Arthur Wardle	1894
Newfoundland Dogs	Louis Aggasiz Fuertes	1918
Newfoundland Dogs	Edwin Herbert Miner	1941
Duke	Edwin Megargee	1942

Paintings

Self-portrait of the Artist with a Newfoundland Dog	Ben Marshall	1811
Chestnut Hack with Two Boys and a Dog	Ben Marshall	2nd Period, 1805-1820

Satan and Piebald Poney	Ben Marshall	2nd Period, 1805-1820
Reproduced as an Engraving by Scott in "The Sporting Magazine," Volume 44, May 1814		
Newfoundland Dog and Ponies	Abraham Cooper	1787-1863
Beauty	Edmund Bristow	
My Pack	Bâteman	
Twa Dogs	Sir Edwin Landseer	1822
Head of Neptune	Sir Edwin Landseer	1824
Lion	Sir Edwin Landseer	1824
A Distinguished Member of the Humane Society	Sir Edwin Landseer	1837
He is Ready	Sir Edwin Landseer	
The Late Duchess of Teck with Newfoundland	Sir Edwin Landseer	
Saved	Sir Edwin Landseer	1856
My Dog—head study for "A Distinguished Member of the Humane Society"	Sir Edwin Landseer	1853
Mme. Charpentiere and Family	Pierre August Renoir	1878
Mrs. G. F. Stratton (Anne D'Ewes)	Sir Thomas Lawrence	1769-1830
Three Children and a Dog	Sir William Beechey	
Boy and Bay Pony and Newfoundland Dog	Alfred De Dreux, France	1810-1860
The Village Post Office	Thomas Waterman Wood, American	1823-1903
Waseeka's Crusoe	Edwin Megargee	1942

Prints, Etchings, and Other Forms of Art

He Is Ready, print	Currier & Ives, N.Y.	
To The Rescue, print	Currier & Ives, N.Y.	
He Is Saved, print	Currier & Ives, N.Y.	
Saved, print	After Landseer, Perry Pictures	1906
Sue, a drawing	Howard Proctor	1944
Newfoundland and Ship, dry point etching	Amos Nattini, Italian	
Newfoundland Retrieving Mallard Duck, etching	French School	
Bookplate for library of the American Kennel Club, Canine Coat of Arms	Edwin Megargee	1935
Club Insignia—Newfoundland Club of America		
Club Insignia—and letterhead, Newfoundland Club of England		

Club Insignia and letterhead, Trenton Kennel Club		
Newfoundlands on Stamps; Various Dates		
Newfoundland China Dogs		circa 1890
Wedgewood Plate with Head of Newfoundland		
Cast Iron Dogs at Woodbury, Conn.	J. L. Mott Iron Works, N.Y.	circa 1890

Illustrations for Literature Section

Reproduction of page from "Beasts" and Children's Book	Osborne Collection, Toronto, Canada	1815
Dandie Counting His Money	Harrison Weir	
Newfoundland Dog and Spaniel	Howitt, from Edward C. Ash's "Dogs, their History and Development"	
Crusoe Proves a Friend in Need	Illustration from Dog Crusoe by Ballantyne	1860
Sancho	Thomas Landseer, from Bingley's Stories for Children	1850
Mme. Tousseau's Wax Figure: Sir Walter Scott and His Newfoundland		
A Little Prayer for Larry, Photostatic reproduction from Honorable Harold Macpherson's Book on the Newfoundland Dog		1937
Carlo, The Roscius of Drury Lane Theatre, colored print	London	1804
The Inundation, an engraving from a painting by the German artist, Kiorhoe		circa 1890

Appendix D

OLDER PEDIGREES

1. Pedigree detail of Ch. Shelton Viking who appears in eleventh generation of Waseeka's Ghostship pedigree.

2. Pedigree detail of Seiger Aegir II von Augsberg who also appears in the eleventh generation showing the close tie which the Swiss dogs have to the English dogs.

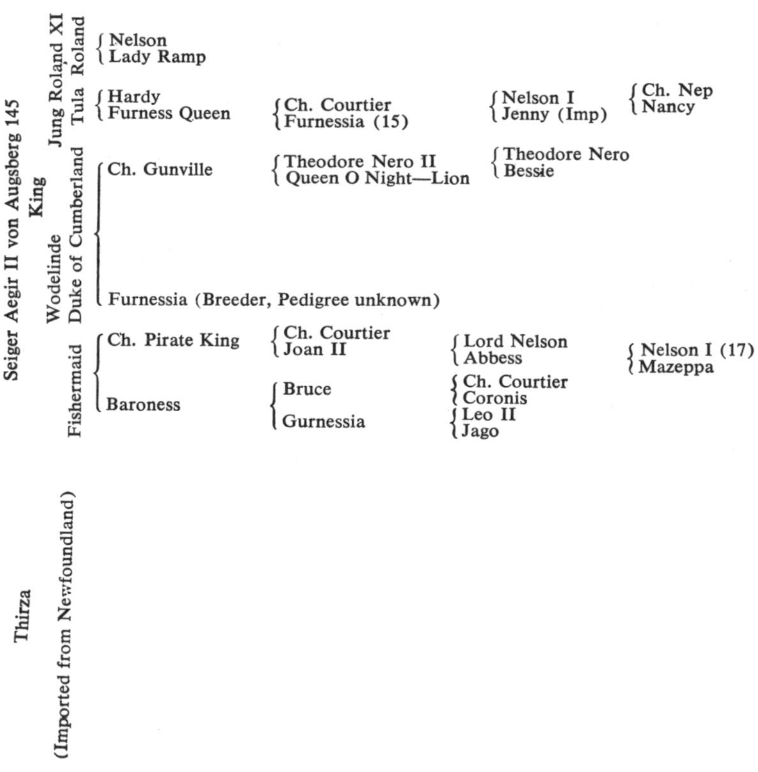

English Champion (Undefeated) Shelton Viking (KC 1724J) 10-19-03

Lord Roseberry
Shelton Madge

Ch. King Stuart
Queenie
Ch. King Stuart
Seaweed

Ch. Wolf of Badenock
Una II
Prince Jack
Queen Ann
Sir Gibbie
Shingle

Ch. Pirate King / Topsy
Ch. Commander / Nell (UNR.)
General Gordon II / Tibby
Charlie / Bell
Ch. Master Jumbo / Shingle (14)
Hematite / Regard

Ch. Courtier / Joan II
Admiral Drake / Vida
Ch. Courtier / Cora
Lion / Ex-Duchess
Lord Nelson (17681) / Cora (16)
Nero XI / Jenney
Alliance / Constance
(15) Ch. Pirate King / Ch. Lady Mayoress

Nelson I / Jenny (Imp)
Lord Nelson (16) / Abbess
Nelson I / Smut
Ch. Cabot / Zella
Ch. Leo / Nell
Nelson I (10672) / Thora
Lord Nelson (16) / Queen
Gunville / Sybil
Gunville / Sybil
Ch. Courtier (16) / Cassandra
Nelson I / Jenny (Imp)

Ch. Nep / Nancy
Nelson I (17) / Mazeppa
Theodore Nero / Rose (Imp)
Ch. Leo (17) / Duchess
Don / Meg of Maldon
Don / Tweed
Nelson (9422) / Empress
Theodore / Queen O Night
Theodore Nero II / Queen O Night
Nelson I (17) / Jenny (17)
Nelson I (17) / Mazeppa

Saul (Imp) / Lorne (Imp)
Bruno / Meg
Hector / - - - - - -
Nelson (2504) / Daughter of Sailor
Theodore Nero / Bessie
Odin / Marchioness

Carlo / - - - - - -

Appendix E

PEDIGREES OF ALL CHAMPIONS FROM 1950 THROUGH 1954

All names marked by an asterisk indicate that dog is either one of the three Siki sired imports from England

Can. Ch. Shelton Cabin Boy
Can. Ch. Baron
Am. Ch. Harlingen Neptune of Waseeka

or that one or more of these imported dogs is found in the pedigree background.

Dog	Parents	Grandparents	Great-grandparents	Great-great-grandparents
Midway O'Lady Sea Romain (CKC 251796)	Ch. Mill Creek Seafarer of Manitou (Sire)	Ch. Viking of Drumnod	*Can. Ch. Shelton Cabin Boy	*Can. Ch. Shelton Cabin Boy
				Lady of Drumnod
			Ch. Thalassa of Drumnod	*Can. Ch. Shelton Cabin Boy
				*Ch. Thalassa of Drumnod
		Ch. Mill Creek Lady II	Ch. Viking of Drumnod	*Can. Ch. Shelton Cabin Boy
				*Ch. Thalassa of Drumnod
			Jewel of Drumnod	*Can. Ch. Shelton Cabin Boy
				*Ch. Thalassa of Drumnod
	Ch. Stubbart's Greetings O'Lady (Dam)	Ch. Mill Creek Seafarer of Manitou	Ch. Viking of Drumnod	*Ch. Viking of Drumnod
			Ch. Mill Creek Lady II	*Jewel of Drumnod
		Ch. Shelton Mermaid Queen Gipsy	Skeena Lynwood's Man O War	*Shelton Baron of Belleville
				*Laurel Brae's Maid of the Sea
			Shelton Queen Juno	*Shelton King Neptune II
				*Shelton Mermaid Queen Bess

Midway Blackledge Sea Raider (W 155607)
Midway Blackledge Lelonga (W 155606)

Parents	Grandparents	Great-grandparents	Great-great-grandparents
Midway O'Lady Sea Romain (See previous detail) (Sire)			
Whodatte of Blackledge (Dam)	Saska of Bracken Brae	Bruce Neleus Toppo	*Westerland Wrestler
			Juanita Topsy
		La Bruin of Garden Acres	*Pilot
			*Lady Roxana
	Shelton Nikita	Shelton Coastguard Boy	*Ch. Coastguard of Laurel Brae
			*Ch. Shelton Sea Queen
		Shelton Queen Juno	*Shelton King Neptune II
			*Shelton Mermaid Queen Bess

Swivy of Camayer (W 87694)	Ch. Oquaga's Sea Pirate (Sire)	Shelton King of V	Shelton King Neptune	*Can. Ch. Baron
				*Shelton Sea Queen
			Shelton Mermaid Queen Bess	*Coast Guard of Laurel Brae
				*Shelton Sea Queen
		Oquaga's Black Beauty	Shelton Sea Diver	*Waseeka's Sea King
				Shelton Queen Bess
			Laurel Brae's Gale	*Shelton Sea Diver
				*Waseeka's Sea Nymph
	Gerry of Camayer (Dam)	Prince of Ayers	Sir Wallace	Dusky Prince
				Queen of the Gipsies
			Perivale's Kings Lassie	*Perivale Coastguard King
				Koch's Rheta of Perivale
		Cleopatra of Camayer	Ch. General	Kenmount Scotch
				Westerland Wendy
			Sally of Camayer	Duke of Camayer
				Sylvia of Camayer

Seaburn Sea Change (W 70227)	Dorken's Prince Charming (Sire)	Ch. Laurel Brae's Life Guard	Ch. Shelton Sea Diver	*Ch. Waseeka's Sea King
				Shelton Queen Bess
			Waseeka's Sea Nymph	*Ch. Harlingen Neptune of Waseeka
				*Waterwich of Drumnod
		Laurel Brae's Reef	Ch. Shelton Sea Diver	*Ch. Waseeka's Sea King
				Shelton Queen Bess
			Laurel's Sea Billow	*Can. Ch. Laurel's Starlight
				*Ch. Waseeka's Sea Nymph
	Salow's Valiant Duchess (Dam)	Larro Commander	Larro Perivale Skipper	*Perivale Coastguard King
				Daventry Grace Darling
			Sue	Sailor II
				Lady Joanna
		Small's Valiant Lady II	Larro Prince Valiant	*Larro Perivale Skipper
				Larro Stewardess
			Small's Valiant Lady	Koch's Danny Boy
				Perivale Sonia

Dryad's Fan (A 981762) Dryad's Admiral (W 20057)	Waseeka's Crusoe (Sire)	Ch. Waseeka's Smuggler	Ch. Waseeka's Sailor Boy	*Ch. Harlingen Neptune of Waseeka
				*Waterwitch of Drumnod
			Ch. Bulwell Aero Flame	Ch. Brave Michael
				The Gift
		Waseeka's Sea Shell	Waseeka's Sea Scout	*Ch. Waseeka's Sea King
				Ch. Waseeka's Sea Maid
			Waterwitch of Drumnod	*Can. Ch. Shelton Cabin Boy
				Lady Cabot
	Ch. Waseeka's Hesperus (Dam)	Ch. Waseeka's Sea Drift	Ch. Waseeka's Sea King	*Ch. Harlingen Neptune of Waseeka
				Vesta of Waseeka
			Ch. Waseeka's Sea Maid	Lifebuoy
				Ch. Tanya
		Waseeka's Clipper Ship	Can. Ch. Coastguard of Laurel Brae	*Can. Ch. Shelton Sea Diver
				*Can. Ch. Waseeka's Sea Nymph
			Ch. Waseeka's Sea Clipper	*Can Ch. Saybrooke Duke
				*Shelton Queen Peggy

Dryad's Lieutenant (W 75051)	Flintridge Rollo (Sire)	Ch. Coastwise Midshipman	Eng. Ch. Midshipman	Brave Michael
				Freya of Avalon
			Ch. Waseeka's Merry Christmas	Ch. Waseeka's Wayfarer
				*Waseeka's Ocean Queen
		Coastwise Seaworthy Sarah	Ch. Waseeka's Skipper	*Ch. Harlingen Neptune of Waseeka
				Vesta of Waseeka
			Coastwise Tugboat Annie	*Ch. Mark Anthony of Waseeka
				*Ch. Cleopatra of Waseeka
	Ch. Dryad's Fan-(See previous detail)			

Bonnavista (W 123755)	Chief Remus (Sire)	Kenmount Eastern Prince	Kenmount Colonel	Westerland Sirius
				*Waseeka's Blarney
			Kenmount Sea Maid	Westerland Sirius
				*Waseeka's Blarney
		Oquaga's Queen Mary	Shelton's King of V	*Shelton King Neptune II
				*Shelton Mermaid Queen Bess
			Oquaga's Black Beauty	*Ch. Shelton Sea Diver
				*Ch. Laurel Brae's Gale
	Black Queen (Dam)	Maine Coast Bucaneer	Moral's Mac A General	*Coastwise Admiral
				Johnson's Judy
			Lady Raveni	Thurston's Masterpiece
				Diana III
		Wee Lassie	General Semeon	*Waseeka's North Wind
				Carlodiana
			Lulla Belle II	Victor
				Lulla Belle

Topsail's Captain Cook (W 186602)	Dorken's Prince Charming (Sire)	Ch. Laurel Brae's Lifeguard	Ch. Shelton Sea Diver	*Ch. Waseeka's Sea King
				Shelton Queen Bess
			Ch. Waseeka's Sea Nymph	*Ch. Harlingen Neptune of Waseeka
				*Waterwitch of Drumnod
		Laurel Brae's Reef	Ch. Shelton Sea Diver	*Ch. Waseeka's Sea King
				Shelton Queen Bess
			Laurel's Sea Billow	*Ch. Laurel's Starlight
				*Ch. Waseeka's Sea Nymph
	Oquaga's Queen Bess (Dam)	Shelton's King of V	Shelton King Neptune II	*Ch. Baron
				*Ch. Shelton Sea Queen
			Shelton Mermaid Queen Bess	*Ch. Coastguard of Laurel Brae
				Ch Shelton Sea Queen
		Oquaga's Black Beauty	Ch. Shelton Sea Diver	*Ch. Waseeka's Sea King
				Shelton Queen Bess
			Laurel Brae's Gale	*Ch. Shelton Sea Diver
				*Waseeka's Sea Nymph

Birchmount Sea Nymph (W 292354)	Winston's Waseeka Blackie (Sire)	Barney Duke	Knight Errant	Black Jumbo
				Maple Queen
			Princess Patricia II	Jack of Oxford
				Black Beauty 4th
		Laurel Brae's Reef	Ch. Shelton Sea Diver	*Ch. Waseeka's Sea King
				Shelton Queen Bess
			Laurel's Sea Billow	*Can. Ch. Laurel's Starlight
				*Ch. Waseeka's Sea Nymph
	Oquaga's Princess Tenna (Dam)	Kenmount Eastern Prince	Kenmount Colonel	Westerland Sirius
				*Waseeka's Blarney
			Kenmount Sea Maid	Westerland Sirius
				*Waseeka's Blarney
		Oquaga's Queen Mary	Shelton King of V	*Shelton King Neptune II
				*Ch. Shelton Sea Queen
			Oquaga's Black Beauty	*Ch. Shelton Sea Diver
				*Laurel Brae's Gale

Perivale Sea Ranger (W 250677)

Parents	Grandparents	Great-grandparents	Great-great-grandparents
Neptune II (Sire)	Prince 5th	Dusky Pilot	Watchman
			Westerland Constance
		Shelton Gipsy Lass	*Can. Ch. Baron
			Shelton Bess
	Mill Creek Mary	Can. Ch. Viking of Drumnod	*Can. Ch. Shelton Cabin Boy
			*Ch. Thalassa of Drumnod
		Can. Ch. Mill Creek Lady II	*Can. Ch. Viking of Drumnod
			*Jewel of Drumnod
Ch. Birchmount Sea Nymph (See detail) (Dam)			

Waseeka's Zunzibar (W 221257)

Parents	Grandparents	Great-grandparents	Great-great-grandparents
Ch. Waseeka's Capstan (Sire)	Waseeka's Blockade Runner	Ch. Barnacle Bill of Waseeka	*Ch. Harlingen Neptune of Waseeka
			*Waterwitch of Drumnod
		Ch. Sea Clipper	*Can. Ch. Saybrooke Duke
			*Shelton Queen Peggy
	Waseeka's Black Chloe	Ch. Waseeka's Smuggler	*Ch. Waseeka's Sailor Boy
			Ch. Bulwell Aero Flame
		Ch. Waseeka's Sea Shell	*Waseeka's Sea Scout
			*Waterwitch of Drumnod
Waseeka Sea Clipper (Dam)	Waseeka's Dauntless	Ch. Waseeka's Square Rigger	*Ch. Waseeka's Smuggler
			*Ch. Waseeka's Sea Song
		Ch. Waseeka's Tern	*Waseeka's Blockade Runner
			*Waseeka's Black Chloe
	Ch. Dryad's Fan (See previous detail)		

Dryad's Decorative Accessory (W 225757)

Parents
Ch. Dryad's Lieutenant (See detail) (Sire)
Dryad's Beacon of Waseeka (Same detail as Waseeka Sea Clipper shown in Waseeka Zunzibar Pedigree) (Dam)

Midway a Sea King (W 59460)
Midway a Sea Queen (W 59467)

- Ch. Stubbart's Stormy Sea (Sire)
  - Mill Creek Seafarer of Manitou
    - Viking of Drumnod
      - *Ch. Shelton Cabin Boy
      - *Ch. Thalassa of Drumnod
    - Mill Creek Lady II
      - *Ch. Viking of Drumnod
      - *Jewel of Drumnod
  - Shelton Mermaid Queen Gipsy
    - Skeena Lynwood's Man O War
      - *Shelton Baron of Belleville
      - *Laurel Brae's Maid of the Sea
    - Shelton Queen Juno
      - *Shelton King Neptune II
      - *Shelton Mermaid Queen Bess
- Kenmount Baroness (Dam)
  - Kenmount Colonel
    - Westerland Sirius
      - Ch. Westerland Sieger
      - Anglo
    - Waseeka's Blarney
      - *Ch. Waseeka's Sea Drift
      - *Waterwitch of Drumnod
  - Kenmount Sea Maid
    - Westerland Sirius
      - Ch. Westerland Sieger
      - Anglo
    - Waseeka's Blarney
      - *Ch. Waseeka's Sea Drift
      - *Waterwitch of Drumnod

Waseeka's Ghost Ship (W 307383)
(See Detail on Inside of Jacket)

Waseeka's King Toxzon (W 183145)

- Waseeka's Capstan (Sire)
  - Waseeka's Blockade Runner
    - Ch. Barnacle Bill of Waseeka
      - *Ch. Harlingen Neptune of Waseeka
      - *Waterwitch of Drumnod
    - Ch. Waseeka's Sea Clipper
      - *Can. Ch. Saybrooke Duke
      - *Shelton Queen Peggy
  - Waseeka's Black Chloe
    - Ch. Waseeka's Smuggler
      - *Ch. Waseeka's Sailor Boy
      - Ch. Bulwell Aero Flame
    - Ch. Waseeka's Sea Shell
      - *Waseeka's Sea Scout
      - *Waterwitch of Drumnod
- Dryad's Sea Spar of Waseeka (Dam)
  - Ch. Coastwise Midshipman
    - Eng. Ch. Midshipman
      - Brave Michael
      - Freya of Avalon
    - Ch. Waseeka's Merry Christmas
      - *Ch. Waseeka's Wayfarer
      - *Waseeka's Ocean Queen
  - Ch. Waseeka's Hesperus
    - Ch. Waseeka's Sea Drift
      - *Ch. Waseeka's Sea King
      - Ch. Waseeka's Sea Maid
    - Waseeka's Clipper Ship
      - *Can Ch. Coastguard of Laurel Brae
      - *Ch. Waseeka's Sea Clipper

Dog	Parents	Grandparents	Great-grandparents	Great-great-grandparents
Coastwise Nan Tucket (W 122030)	Dryad's Coastwise Sailor Boy (Sire)	Waseeka's Crusoe	Ch. Waseeka's Smuggler	*Ch. Waseeka's Sailor Boy
				Ch. Bulwell Aero Flame
			Waseeka's Sea Shell	*Waseeka's Sea Scout
				*Waterwitch of Drumnod
		Ch. Waseeka's Hesperus	Ch. Waseeka's Sea Drift	*Ch. Waseeka's Sea King
				Ch. Waseeka's Sea Maid
			Waseeka's Clipper Ship	*Can. Ch. Coastguard of Laurel Brae
				*Ch. Waseeka's Sea Clipper
	Coastwise Marina (Dam)	Shelton Baron Monty	Ch. Skeena Lynwood's Man O War	*Shelton Baron of Belleville
				*Laurel Brae's Maid of the Sea
			Shelton Queen Juno	*Shelton King Neptune II
				*Shelton Mermaid Queen Bess
		Mill Creek Manitous Honey Chile	Can. Ch. Viking of Drumnod	*Can. Ch. Shelton Cabin Boy
				*Ch. Thalassa of Drumnod
			Can. Ch. Mill Creek Lady II	*Ch. Viking of Drumnod
				*Jewel of Drumnod

Dog	Parents	Grandparents	Great-grandparents	Great-great-grandparents
Skippers Star (W 87004)	Olsons Andy Boy (Sire)	General Semeon	Waseeka's Northwind	Ch. Waseeka's Wayfarer
				*Ch. Waseeka's Louise
			Carlodiana	Siki's Carlo
				Westerland Diana
		Carlodiana	Siki's Carlo	Siki II
				Saratoga Betsy
			Westerland Diana	Westerland Sirius
				*Laurel Foam
	Cindy of Kenmount (Dam)	Duke of Kenmount	Kenmount Sebastian	Westerland Sirius
				Corona
			Lulla Belle II	Victor
				Lulla Belle
		Admirable Black Dixie	Caesar Wah-ee-na	Tiger Boy
				Ten-Day Pee Wee
			Beauty VI	Dusky Laddy
				Gypsy Pee Chee

Claverie Barnacle (W 295119)

- Seth's Guilford Viking (Sire)
  - Midway Baron O Coastal Sea
    - Shelton Baron Monty
      - *Skeena Lynwood's Man O War
      - *Shelton Juno
    - Mill Creek Manitous Maid O War
      - *Ch. Viking of Drumnod
      - *Ch. Mill Creek Lady II
  - Midway Angil of Canochee
    - Ch. Mill Creek Seafarer of Manitou
      - *Ch. Viking of Drumnod
      - *Ch. Mill Creek Lady II
    - Ch. Stubbarts Angel Girl
      - *Shelton Baron Monty
      - Ch. Mill Creek Manitous Dark Angel
- Blackledge Kaola (Dam)
  - Saska of Bracken Brae
    - Bruce Neleus Toppo
      - Westerland Wrestler
      - Juanita Topsy
    - La Bruin of Garden Acres
      - Pilot
      - Lady Roxanna
  - Shelton Tamara
    - Shelton Coastguard Boy
      - *Ch. Coastguard of Laurel Brae
      - *Ch. Shelton Sea Queen
    - Shelton Queen Juno
      - *Ch. Shelton King Neptune II
      - *Shelton Mermaid Queen Bess

Midway Sea Raider (W 177685)

- Ch. Midway Blackledge Sea Raider (See Previous Detail) (Sire)
- Daniel's Bouncing Gale (Dam)
  - Shelton's King of V
    - Shelton King Neptune II
      - *Can. Ch. Baron
      - *Ch. Shelton Sea Queen
    - Shelton Mermaid Queen Bess
      - *Ch. Coastguard of Laurel Brae
      - *Ch. Shelton Sea Queen
  - Oquaga's Black Beauty
    - Ch. Shelton Sea Diver
      - *Ch. Waseeka's Sea King
      - Shelton Queen Bess
    - Laurel Brae's Gale
      - *Ch. Shelton Sea Diver
      - *Ch. Waseeka's Sea Nymph

Little Bear's Merasheen (W 284104)
Little Bear's Seldom Come By (W 284103)

- Ch. Dryad's Lieutenant (See Previous Detail) (Sire)
- Ch. Bonnavista (See Previous Detail) (Dam)

Little Bear's Isolt of Irwin-Dyl (W 334421)
Little Bear's James Thurber (W 318946)
Little Bear's Gander (W 330208)

Ch. Midway Blackledge Sea Raider (See previous detail)
(Sire)

Ch. Bonnavista (See previous detail)
(Dam)

Carbonear Newf (W 180744)	Westerland Uno (Sire)	Kenmount Colonel	Westerland Sirius	Ch. Westerland Sieger
				Anglo
			Waseeka's Blarney	*Ch. Waseeka's Sea Drift
				*Waterwitch of Drumnod
		Limsie Lorne	Ch. Water Rat	Eng. Ch. Brave Michael
				Judith Van de Negerhut
			Limb of Chinnor	Uz
				Esther
	Waseeka's Manatee (dam)	Waseeka's Dreadnaught	Ch. Waseeka's Square Rigger	*Ch. Waseeka's Smuggler
				*Ch. Waseeka's Sea Song
			Ch. Waseeka's Tern	*Ch. Waseeka's Blockade Runner
				*Waseeka's Black Chloe
		Waseeka's Kyle	Skeena Lynwood's Man O War	*Shelton Baron of Belleville
				*Laurel Brae's Maid of the Sea
			Waseeka's Black Chloe	*Ch. Waseeka's Smuggler
				*Ch. Waseeka's Sea Shell

Perivale Rocky Shore (W 250693)	Neptune II (Sire)	Prince 5th	Dusky Pilot	Watchman
				Westerland Constance
			Shelton Gipsy Lass	*Can. Ch. Baron
				Shelton Bess
		Mill Creek Mary	Ch. Viking of Drumnod	*Can. Ch. Shelton Cabin Boy
				*Ch. Thalassa of Drumnod
			Ch. Mill Creek Lady II	*Ch. Viking of Drumnod
				*Jewel of Drumnod
	Can. Ch. Coastwise Shore Leave (Dam)	Dryad's Coastwise Sailor Boy	Waseeka's Crusoe	*Ch. Waseeka's Smuggler
				*Ch. Waseeka's Sea Shell
			Ch. Waseeka's Hesperus	*Ch. Waseeka's Sea Drift
				*Waseeka's Clipper Ship
		Banshee of Big Bear	Flintridge Rollo	*Ch. Coastwise Midshipman
				*Coastwise Seaworthy Sarah
			Tug Boat Annie of Big Bear	Harlingen Boatswain
				Klondike Annie

Dog	Parents	Grandparents	Great-grandparents	Great-great-grandparents
Midway Black Ace (W 177574)	Ch. Stubbart's Nelson (Sire)	Mill Creek Seafarer of Manitou	Ch. Viking of Drumnod	*Ch. Shelton Cabin Boy
				*Ch. Thalassa of Drumnod
			Mill Creek Lady II	*Ch. Viking of Drumnod
				*Jewel of Drumnod
		Daniel's Bouncing Gale	Shelton's King of V	*Shelton King Neptune II
				*Shelton Mermaid Queen Bess
			Oquaga's Black Beauty	*Shelton Sea Diver
				*Laurel Brae's Gale
	Midway A Sea Countess (Same detail as Midway A Sea King) (Dam)			

Dog	Parents	Grandparents	Great-grandparents	Great-great-grandparents
Spinnaker's Sinbad (W 274187)	Ch. Topsail's Captain Cook (See Detail) (Sire)			
	Lady Jetina of Oakwood C. D. (Dam)	Barrett's Bing	Captain Bing	*Waseeka's Topsail
				Lady Tipton
			Diana III	King VI
				Queen VII
		Queen Jillina of Butternut	Moral's Captain Bing	*Captain Bing
				Dixie Alice
			Glenmuir Lady Patton	*Waseeka's Jolly Pirate
				Glenmuir Sea Wind

Dog	Parents
Midway Lady Baldor (W 308229)	Ch. Dryad's Admiral (See detail) (Sire)
	Midway a Sea Princess (Same detail as Midway A Sea King) (Dam)

Little Bear's Big Chance (W 303679)

- Ch. Midway Blackledge Sea Raider (See Detail) (Sire)
- Ch. Stubbart's Greetings O'Lady (Dam)
  - Mill Creek Seafarer of Manitou
    - Viking of Drumnod
      - *Ch. Shelton Cabin Boy
      - *Ch. Thalassa of Drumnod
    - Mill Creek Lady II
      - *Ch. Viking of Drumnod
      - *Jewel of Drumnod
  - Shelton Mermaid Queen Gipsy
    - Skeena Lynwood's Man O War
      - *Shelton Baron of Belleville
      - *Laurel Brae's Maid of the Sea
    - Shelton Queen Juno
      - *Shelton King Neptune II
      - *Shelton Mermaid Queen Bess

Dryad's Cherie of Spinnaker (W 371142)

- Ch. Dryad's Pilot (Sire)
  - Ch. Dryad's Lieutenant
    - Flintridge Rollo
      - Ch. Coastwise Midshipman
      - *Coastwise Seaworthy Sarah
    - Ch. Dryad's Fan
      - *Waseeka's Crusoe
      - *Ch. Waseeka's Hesperus
  - Ch. Coastwise Nan Tucket
    - Dryad's Coastwise Sailor Boy
      - *Waseeka's Crusoe
      - *Ch. Waseeka's Hesperus
    - Coastwise Marina
      - *Shelton Baron Monty
      - *Mill Creek Manitous Honey Chile
- Dryad's Beacon of Waseeka (Dam)
  - Waseeka's Dauntless
    - Ch. Waseeka's Square Rigger
      - *Ch. Waseeka's Smuggler
      - *Ch. Waseeka's Sea Song
    - Ch. Waseeka's Tern
      - *Waseeka's Blockade Runner
      - *Waseeka's Black Chloe
  - Ch. Dryad's Fan (See previous detail)

Irwindyl's Sir Aliking (W 423920)
Irwindyl's Lady Beale Isoud (W 419525)

- Perivale Lifeguard (Sire)
  - Neptune II
    - Prince V
      - Dusky Pilot
      - *Shelton Gipsy Lass
    - Mill Creek Mary
      - *Can. Ch. Viking Drumnod
      - *Can. Ch. Mill Creek Lady II
  - Can. Ch. Coastwise Shore Leave
    - Dryad's Coastwise Sailor Boy
      - *Waseeka's Crusoe
      - *Ch. Waseeka's Hesperus
    - Banshee of Big Bear
      - *Flintridge Rollo
      - Tug Boat Annie of Big Bear
- Ch. Skipper's Star (Dam)
  - Olson's Andy Boy
    - General Semeon
      - *Waseeka's Northwind
      - Carlodiana
    - Carlodiana
      - Siki's Carlo
      - *Westerland Diana
  - Cindy of Kenmount
    - Duke of Kenmount
      - Kenmount Sebastian
      - Lulla Belle II
    - Admirable Black Dixie
      - Caesar Wah-ee-na
      - Beauty V

INDEX

D

I

J

K

L

M

N

O

P

Q

R

S

T

U

W